POLITICS AFTER HOPE

◊

THE RADICAL IMAGINATION
SERIES

Edited by Henry A. Giroux
and Stanley Aronowitz

POLITICS AFTER HOPE

Barack Obama and the Crisis of Youth, Race, and Democracy

HENRY A. GIROUX

Paradigm Publishers
Boulder • London

Copyright © 2010 Paradigm Publishers

Published in the United States by Paradigm Publishers, 2845 Wilderness Place, Suite 200, Boulder, CO 80301 USA.

Paradigm Publishers is the trade name of Birkenkamp & Company, LLC, Dean Birkenkamp, President and Publisher.

Library of Congress Cataloging-in-Publication Data

Giroux, Henry A.
  Politics after hope : Barack Obama and the crisis of youth, race, and democracy / Henry A. Giroux.
    p. cm. — (The radical imagination series)
  Includes bibliographical references and index.
  ISBN 978-1-59451-852-2 (hardcover : alk. paper) — ISBN 978-1-59451-853-9 (pbk. : alk. paper)
  1. United States—Politics and government—2009–. 2. Youth—Political activity—United States. 3. Youth—Government policy—United States. 4. Children—Government policy—United States. 5. United States—Race relations—Political aspects. 6. Education and state—United States. 7. Obama, Barack. I. Title.
  JK1764.G57 2010
  320.60973—dc22

                                                          2010000836

Printed and bound in the United States of America on acid-free paper that meets the standards of the American National Standard for Permanence of Paper for Printed Library Materials.

Designed and Typeset by Straight Creek Bookmakers.

14 13 12 11 10   1 2 3 4 5

To Victoria Harper, who takes seriously what it means to be a public intellectual working to make the world a more just and better place. I am forever grateful for her courage, patience, generosity, and belief that my work mattered.

To Susan, who has filled my life with so much joy and love.

Contents

❧

Acknowledgments

＋⊖

This book would not have been written if I had not been asked by Victoria Harper to contribute articles to the online news magazine *Truthout*. She not only provided me with a new audience, but she also allowed me to demonstrate that there is no contradiction between theoretical rigor and clarity, on the one hand, and academic work and public life, on the other. She has been invaluable in encouraging me to write for *Truthout* and for pushing my work in a new direction. She is one of the best editors I have ever worked with and is an exemplary model for what it means to take seriously the political and civic relationship among writing, research, and the demands of democratic public life.

Moreover, her invitation to contribute to *Truthout* came just at the right time. Not only was the United States going through a major political transition with the election of Barack Obama to the presidency, but this also was a historic moment in which a new space for publicly engaged work seemed to be opening up as progressives across the country increasingly used the new media to support Obama's bid for the presidency and to mount a counterresponse to the suppression of dissent that had become the hallmark of the Bush-Cheney regime. Power was once again being held accountable, or at least for that moment in time it seemed possible once again to theorize politics from the space of a more open, humane, and just location. Existing neoconservative and neoliberal paradigms, especially those fostered during the Bush-Cheney years, organized around various poisonous species of religious, economic, and military fundamentalism seemed to be out of place, out of whack, and open to new interrogations and modes of analysis. The right-wing media's largely unchecked and relentless efforts to lie, misrepresent, and produce endless falsehoods in support George W. Bush's policies along with other forms of ideologically slanted public discourse seemed to weaken as a climate of manufactured fear, rabid nationalism, and an ongoing assault on critical thought and civil liberties appeared to ease up with Obama's election and his call for a new kind of politics.

A disparate array of issues related to gender, militarism, poverty, starvation, war, casino capitalism, ecological destruction, economic inequalities, and state terrorism were increasingly addressed critically by a growing number of discerning writers, artists, and journalists as the numbing and paralyzing charges of treason or anti-Americanism aimed at almost any form of dissent seem to lose their credibility and force. And yet in the midst of this new space of public debate and criticism, key elements of a truly transformative agenda went missing. There was a deadening silence from liberals and progressives about crucial issues such as the relationship between democracy and the fate of youth, the persistence of racism, and the central importance of education in providing a formative culture for social responsibility, engaged citizenship, and public values. *Politics After Hope* attempts to rupture the silence on such issues.

It also addresses another kind of silence. Just as the new critical media journalism seemed to gain some attention, far too many academics became more disengaged from public life. They hid behind the traditional firewall of jargon, staged forms of academic neutrality and professionalism, or eagerly offered their services to the rapidly growing military-industrial-academic complex.

Politics After Hope is, in part, about what Michel Foucault in much of his work referred to as "the critical history of the present." Offering up an analysis of the first year of the Obama presidency, *Politics After Hope* also reaches back into history to engage a series of problems that have led up to the current historical conjuncture and have left a deep imprint on how politics is currently being defined and mobilized to shape the future. We live at a time when it is imperative for parents, academics, artists, cultural workers, and others to speak beyond the immediacy of their own identities, localities, and experiences. In particular, this means that anyone who cares about democracy has to take responsibility for making power accountable, has to embrace the totality of the problems that connect us all, and has to speak beyond the confines of the academy, union halls, workplaces, places of worship, homes, and often isolated communities. This book is also a call for academics to become public intellectuals and use their voices to raise the bar of intellectual critique and civic engagement.

Given these larger concerns, *Politics After Hope* is about more than a critical engagement with Obama's presidency and its increasing adoption of the Bush administration's conservative policies; it is also about trying to elevate the public conversation to a new level of self-consciousness and awareness by speaking to a diverse and broad number of audiences. The book speaks to political and moral issues often associated with those marginalized by class, age, and race. That is, it attempts to reclaim a certain visibility for those individuals and groups who are often left out of political debates across the ideological spectrum. These are poor whites and disenfranchised minority youth too often considered disposable and erased from dominant discourses and a society in which they are rendered "excess" because they are considered useless workers, bad consumers, or, worse yet, a pathologized and dangerous threat to be contained. *Politics After Hope* attempts the hard work of critical analysis and moral judgments by attempting to think critically about how domestic politics toward the young especially have been shaped by the wider aims of a market-driven fundamentalism, a permanent war economy and culture, and a politics of disposability that registers something new and utterly antidemocratic and authoritarian about the nature of politics and casino capitalism and about the country we have become. Matters concerning youth, education, democracy, and race are central to understanding both the past and the future of the Obama regime, and yet these issues in their related complexities and mutual determinations are often ignored by many conservative and liberal critics of the new administration. *Politics After Hope* selectively focuses on the Obama's administration policies toward youth, race, democracy, and education, all of which get little attention from progressives or the mainstream press.

We live at a time when markets drive politics, entire populations become expendable because they are considered economic liabilities, and a ruthless culture of cruelty, greed, and unabashed arrogance views civic values, social responsibility, and democracy itself with utter disdain. Economic life is now consumed by a value system in which acquiring money, things, and status at the expense of others has become so normalized that almost any reference to some kind of moral index by which to judge our actions seems either quaint or absurd. Obama railed against this type of economic Darwinism and culture of cruelty when he first ran for office, but that discourse has turned into empty rhetoric as he has surrounded himself with the moneylenders, bankers, and financial experts that produced the grave economic, political, and social crises the United States faces currently. *Politics After Hope* is an attempt to understand these issues in light of both the emerging policies of the Obama administration and the legacy of problems that preceded Obama's entry into the White House.

But this book engages these issues not simply through the often raw categories of power and politics, but also through an analysis of the pedagogical and formative culture that produced the agents that supported an imperial presidency, a permanent war economy, and a state that officially supports torture, indefinite detention, the USA PATRIOT Act, and other sundry elements of a creeping authoritarianism. Public pedagogy or the educational force of the larger culture looms large in this book because it assumes that the production of identities, values, desires, modes of intelligibility, and visual maps of meaning is central to the construction of agency and the modes of politics and power such a pedagogy deploys, reproduces, and legitimates.

At the very least, *Politics After Hope* attempts to illuminate how important it is at this historical conjuncture to view hope as a precondition of politics, if not of critical agency itself. But politics after hope becomes meaningful only if pedagogy becomes central to our understanding of how knowledge, values, and social relations are constructed within a wide variety of sites extending from the family to the old and new media to the schools. It is precisely within such sites that diverse individuals and social groups can once again struggle critically for those values, issues, and problems that open the possibility for connecting theory with practice, moral outrage with political transformation, ideology with institutional transformation, and education with the possibility of critical and engaged social change.

This book would not have been written without the help of many friends who offered invaluable criticisms and support. I want to especially thank David Clark, Ira Shor, Sophia McClennen, Christopher Robbins, Ken Saltman, Roger Simon, Stanley Aronowitz, Tolu Olorunda, Peter Mayo, Doug Morris, and Donaldo Macedo. I am grateful to Michael Peters for publishing some of my *Truthout* articles in *Policy Future in Education*. As usual, I am deeply indebted to Grace Pollock, my research assistant and colleague, who edited every page of this manuscript and greatly improved the quality of the overall project. Once again, my incredible administrative assistant, Maya Sabados, went far beyond any standard measure of excellence in helping me put this book together. She was invaluable in aiding me with the research, typing, and editing. I also want to thank my good friend Dean Birkenkamp for supporting this project right from the beginning and for encouraging me to publish it with Paradigm Publishers, a truly wonderful and courageous press. Susan Searls Giroux was an invaluable source of insightful and critical ideas; she put up with endless conversations about the material, edited with great insight every chapter, and improved greatly upon every idea and word in this manuscript. I could never have written *Politics After Hope* without her support, warmth, and love. My canine companions, Kaya and Miles, managed to lower my blood pressure and provided much comfort and joy in the increasingly dark times in which this book was written.

I also want to thank *Harvard Educational Review* for permission to publish Henry A. Giroux, "Obama's Dilemma: Postpartisan Politics and the Crisis of American Education," *Harvard Educational Review* 79, no. 2 (Summer 2009): 250–266. Copyright © by the President and Fellows of Harvard College. All rights reserved.

I
Introduction

Introduction

Barack Obama and the "Fierce Urgency of Now"

꘎

We have also come to this hallowed spot to remind America of the fierce urgency of now. This is no time to engage in the luxury of cooling off or to take the tranquilizing drug of gradualism. Now is the time to make real the promises of democracy. Now is the time to rise from the dark and desolate valley of segregation to the sunlit path of racial justice. Now is the time to lift our nation from the quicksands of racial injustice to the solid rock of brotherhood. Now is the time to make justice a reality for all of God's children.
　　　　　　　　　　　　　　　　　　　　—Martin Luther King Jr.[1]

In a speech delivered in South Carolina on November 3, 2007, Barack Obama told his audience that he was running for the presidency of the United States because, like Dr. Martin Luther King Jr., he believed in the "fierce urgency of now" and that "there is such a thing as being too late."[2] This was a speech marked not merely by an appeal to lofty ideals, a signature trait of Obama's rhetorical style, but also by a carefully constructed criticism of the Bush administration and its descent into a deep abyss of corruption. He used the occasion to renounce what he designated "the politics of fear and cynicism," promising to repair "the enormous damage" of the dismal Bush years, which included the debacle of Hurricane Katrina, violations of numerous civil liberties such as the use of warrantless wiretaps, and war crimes; he stated, "We are not a nation that makes excuses for torture, we are a nation that rejects it."[3] He railed against corporate lobbyists for "setting the agenda in Washington" and insisted that he would stop "passing bills called No Child Left Behind" while jettisoning educational traditions that narrowly favor "just teaching to the test."[4] He also combined this language of critique with a language of hope, insisting that he would build a world in which "my children and their children have the same chances that someone, somewhere gave me."[5]

Almost exactly a year later in his victory speech in Chicago, Obama once again stressed a politics of hope by claiming that his own election as an African American pointed to an "America where all things are possible." But he also grounded his narrative of hope and what it had accomplished in the struggles of everyday people who had supported his campaign. For example, he lauded "working men and women who [had] dug into what little savings they had to give $5 and $10 and $20 to the cause." He enthused over the civic energy of young people who had rallied in great numbers to his cause and whose actions had thoroughly discredited the stereotype of youth as apathetic slackers. He also pointed to an older generation of Americans "who [had] braved the bitter cold and scorching heat to knock on the doors of perfect strangers" on his behalf. And, again, he linked the fate of young people to a coming era of responsibility, rallying his audience to imagine great possibilities "if our children should live to see the next century, if my daughters should be so lucky to live as long as Ann Nixon Cooper [a 106-year-old African American woman singled out by Barack Obama as someone who embodied the spirit of his election victory because she had overcome personal hardships and courageously served her family and community], what change will they see? What progress will we have made?"[6]

These themes enlivened his inaugural address when Obama, once again, called upon the American people to choose hope over fear and reject "worn-out dogmas that for far too long have strangled our politics." He reminded his listeners that politics and government must return to a "new era of responsibility" as the price of democratic citizenship. And he repeated his reference to young people as a measure of such responsibility, invoking the obligation "of carrying forth the great gift of freedom" and delivering it safely "to future generations."[7]

As the iconic harbinger of hope and a more democratic future, Obama's appeal to the fierce urgency of now was evident once again in his speech to the NAACP in July 2009. Yet unlike dozens of his other speeches, this address incorporated a number of ideological positions that implied a shift in his commitment to redressing the

4

grievous missteps of the Bush years to less firm ground than he had previously suggested. In the NAACP speech, he acknowledged the evils of racism, citing the disproportionate influence of the wealth gap, unemployment, spiraling health care costs, HIV/AIDS, the housing crisis, and the effects of the economic meltdown on African Americans. And he spent a considerable amount of time talking about the ways in which public education does a horrible disservice to the needs of poor minority students, which he correctly identified as both an African American problem and an American problem. He cited the legacy of Jim Crow and how it continues to structure high unemployment, the housing crisis, and the energy crisis, all to the detriment of African Americans. Obama ably demonstrated his working knowledge of African American history and culture and praised W. E. B. Du Bois and Martin Luther King Jr. for their "fierce passion for justice" and for how they both worked to critically educate the public about the evils of racism, make the machinery of power visible, and forge antiracist struggles into broad social movements. As he put it:

> From the beginning, these founders understood how change would come—just as King and all the civil rights giants did later. They understood that unjust laws needed to be overturned; that legislation needed to be passed; and that Presidents needed to be pressured into action. They knew that the stain of slavery and the sin of segregation had to be lifted in the courtroom, and in the legislature, and in the hearts and the minds of Americans. They also knew that here, in America, change would have to come from the people. It would come from people protesting lynchings, rallying against violence, all those women who decided to walk instead of taking the bus, even though they were tired after a long day of doing somebody else's laundry, looking after somebody else's children. It would come from men and women of every age and faith, and every race and region—taking Greyhounds on Freedom Rides; sitting down at Greensboro lunch counters; registering voters in rural Mississippi, knowing they would be harassed, knowing they would be beaten, knowing that some of them might never return.[8]

But then his address took an oddly conservative turn when he concluded by urging black Americans to assume a sense of personal responsibility, claiming "government programs alone won't get our children to the Promised Land."[9] Echoing many of his right-wing detractors, he urged parents in particular to work with their children to ensure they stay in school, while failing to acknowledge the insidious zero tolerance policies that push so many youth into the streets or the criminal justice system, often for trivial behavioral infractions. He exhorted parents to raise expectations for their children, but then only made a passing reference to a prison-industrial complex that profiles and incarcerates many black youth in staggeringly disproportionate numbers and to the lack of public services and employment opportunities ravaging many African American communities. He urged parents to read to their kids at night, assuming they did not have to work, assuming that functional illiteracy was not this generation's problem. And he said nothing about schools that fail to teach kids how to read because these schools lack resources and good teachers and are overcrowded. Young people were chastisingly told that to get ahead, they would have to turn off the television, pull up their pants, and do their homework. Lost in a glaring understatement of what Cornel West calls "the very ugly realities of poor and working class people" was any reference to a market society that defines their needs largely as consumers or to a system of neoliberal finance and speculation that turns society into a nation of debtors.[10] Obama invoked history only to forget history, shifting the burden of social problems to the limited realm of private pursuits and "onto the shoulders of individuals who are now expected to be 'free choosers' and to bear in full the consequences of their choices."[11]

Gesturing to the ideological right, Obama resorted to telling young people that they have to use their own wits and resources to get jobs, stay in school, and take on a measure of social and moral responsibility. At the same time, Obama's call to personal responsibility failed to say anything about the Wall Street elites whose greed and corruption caused a worldwide financial meltdown and who were rewarded for their lack of personal and social responsibility with billions of dollars in taxpayer-funded bailouts.

But beyond a fatal hypocrisy, the privatizing message of personal responsibility has a long history as a vicious racial code for denying and evading the myriad of structural forces that promote discriminatory lending and zoning policies, segregated schools, diversion of federal funds from much needed social programs to dysfunctional tax cuts for the rich, exploitation of people whose economic choices are limited by predatory financial institutions, an economic Darwinism that destroys any vestige of the public good, and corporate-controlled dominant media that endlessly blame poor minorities of color and class for their fate.[12] The message was all too tragically clear: "individual initiative" and "personal responsibility" for the poor, bailouts for the rich.

But personal responsibility is empty rhetoric in a society that collapses social problems into private issues (other than to suggest

6

it has washed its hands of the misery and "misfortunes its members may suffer").[13] Obama has, for the most part, turned his back on the perils of an overly deregulated, privatized, and corporatized social order. As *New York Times* columnist Bob Herbert points out, Obama seems clueless when it comes to recognizing and correcting the fact that "we've spent the last few decades shovelling money at the rich like there is no tomorrow. We abandoned the poor, put an economic stranglehold on the middle class and all but bankrupted the federal government—while giving the banks and megacorporations and the rest of the swells at the top of the economic pyramid just about every thing they've wanted."[14] Obama seems to think that giving Wall Street billions of dollars in bailouts somehow puts a check on its unrestrained greed, arrogance, and abuse of power. At the same time, he rightly exhibits disdain for the billions of dollars in bonuses paid out by government-rescued banks to their employees. Unfortunately, his disdain for Wall Street's arrogance is not matched by the compassion and courage necessary to promote legislation that might effectively address the hardships of millions of Americans struggling to stay in their homes, keep their jobs, and keep food on the table. Against the gravity of such social problems, the appeal to individual responsibility seems almost irresponsible.

Obama has chosen to ignore what Zygmunt Bauman identifies as a society in which "citizens are now abandoned to their own cunning and guts while held solely responsible for the results of their struggles against adversities not of their making" and those who are poor and powerless are deemed superfluous, redundant, and disposable.[15] Obama's endorsement of the tough love ideology more typically issued from the far right Manhattan Institute suggests that he is reluctant to implement the lofty ideals that have shaped so many of his own speeches. The courage to take on predatory capitalism, state violence, the reach of the prison-industrial complex, and the rise of the crime complex governing much of the everyday existence of poor minority youth meekly gave way to the force of individual responsibility—absurdly plunging massive systemic abuse into the shallow waters of individual character. Black pathology, given its mythic power in American history, once invoked, serves, once again, to nullify those economic, political, and social forces that undermine democracy in the United States.

In this discourse, the fierce urgency of now is traded for the apparently more fierce urgency of popular poll ratings (though they are dropping) and a shot at a second term in office. All the while a form of social amnesia regarding the history of repression is tacitly sanctioned and approved. Ultimately, the transformative power of the fierce urgency of now relies upon personal shame, rather than a collective struggle to take back democracy, which could raise individual awareness and promote real structural transformation. Under such circumstances, Obama's notion of hope appears to have less affinity with Martin Luther King Jr. than with the upper-middle-class African American and decidedly postracial made-for-television Huxtable family headed by fellow conservative Bill Cosby.

All of Obama's public addresses share another common thread. They refer to aspects of the president's politics that are rarely talked about in the mainstream media, which include his focus on the promise of democracy, the well-being of young people, and the importance of education, equality, and racial justice. Many of the speeches by Obama from which I have drawn here embody the very contradictions that now shape Obama's leadership in the White House. They register the promise of real change, on the one hand, and a willingness to undermine such change, on the other, by refusing to take seriously Martin Luther King Jr.'s warning about avoiding the drug of gradualism in order "to make real the promises of democracy."[16] At the same time, Obama's rhetorical gestures make visible an understanding of his view of hope as not only a crucial reference point for imagining a better world, but also a central dynamic for infusing politics with both a commitment to justice and a willingness to intervene in the world to change it for the better. Hope in this discourse, like the promise of democracy itself, is neither romanticized nor divorced from material relations of power and the necessity of social struggle. In fact, Obama's notion of hope, expressed repeatedly in his public addresses and books, provides an important measure against which to assess the distance between his commitment to a fully emancipatory notion of hope and the oddly conservative agenda he has actually pursued through the executive branch.

For the most part, the mainstream media have focused on five crises that mark the contemporary moment—the economic crisis, the war on terror, the health care crisis, climate change, and the escalating war effort in Afghanistan. How the current administration deals with each of these has become the measure that will ascertain the success of Obama's government. Obama has taken on each of these crises in turn, yet his decisions, his choice of advisers, and his proposed policies suggest that his notion of hope is not merely in retreat, but is also being utterly stripped of its emancipatory possibilities. By the beginning of 2010, it had become evident that Obama had moved closer to the right wing of the Democratic Party. He had surrounded himself with advisers who were perpetrators in the financial crisis, compromised with pharmaceutical companies in constructing health care legislation, allowed lobbyists to shape climate change legislation to benefit corporate polluters, and escalated the war in Afghanistan against the wishes of a large segment of the American public as well as a significant number of other Democratic Party members.

Even mainstream and popular liberals such as *New York Times* writers Paul Krugman, Bob Herbert, and Frank Rich seem to be disillusioned with Obama. Krugman is baffled as to why the Obama administration would oppose a House bill "setting rules for pay packages at a wide range of financial institutions," observing a troubling collusion with the dubious principle that "what's good for Wall Street is good for America."[17] After the Henry Louis Gates debacle in which the distinguished African American Harvard professor was arrested for expressing anger at police officers who barged uninvited into his home, Bob Herbert remarked that Obama would prefer to "walk through the fire" than spend his time addressing racial problems.[18] But Herbert does not restrict his criticism to either the politics of race or the ever-prevalent economic crisis—he goes right to the heart of Obama's retreat from his trademark hope in pointing to the administration's dismal policies extending Bush-era attempts to undermine basic civil liberties. Herbert cites Obama's support for preventive detention and the state secrets privilege, a refusal to release "photos of American soldiers engaged in the brutal abuse of prisoners in Iraq and Afghanistan," and a continuation of what is essentially a cleaned-up version of extraordinary rendition.[19] Herbert could have also made reference to Obama's embrace of the Bush policy of issuing signing statements, which are used by a president to alter the meaning of enacted laws, and his support for detention camps and "black sites" in Afghanistan that illegally hold detainees while preventing access to lawyers and to the International Committee of the Red Cross.[20] Frank Rich warns us that the biggest thing to fear about Obama is not that he is a socialist, as the loony wing of the Republican Party claims, but "that he is a corporatist."[21]

These security policies, launched by the Bush administration and threatening to erode the very foundations of our civil liberties, have been examined in great detail by many on the left as well as by some moderate progressives. The American Civil Liberties Union, Glenn Greenwald, David Cole, Bill Moyers, and a host of prominent writers have joined the fray in criticizing Obama for not only extending but also reinforcing many of the egregious policies instituted by George W. Bush as part of the "war on terror." Other progressives have pointed to Obama's refusal to support the most empowering elements of the Employee Free Choice Act, thus undermining the right of workers to form unions.[22] Moreover, many liberals and leftists have been alarmed over Obama's continuation of the tough crackdown on immigrants initiated by the Bush administration.[23] In all of these cases, there has been a profound discrepancy between Obama's soaring rhetoric and his limited, even disingenuous, political actions. Chris Hedges is particularly insightful in capturing the contradictions and false promises at the heart of the Obama administration:

> The American empire has not altered under Barack Obama. It kills as brutally and indiscriminately in Iraq, Afghanistan and Pakistan as it did under George W. Bush. It steals from the U.S. treasury to enrich the corporate elite as rapaciously. It will not give us universal health care, abolish the Bush secrecy laws, end torture or "extraordinary rendition," restore habeas corpus or halt the warrantless wiretapping and monitoring of citizens. It will not push through significant environmental reform, regulate Wall Street or end our relationship with private contractors that provide mercenary armies to fight our imperial wars and produce useless and costly weapons systems.[24]

Hedges has responded to Obama's retreat from the politics of hope and real change by arguing that "our last hope is to step outside of the two-party system and build movements that defy the Democrats and the Republicans. If we fail to do this, we will continue to undergo a corporate coup d'état in slow motion that will end in feudalism."[25] Hedges has no desire to try to influence the power elite simply from within. He believes that only a mass movement unequivocally on the side of socialism will be capable of mounting the collective struggles for change necessary to reclaim the power and the tools for a viable democracy.

With the election of Obama, hope, for many progressives, seems to have exhausted itself, as if it had found its final resting place in the election of an African American president. Yet Peter Dreier argues that, even though there is considerable anger among the American public over a number of Obama's policies, extending from health care reform to the war in Afghanistan, such anger is meaningless unless it is mixed with hope and collective action. And as he rightly puts it, "To be effective politically that hope has to be mobilized through collective action—in elections, meetings with elected officials, petitions, e-mail campaigns, rallies, demonstrations and even, at times, civil disobedience."[26]

But hope never ends, because no society has perfected democracy or is democratic enough that the fierce urgency of now becomes either outdated or irrelevant. Hope needs both a discourse and a sense of possibility, just as it demands a concerted effort on the part of individuals and social movements to combine the pedagogical conditions for creating an informed citizenry with a sense of urgency that demands informed and coordinated action. At the heart of this struggle, implicit though unmentioned by Hedges or Dreier, is the need to make the crisis of agency visible through the crisis of education—to understand that both are central to such a politics. A democratic politics demands an informed and critically literate citizenry, especially at a time when citizenship has been reduced to consumerism, and politics and agency appear largely drained of any substance. Democracy cannot exist without an informed and engaged public, which is dependent on the existence of a formative, open, and critical culture. Obama defied the onset of cynicism for a short time, and I feel compelled to ask the question, How did he successfully resurrect in his presidential campaign the issue of agency through modes of education that helped defeat John McCain? Put more specifically, what does his victory suggest about the role that intellectuals, unions, educators, workers, parents, youth, and others might play in rethinking how the media, schools, Internet, newspapers, and any other communication sites can be utilized as important pedagogical spheres that become central sites of struggle? Such a struggle will need to create a sense of public urgency, affirm democratic public values, and provide the conditions for the growth of ready and willing individual and collective agents for change.

Ironically, Obama himself has provided both a language for and an example of how this might be done. In the run-up to the 2008 election, he used the new media to spread a message of hope, he made clear that the Bush administration had created a nightmarish crisis of such proportions that the very nature of democracy was in peril, and he masterfully reached out and educated a wide range of constituents about his platform and the need to support his candidacy. His call for people to educate themselves in the spirit of citizen activism, find cracks in the system, put pressure on politicians (including presidents), and take to the streets for the causes they believed in can be found in many of his speeches—and can be read in retrospect as both a plea and a blueprint within the current historical moment to create new mass movements to continually challenge Obama himself, pushing him to move away from his centrist tendencies and the conservative pressures of corporate-driven party politics.

The new era of responsibility that Obama talks about found resonance in his own attempts, against great odds, to inspire people to take chances, assume risks, and exercise civic courage in order to deepen and expand the possibilities of a substantive democracy. But that responsibility was not intended to be either privatized or romanticized, nor was it meant to be relegated to a strictly individual task that depoliticized politics and furthered the myth of Obama as the iconic, solitary, heroic symbol of a new future. On the contrary, it is a discourse of responsibility Obama forged in the heat of politics, power, and struggle, one in which matters of agency and politics transcended the space of the privatized individual.

But once Obama assumed the office of the presidency and surrounded himself with the captains of corporate power and the same business elites that had created the global financial crisis, his call to responsibility was fueled by a notion of hope that downplayed its emancipatory potential.[27] Politics after hope was sabotaged by a movement of centrists, lobbyists, market fundamentalists, militarists, and right-wing ideologues who believed that there was no longer any need for either hope or struggle once their expertise was called upon. And it is precisely this bankrupt notion of responsibility and politics that must be challenged by those who imagine a very different politics from both the Obama administration and from emerging social movements. In opposition to a hope decoupled from a viable radical democratic politics, there is a need to forge a notion of possibility motivated by the collective responsibility of a mass movement that is capable of creating and sustaining a new kind of politics, one that does not end with Obama's election but sees it as a starting point for a new level of mass protest, collective struggle, and movement building. Martin Luther King Jr.'s call for the fierce urgency of now suggests the need to forge organized collectivities that can push Obama further to the left and begin the long, difficult, but necessary task of developing a third political party.

There are too many people suffering both in the United States and abroad at the current moment to put all of our efforts toward the one goal of building a third party—we need both short-term and long-term strategies for change. Expanding the safety net for the poor, providing jobs for the millions of unemployed, putting families back into their homes, offering shelter to the homeless, ensuring that everyone has decent health care, making sure that the millions who go to bed hungry have food—these are issues that cannot wait, and the Obama administration must be pushed to enact policies that provide these services. We need to move from a "foreclosure society" to a democratic society, just as we need social movements to struggle for sharp reductions in military spending so that resources can be invested in urgent social concerns, extending from health care to the energy crisis to problems facing urban centers. A politics that addresses the fierce urgency of now cannot wait because the suffering many people are now facing is too great and the stakes are too high. But in the long run a third party has to be understood as a necessary precondition for saving an aspiring democracy from its descent into financial ruin, political corruption, and moral irresponsibility. Gradualism and political centrism offer a politics that benefits only those in power. The result is not thoughtfulness and dialogue but compromise and moral cowardice. Obama urgently needs to be pushed into reclaiming his democratic sensibilities and attentiveness to the suffering of those most disenfranchised by the dominant society. But there is still one even more foundational, and therefore more pressing, task than calling for bold action from Obama, new social movements, and a radical third party.

What is most needed in the present historical moment is a concerted effort to create the educational and political conditions necessary to resurrect a new kind of citizenry capable of thinking through and acting on the problems that threaten to destroy both the United States and the planet. This political precondition suggests that central to any viable notion of political agency is the issue of education and the multifaceted role it must play in developing both the spaces for a new kind of civic and critical subjectivity and the tools and tactics necessary to support a social movement capable of challenging official power while maintaining the sense of urgency needed for restructuring the entire economic, social, and political order in an effort to overcome the current crisis of democracy. This civic culture can then provide the foundation for the emergence of a mass movement that struggles to educate and push Obama in a new direction while at the same time opening up new public spheres for alternative political parties and social movements. There is a dire need for a social movement that not only demands fundamental structural changes but is also capable of connecting diverse struggles as part of a larger movement for political, economic, and social transformation. This is not a question of ignoring particular agendas and often isolated struggles but of affirming and reaching beyond them to a set of common interests that both strengthen their democratic possibilities and broaden their struggle for a radical democracy. We need a politics that recognizes the local but is also capable of connecting it with the totality of interrelated and myriad projects that constitute a truly democratic project. At the same time, there is a need for social movements not only to provide a larger context for connecting the various agendas they address—from joblessness to the ecological crisis—but also to connect broader structural and ideological issues to the issues that affect people's lives on a daily basis.

Focusing on the economic crisis through the discourse of finance is important, as is understanding America's two wars through the discourse of empire, but it is not enough. Social movements, academics, community organizers, educators, public intellectuals, and other cultural workers need a language that speaks to people on the ground—a language that addresses in concrete terms the black unemployment rate, the 2.3 million people incarcerated as part of the prison binge, the millions of children suffering under zero tolerance policies in the public schools, the 37 million who go to bed hungry every night, the housing and food crisis, the fears and anxieties of unemployed workers, and the diminishing quality of life for older people on a fixed income. Under the regime of free-market fundamentalism, these issues are often mystified because they are coded as matters of character, reduced to individual issues, and stripped of their public content. Clearly, any individual or social effort toward a radical transformation of the economy and society that does not address the serious issue of translating private problems into public issues will be dead on arrival. As C. Wright Mills argued in *The Sociological Imagination*, intellectuals must not only locate themselves in the sociohistorical structure of their times; they must also reclaim the discourse of public values and, in doing so, work "continually to translate personal troubles into public issues, and public issues into the terms of their human meaning for a variety of individuals."[28]

Obama offered hope, but he has instead embraced corporate and military power. As a consequence, he has put the democratic connection between hope and politics in jeopardy. Obama's notion of hope has succumbed to a politics that has lost its hold on the present. His actions demonstrate little interest in alleviating the sufferings of everyday people, protesting injustice, and disrupting the workings of empire. At this early stage in his presidency, the cracks and contradictions are clear, but so are the possibilities for a different kind of politics after hope, one that suggests that history is open and power is not confined to the elites and power brokers in the military, financial sector, or government. The passage from passivity to anger to engagement can begin by our recognizing the gap between Obama's inspiring calls for change and the actual policies he has put into place. Glenn Greenwald offers an incisive example of the contradictions that now plague the Obama administration:

> The central pledges of the Obama campaign were less about specific policy positions and much more about changing the way Washington works—to liberate political outcomes from the dictates of corporate interests; to ensure vast new levels of transparency in government; to separate our national security and terrorism approaches from the politics of fear. After being in office for one year, it is clear that with some mild exceptions, those pledges have been repeatedly violated. For example, negotiating his health care reform plan in total secrecy and converting it into a gigantic gift to the pharmaceutical and insurance industries—which is exactly what a plan with (1) mandates, (2) no public option and (3) a ban on bulk negotiations for drug prices would be—would constitute yet another core violation of those commitments, yet another bolstering (a major one) of the very power dynamic he vowed to subvert.[29]

It is precisely in the space of this tension between what is and what ought to be that politics can be reinvigorated through education of the public with the very same words that inspired a majority of people to vote for Obama in the first place. The success of such an education does not rest by pointing to the swindle of fulfillment that followed the election, but asks what can now be done to go back to a politics in which hope is only the beginning, not the end, of what it means to see and act otherwise.

Hope provides the conditions for humans to imagine how things can be different from what they are in the present. It combines reason with not merely a lofty vision of possibility but also a real sense of limits and taps into our deepest experiences concerning the demands of individual responsibility and the obligations of social and economic justice. When armed with knowledge, people can link the power of judgment to the urge to change the world around them. When dismantled in the discourse of cynicism, perfection, or finality, hope loses a sense of possibility, dissolving into a world where tensions fade away and conflicts and contradictions cease to exist. As the Obama administration moves into its second year in office, his politics of hope has increasingly been transformed into a politics of accommodation and his quest for pragmatism and realism has become a weakness rather than a strength. Obama's earlier paean to progressive politics is increasingly viewed by many progressives as a caricature of sorts as he seems more than willing, if not eager, to pander to those powerful "special interests and lobbyists" whom he claims "are invested in the old way of doing business" and have "run Washington for far to long."[30] As Obama's efforts at reform unfold, the interests of big business once again trump the public interest. Deals are now made between the White House and the big pharmaceutical companies; insurance companies are driving health care policies; the major financial industries receive billions from taxpayers and celebrate by paying out exorbitant bonuses to their executive employees. The cynical and exploitative politics of Reaganism, far from being challenged by Obama, appears to be alive and well as the private sector once again defeats any attempt at real regulation and ends up committing the same abuses that led to the current financial meltdown.

In this instance, the language of possibility has been removed from the discourse of critique and hope appears to be stuck in reverse, if not hovering on life support. Politics after hope recognizes that hope is never finished; it always remains uneasy in the face of unchecked and unaccountable power and never stops its quest for equality and justice. Moreover, politics after hope recognizes that the fate of the future is never settled and that democracy is always a process of becoming rather than a state of being. This book responds to the challenge of politics after hope by focusing on those areas where Obama grounded his own sense of hope: the well-being and future of young people, the necessity to overcome racial injustices, the importance of abiding by the promise of a democracy to come, and the indisputable value of education if democracy is to be reclaimed in our lifetimes. These four considerations provide the ethical and political starting points for enabling hope to live up to its promises, while making civic responsibility and education central to a movement that takes radical democracy seriously.

II
YOUTH

Chapter I
War Talk, the Death of the Social, and Disappearing Children
A Lesson for Obama

⌖

Under the Bush administration, the language of war entered a distinctly new register, becoming more expansive in both its meaning and its consequences. War no longer needed to be ratified by Congress because it was now waged by various government agencies that escaped the need for official approval. War became a permanent condition adopted by a nation-state that was largely defined by its repressive functions, which were a response to its powerlessness to regulate corporate power, provide social investments for the populace, and guarantee a measure of social freedom. This has been evident not only in the all-embracing militarization of public life that emerged under the combined power and control of neoliberal zealots, religious fanatics, and far right–wing conservatives but also in the destruction of a liberal democratic political order and a growing culture of surveillance, inequality, and cynicism.

The concept of war occupies a strange place in the current lexicon of foreign and domestic policy. It no longer simply refers to a war waged against a sovereign state such as Iraq, nor is it merely a moral referent for engaging in acts of national self-defense. The concept of war has been both expanded and inverted. It has been expanded in that it has become one of the most powerful concepts for understanding and structuring political culture, public space, and everyday life: Wars are now waged against crime, labor unions, drugs, terrorism, and a host of alleged public disorders. Wars are declared not only against foreign enemies, but also against alleged domestic threats. The concept of war has been inverted in that is has been removed from any concept of social justice—a relationship that emerged under President Lyndon Johnson and was exemplified in the war on poverty. War is now defined almost exclusively as a punitive and militaristic process. This can be seen in the ways in which social policies have been criminalized so that the war on poverty developed into a war against the poor, the war on drugs became a war waged largely against youth of color, and the war against terrorism continues as a war against immigrants, domestic freedoms, and dissent itself.

In the Bush-Cheney view of terrorism, war is individualized as every citizen becomes a potential terrorist who has to prove that he or she is not dangerous. Under the rubric of the ever-present state of emergency and its government-induced media panics, war provides the moral imperative to collapse the "boundaries between innocent and guilty, between suspects and non-suspects."[1] War provides the primary rhetorical tool for articulating a notion of the social as a community organized around shared fears rather than shared responsibilities and civic courage. War is now transformed into a slick Hollywood spectacle designed to glamorize a notion of hypermasculinity fashioned in the conservative oil fields of Texas and fill public space with celebrations of ritualized militaristic posturing touting the virtues of either becoming part of "an Army of one" or indulging in commodified patriotism by purchasing a new (hybrid) Hummer.

War as spectacle easily combines with the culture of fear to divert public attention away from domestic social problems, define patriotism as consensus, enable the emergence of a deeply antidemocratic state, and promote what *Salon* blogger Glenn Greenwald calls the "war on the constitution."[2] The political implications of the expanded and inverted use of war as a metaphor can also be seen in the war against "big government," which is really a war against the welfare state and the social contract itself—that is, a war against the notion that everyone should have access to decent education, health care, employment, and other public services. One of the most serious issues to be addressed in the debate about George W. Bush's concept of permanent war is the effect it is having on one of our most vulnerable populations—children—and the political opportunity this issue holds for articulating a language of both opposition and possibility.

Wars are almost always legitimated to make the world safe for "our children's future," but the rhetoric belies how that future is often denied by the acts of aggression put into place by a range of ideological state apparatuses that operate on a war footing. This would include the horrible effects of the militarization of schools, the use of the criminal justice system to redefine social issues such as poverty and homelessness as violations of the social order, and the subsequent rise of a prison-industrial complex as a way to contain as a generation of suspects those youth for whom class and race loom large. Under the rubric of war, security, and antiterrorism, children are "disappeared" from the most basic social spheres that provide the conditions for a sense of agency and possibility, as they are rhetorically excised from any discourse about the future. Children now pass easily from school to the criminal justice system to the prison. Unemployed youth disappear from the discourse of social concern only to reappear in the demonizing and punishing rhetoric of the criminal, drug addict, and thug.

One particularly repugnant example of the disappearing of children was made clear in a report issued by the Equal Justice Initiative in 2007. The report states that "in the United States, dozens of 13- and 14-year-old children have been sentenced to life imprisonment with no possibility of parole after being prosecuted as adults."[3] In this case, the United States has the dubious distinction of being the only country in the world "where a 13-year-old is known to be sentenced to life in prison without the possibility of parole."[4] What is to be said about a country that is willing to put young children behind bars until they die? These alleged criminals are not adults; they are immature and underdeveloped children who are too young to marry, drive a car, get a tattoo, or go to scary movies, but not too old to be put in prison for the rest of their lives. According to a recent Equal Justice Initiative report, "At least 2225 people are serving sentences of death in prison for crimes they committed under the age of 18."[5] Even more disturbing is the fact that "73 children sentenced to die in prison ... are either 13 or 14 years old."[6] Moreover, on any given day in the United States, "9500 juveniles under the age of 18 are locked up in adult penal institutions."[7] At the current time, forty-four states and the District of Columbia can try fourteen-year-olds in the adult criminal system.[8]

The Bush administration's aggressive attempts to reduce the essence of democracy to profit making, shred the social contract, elevate property rights over human rights, privatize and corporatize public schools, and promote tax cuts that benefit the rich and destroy social programs and public investments failed when applied to the vast majority of citizens, but especially when applied to children. And yet children provide one of the most important referents for exposing and combating such policies. Making visible the suffering and oppression of children cannot help but challenge the key assumptions of "permanent war" and market-driven policies designed to destroy public institutions and prevent government from providing important services that ameliorate ignorance, poverty, racism, inequality, and disease. Children offer a crucial rationale for engaging in a critical discussion about the long-term consequences of current policies. Any debate about war, regime change, and military intervention is both unethical and politically irresponsible if it does not recognize how such policies affect children.

For the Obama administration, the focus on children may be the one crucial place to begin developing an ethical referent and a unifying rallying point of struggle in order to convince a broader public that a permanent war culture and economy, and an ongoing politics of militarization and empire building, do not promote democracy either abroad or at home. A permanent culture of war and militarization has little to do with either justice or democracy and can best be understood in the hard currency of human suffering that children all over the globe are increasingly forced to pay as a result of the violence promoted by these policies.

Chapter 2
Hard Lessons

Neoliberalism, Education, and the Politics of Disposability

ᴔ

In spite of the almost unprecedented financial and credit crises gripping the United States, the legacy of jaded excess lives on as both a haunting memory and an ideological register that continue to shape contemporary politics. After all, it was only a few years ago that pundits widely proclaimed, if not celebrated, the return of a New Gilded Age and its updated "'dreamworlds' of consumption, property, and power" to the United States with a vengeance.[1] The exorbitantly rich along with their conservative ideologues publicly invoked and lionized that bygone period in nineteenth-century American history when corporations ruled political, economic, and social life and an allegedly heroic entrepreneurial spirit brought great wealth and prosperity to the rest of the country.

Even with the economic blowout and its now visible register of corruption and greed on the part of Wall Street bankers and traders, the dominant press cannot relinquish its love affair with the super-rich, regardless of how greedy they appear. How else can we explain stories about how the rich are going through hard times as exemplified in their either moving out of their high-priced mansions into more modest million-dollar condos or being forced to give up riding in limos for more discreet modes of transportation? In some cases, these high-flying entrepreneurs of the now-devalued Gilded

Age are celebrated because of their unmitigated belief in the gospel of wealth and their sheer courage to spend in tough times. Or as the *New York Times* puts it, "When the times get tough, the smart spend money."[2] And while tent cities are emerging all over the country, the ultrarich provide a lesson in what it means to be "smart," capitalizing on their spending habits by buying $14 million condos in New York City, dishing out $3,000 at the Goldbar Lounge for a bottle of Louis XIII Cognac, or paying $656,000 for a Rolls Royce Phantom convertible.[3] What these stories often forget to mention is the legacy of corporate swindling, corruption, and financial adventurism that was responsible for bankrupting the country.

There is more at work in these examples of Gilded Age excess than a predatory narcissism, a zany hubris, and a neofeudal worldview in which self-interest and the laws of the market are seen as the only true measures of politics. There is also an attack on the idea of the social contract—the state's provision of minimum guarantees of security—and the very notion of democratic politics. Moreover, in this freewheeling, deregulated market society, the citizen is reduced to a consumer or, if labeled as a flawed consumer, rendered as excess, redundant, and disposable. Rampant greed, market deregulation, and cutthroat individual competition, lauded in this world of free-market fundamentalism, have produced during the last thirty years an unparalleled degree of social inequality in the United States, along with massive dislocations in the basic foundations of society. Clearly, any understanding of the present financial crisis and its disastrous effects has to include a consideration of free-market fundamentalism, or *neoliberalism*, and the ideologies, cultural formations, and modes of political irresponsibility that produced it. Discussions about the economic meltdown are largely focused on economics or, as Paul Krugman puts it, "the market mystique—the magic of the financial marketplace and [the fraudulent and corrupt] wizards who perform that magic."[4]

Almost nothing is said about the public values, ideologies, modes of rationality, and commonsense assumptions that produce both neoliberal beliefs and the subjects who unquestionably accept such views. Characteristic of many current critiques of the financial crisis is a disconnect between analyses of the destruction produced by the economic meltdown and a silence regarding the market-driven values underlying its sordid vision of the world. Neoliberalism has not only altered economic agendas throughout the world but has also transformed politics, restructured social relations, and produced an array of reality narratives and disciplinary measures that normalize its perverted view of citizenship, the state, and the supremacy of market relations. Clearly, the crisis of free-market fundamentalism and the economic Darwinism that functions as its counterpart are as much educational issues as they are economic and political problems.

The varied populations suffering and made increasingly disposable under neoliberalism can attribute their oppression to a reactionary politics in which the categories of "citizen" and "democratic representation," once integral to national politics, are no longer recognized. In the past, people who were marginalized by class and race could at least expect a modicum of support from the social state, either through an array of limited social provisions or from employers who recognized that the marginalized still had some value as part of a reserve army of unemployed labor. This is no longer true. Under the ruthless dynamics of free-market fundamentalism, there has been a shift away from the goals of living a life of dignity and working for economic independence and a move toward the much more deadly task of struggling to stay alive—or keeping one step away from becoming part of the growing army of humans considered utterly disposable and redundant.

Disposable populations have historically been relegated to the frontier zones of society as part of an ongoing effort to hide them from public view. Until recently, such populations were warehoused in schools that resembled boot camps,[5] dispersed to dank and dangerous workplaces far from the enclaves of the tourist industries, incarcerated in prisons that privileged punishment over rehabilitation, and consigned to the status of the permanently unemployed. But such populations now seem to be an everyday part of the American landscape, glaringly visible in the burgeoning tent cities, revealed in dominant media reports about families being evicted from their homes, and evident in cars and RVs that now line up in parking areas and serve as many people's only shelter. Rendered redundant as a result of the collapse of the welfare state, a pervasive racism, a growing disparity in income and wealth, and a set of take-no-prisoners market principles, an increasing number of individuals and groups are suffering from what Orlando Patterson in his discussion of slavery calls "social death."[6] The young, working poor, unemployed, disabled, and homeless increasingly share a common fate as more and more people become victims of the socially strangulating culture of hyperindividualism, self-interest, corporate corruption, and viral consumerism that now governs the political sphere as well as the realm of everyday life in accordance with the organizing principles of free-market fundamentalism.

Under neoliberalism, social problems such as poverty become utterly privatized and removed from public discourse. Principles of communal responsibility are derided in favor of narrowly defined individual satisfactions, largely measured through the acquisition and disposability of consumer goods. In this highly privatized universe, visions of the good society are cast aside, replaced by "the perpetual search for bargains" and maximum consumer satisfaction.[7] The consequences involve not only the undoing of social bonds and the dismissal of shared responsibilities but also the endless reproduction of the much-narrowed registers of character and individual self-reliance as substitutes for any rigorous analyses of the politics, ideologies, and mechanisms of power at work in the construction of socially created problems. All problems are now laid on the doorstep of the individual, regardless of how unlikely the individual might have been involved in creating them. This makes it more socially acceptable to blame the poor, homeless, uninsured, jobless, and other disadvantaged individuals and groups for their problems, while reinforcing the merging of the market state with the punishing state. This is the central discourse of Fox News, which apparently believes that the mortgage crisis was due to financially irresponsible home buyers and not to the unabashed corruption and unchecked power of the deregulated banking and mortgage industries.

What is often ignored by studies conducted on the rise of neoliberalism in the United States is that it is not only a system of economic power relations but also an educational project, intent on producing new forms of subjectivity and on sanctioning particular modes of conduct.[8] We get a sense of what kind of conduct is promoted by neoliberalism from an insight provided by British media theorist Nick Couldry, who insists that "every system of cruelty requires its own theater," one that draws upon the rituals of everyday life in order to legitimate its norms, values, institutions, and social practices.[9] Neoliberalism represents one such system of cruelty that is reproduced daily through a regime of common sense and that now serves as a powerful pedagogical force shaping our lives, memories, and daily experiences while attempting to erase everything critical and emancipatory about history, justice, solidarity, freedom, and the meaning of democracy. Undoubtedly, neoliberal norms, practices, and social relations are being called into question to a degree unwitnessed since the 1930s. Yet despite the devastating impact of a financial meltdown, neoliberalism's potent market-driven ideology is far from bankrupt and is still a powerful cultural and educational force to be reckoned with. How else could we explain the lack of critical discourse about the expanding number of mainstream public institutions that legitimate and normalize the values underpinning free-market fundamentalism?

Under the administration of George W. Bush, democracy was viewed with contempt, young people were not considered worthy investments, and the rich were given $2 trillion in tax breaks. For many young people and adults today, the private sphere has become the only space in which to imagine any sense of hope, pleasure, or possibility. Culture as an activity in which young people actually produce the conditions of their own agency through dialogue, community participation, public stories, and political struggle is being eroded. In its place, we are increasingly surrounded by a "climate of cultural and linguistic privatization" in which the only obligation of citizenship is to consume and shop.[10] Even though an unfolding economic crisis should discredit the language of the free market, there is nothing yet to substitute in its place.

It is imperative that we develop a new language, especially for young people, one that recognizes how individual problems are related to social concerns. Living in a real democracy means finding collective ways of dealing with the most pressing social and economic problems facing future generations, including ecological destruction, extreme poverty, economic inequality, persistent racism, and the necessity for a vibrant social state. We need to reclaim the meaning of democracy and give it some substance by recognizing, as Bill Moyers points out, that democracy is not just about the freedom to shop, formal elections, or a two-party system: It is about discovering "the means of dignifying people so they become fully free to claim their moral and political agency."[11] The problems currently faced by the United States are not merely economic. They are also political and educational and demand solutions that can address the combination of forces that have produced a rampant culture of neoliberalism to the detriment of democratic public life.

To strengthen the public sphere, we must use its most widespread institutions, undo their degeneration into means of commodification and control, and reclaim them as democratic spaces. Schools, colleges, and universities come to mind—because of both their contradictions and their democratic potential, their reality and their promise, though, of course, they are not the only sites of potential resistance. This democratic transformation must involve more than a simple appeal to thoughtfulness, critique, and dialogue; it must assert what kind of education matters to a democracy and restate a commitment to public and higher education in terms of its value for political culture and democratic public life.

One of the most important challenges facing education in the Obama era is the reintroduction of educational policies, values, and social practices that help produce civic identifications and commitments, teach young people how to participate in and shape public life and exercise critical judgment, and provide the pedagogical conditions that enable them to exercise civic courage. The Obama administration to date has been of little help here and largely supports a notion of education that is tied to a business culture, one that validates charter schools, high-stakes testing, students defined less as citizens than as potential workers, and profit incentives to reward student achievement—a model of education not unlike what the Bush administration supported. The shortcomings of Barack Obama's philosophy of education and its uncritical acceptance of neoliberal values, especially in light of his vociferous indignation over Wall Street corruption and bonuses, are difficult to understand and even more difficult to accept. Nowhere is the disconnect between Obama's call for change and his love of markets more pronounced than in his educational policies.[12]

If we are to move beyond the limited strategy and language of bailouts—a code word for helping the wealthy and asking the poor to make more sacrifices—the larger public dialogue needs to focus on how we view, represent, and treat young people and others marginalized by class, race, disability, and age. This dialogue needs to be about how to imagine and struggle for a democratic future. The potential for a better future further increases when critical education and democratically inspired modes of literacy become central to any viable notion of politics. Education in this instance becomes both an ethical and a political referent: It furnishes an opportunity for adults to provide the conditions for themselves and young people to become critically engaged social agents who value democratic values over market values and who take seriously the notion that when human beings recognize the causes of their suffering, they are in a better position to bring to a halt the misery caused by market fundamentalism and other antidemocratic tendencies. Similarly, a critically informed pedagogy points to a future in which public schools and higher education, in part, play a fundamental role in providing the conditions for each generation of youth to struggle anew to sustain the promise of a democracy that must be continually expanded into a world of new possibilities and opportunities for keeping justice and real hope alive.

This may sound a bit utopian given the political and economic crisis we are facing in both the United States and Canada, but we have few choices if we are going to fight for a future that does a great deal more than endlessly repeat the present. I think it is all the more crucial to take seriously Hannah Arendt's admonition that living in dark times requires believing that history never reaches an endpoint and that the space of the possible is always larger than the one on display.[13]

Chapter 3
Commodifying Kids
The Forgotten Crisis

 ↭

As the United States and the rest of the world enter into an economic free fall, the current crisis offers an opportunity to question the politics of free-market fundamentalism, the destruction of the social state, the dominance of economics over politics, and the subordination of justice to the laws of finance and the accumulation of capital. But this crisis does more. It also provides an opportunity for the American public to analyze the ways in which children's culture has been corrupted by rampant commercialization, commodification, and consumption. There is more at stake in this crisis than stabilizing the banks, shoring up employment, and fixing the housing market, though these are important problems for the nation to solve. There is also the issue of what kind of public spaces and values we want to make available, outside of those provided by the market, for children to gain the knowledge, skills, and experiences they need to confront the myriad problems facing the twenty-first century. The road to recovery cannot be simply about returning to modified free-market capitalism and a reestablished, utterly bankrupt consumer society. Given all the pain and suffering that the vast majority of Americans have endured, we should ask ourselves if there is a teachable moment here. What kind of society and future do we want for our children given how obviously unsustainable and exploitative the now-failed market-driven system has proved to be?

In a society that measures its success and failure solely through the economic lens of the gross national product (GNP), it becomes difficult to define youth outside of market principles determined largely by criteria such as the rate of market growth and the accumulation of capital. The value and worth of young people in this discourse are largely determined through the bottom-line cost-benefit categories of income, expenses, assets, and liabilities. The GNP does not measure justice, integrity, courage, compassion, wisdom, and learning, among other values vital to the interests and health of a democratic society. Nor does the GNP address the importance of civic literacy, social responsibility, a critically engaged citizenry, public goods, and the fostering of democratic institutions. In a society driven entirely by market mentalities, moralities, values, and ideals, consuming, selling, and branding become the primary modes through which to define agency and social relations—intimate and public—and to shape the sensibilities and inner lives of adults as well as how society defines and treats its children.

Even though the "empire of consumption" has been around for a long time,[1] American society in the last thirty years has undergone a sea change in the daily lives of children—one marked by a major transition from a culture of innocence and social protection, however imperfect, to a culture of commodification. This is culture that does more than undermine the ideals of a secure and happy childhood; it also exhibits the bad faith of a society in which, for children, "there can be only one kind of value, market value; one kind of success, profit; one kind of existence, commodities; and one kind of social relationship, markets."[2] Children now inhabit a cultural landscape in which they can recognize themselves only in terms preferred by the market.

Subject to an advertising and marketing industry that spends more than $17 billion a year on shaping children's identities and desires,[3] American youth are commercially carpet bombed through a never-ending proliferation of market strategies that colonize their consciousness and daily lives. Multibillion-dollar corporations, with the commanding role of commodity markets as well as the support of the highest reaches of government, now become the primary educational and cultural force in shaping, if not hijacking, how young people define their interests, values, and relations to others. Juliet Schor, one of the most insightful and critical theorists of the commodification of children, argues that "these corporations not only have enormous economic power, but their political influence has never been greater. They have funneled unprecedented sums of money to political parties and officials.... The power wielded by these corporations is evident in many ways, from their ability to eliminate competitors to their ability to mobilize state power in their interest."[4]

As the sovereignty of the market displaces state sovereignty, children are no longer viewed as an important social investment or as a central marker for the moral life of the nation. Instead, childhood ideals linked to the protection and well-being of youth are transformed—decoupled from the "call to conscience [and] civic engagement" and redefined through what amounts to a culture of cruelty, abandonment, and disposability.[5] Childhood ideals increasingly give way to a market-driven politics in which young people are prepared for a life of objectification while simultaneously drained of any viable sense of moral and political agency. Moreover, as the economy implodes, the financial sector is racked by corruption and usury, the housing and mortgage markets are in free fall, and millions of people lose their jobs, the targeting of children for profits takes on even more insistent and ominous tones. This is especially true in a consumer society in which children more than ever mediate their identities and relations to others through the consumption of goods and images. No longer imagined within the language of responsibility and justice, childhood begins with what might be called the scandalous philosophy of money—that is, a logic in which everything, including the worth of young people, is measured through the potentially barbaric calculations of finance, exchange value, and profitability. And this is part of the economic crisis that is barely mentioned in the mainstream media.

What is distinctive about this period in history is that the United States has become the most consumer-oriented society in the world. Kids and teens, because of their value as consumers and their ability to influence spending, are not only at "the epicenter of American consumer culture" but are also the major targets of those powerful marketing and financial forces that service big corporations and the corporate state.[6] In a world in which products far outnumber shoppers, youth have been unearthed not simply as another expansive and profitable market but also as the primary source of redemption for the future of capitalism—even as it implodes. Erased as future citizens of a democracy, kids are now constructed as consuming and salable objects. New Gilded Age corporations, however devalued, and their army of marketers, psychologists, and advertising executives now engage in what Susan Linn calls a "hostile takeover of childhood,"[7] poised to take advantage of the economic power wielded by kids and teens. With spending power increasing to match that of adults, the children's market has greatly expanded in the last few decades in terms of both direct spending by kids and their influence on parental acquisitions.

Although figures on direct spending by kids differ, Benjamin Barber claims that "in 2000, there were 31 million American kids between twelve and nineteen already controlling $155 billion consumer dollars. Just four years later, there were 33.5 million kids controlling $169 billion, or roughly $91 per week per kid."[8] Alex Molnar and Faith Boninger cite figures indicating that preteens and teenagers command "$200 billion in spending power."[9] Schor argues that "children age four to twelve made ... $30.0 billion" in purchases in 2002, while kids aged twelve to nineteen "accounted for $170 billion of personal spending."[10] Young people are attractive to corporations because they are big spenders, but that is not the only reason. They also exert a powerful influence on parental spending, offering up a market in which, according to Anup Shah, "children (under 12) and teens influence parental purchases totaling over ... $670 billion a year."[11]

One measure of the corporate assault on kids can be seen in the reach, acceleration, and effectiveness of a marketing and advertising juggernaut that attempts to turn kids into consumers and childhood into a salable commodity. Every child, regardless of how young, is now a potential consumer ripe for being commodified and immersed in a commercial culture defined by brands. According to Lawrence Grossberg, children are introduced to the world of logos, advertising, and the "mattering maps" of consumerism long before they can speak: "Capitalism targets kids as soon as they are old enough to watch commercials, even though they may not be old enough to distinguish programming from commercials or to recognize the effects of branding and product placement."[12] In fact, American children from birth to adulthood are exposed to a consumer blitz of advertising, marketing, education, and entertainment that has no historical precedent. There is even a market for videos for toddlers as young as four months. One such baby video, called *Baby Gourmet*, alleges to "provide a multi-sensory experience for children designed to introduce little ones to beautiful fruits and vegetables ... in a gentle and amusing way that stimulates both the left and right hemispheres."[13] This would be humorous if Madison Avenue were not deadly serious in its attempts to sell this type of hype—along with other baby brands such as *Baby Einstein, Brainy Baby, Sesame Street Baby*, and Disney's *Winnie the Pooh Baby*—to parents eager to provide their children with every conceivable advantage over the rest. Not surprisingly, this is part of a growing $4.8 billion market aimed at the youngest children.[14] Schor captures perfectly the omnipotence of this machinery of consumerism as it envelops the lives of very young children:

At age one, she's watching *Teletubbies* and eating the food of its "promo partners" Burger King and McDonald's. Kids can recognize logos by eighteen months, and before reaching their second birthday, they're asking for products by brand name. By three or three and a half, experts say, children start to believe that brands communicate their personal qualities, for example, that they're cool, or strong, or smart. Even before starting school, the likelihood of having a television in their bedroom is 25 percent, and their viewing time is just over two hours a day. Upon arrival at the schoolhouse steps, the typical first grader can evoke 200 brands. And he or she has already accumulated an unprecedented number of possessions, beginning with an average of seventy new toys a year.[15]

Complicit, wittingly or unwittingly, with a politics defined by market power, the American public offers little resistance to children's culture being expropriated and colonized by Madison Avenue advertisers. Eager to enthral kids with invented fears and lacks, these advertisers also entice them with equally unimagined new desires to prod them into spending money or to influence their parents to spend it in order to fill corporate coffers. Every child is vulnerable to the many advertisers who diversify markets through various niches, one of which is based on age. For example, the DVD industry sees toddlers as a lucrative market. Toy manufacturers now target children from birth to ten years of age. Children aged eight to twelve constitute a tween market and teens an additional one. Children visit stores and malls long before they enter elementary school, and children as young as eight make visits to malls without adults. Disney, Nickelodeon, and other megacompanies now provide Web sites such as "Pirates of the Caribbean" for children under ten years of age, luring them into a virtual world of potential consumers that reached 8.2 million players in 2007; this electronic mall is predicted to include 20 million children by 2011.[16] Moreover, as Brook Barnes points out in the *New York Times*, these electronic malls are hardly being used for either innocent entertainment or educational purposes. On the contrary, she states, "media conglomerates in particular think these sites—part online role-playing game and part social scene—can deliver quick growth, help keep movie franchises alive and instill brand loyalty in a generation of new customers."[17]

Using the new media and eye-catching graphics, companies often promote their products directly to children "without the knowledge of parents."[18] For instance, the food industry spends millions of dollars on digital marketing campaigns conducted through the

Internet, cell phones, flashy video games, and social networking sites in order to market junk food to children that includes everything from sugary drinks and calorie-laden candies to fat-laden meals. In this instance, matters of profit and fealty to the bottom line trump the health danger—such as diabetes and obesity—these products pose to the lives of young people. But there is more at stake here than making money, endangering the health and lives of young people, and promoting brand loyalty among young children. There is also the construction of particular modes of subjectivity, identification, and agency organized around market-based values and an endless desire to consume.

Some of these identities are on full display in advertising aimed at young girls. Market strategists are increasingly using sexually charged images to sell commodities, often representing the fantasies of an adult version of sexuality. For instance, Abercrombie & Fitch, a clothing franchise for young people, has earned a reputation for its risqué catalogs filled with promotional ads of scantily clad kids and its over-the-top sexual advice columns for teens and preteens; one catalog featured an ad for thongs for ten-year-olds with the words "eye candy" and "wink wink" written on them.[19] Another clothing store sold underwear geared toward teens with "'Who needs Credit Cards ... ?' written across the crotch."[20] Children as young as six are being sold lacy underwear, push-up bras, and "date night accessories" for their various doll collections. In 2006, the Tesco department store chain sold a pole-dancing kit designed for young girls to unleash the sex kitten inside. Encouraging five- to ten-year-old children to model themselves after sex workers suggests the degree to which matters of ethics and propriety have been decoupled from the world of marketing and advertising, even when the target audience is young children. The representational politics at work in these marketing and advertising strategies connects children to a reductive notion of sexuality, pleasure, and commodification, while depicting children's sexuality and bodies as nothing more than objects for voyeuristic adult consumption and crude financial profit.

For the last few decades, critics such as Thomas Frank, Kevin Phillips, and David Harvey have warned us, and rightly so, that right-wing conservatives and free-market fundamentalists have been dismantling government by selling it off to the highest or "friendliest" bidder. But what they have not recognized adequately is that what has also been sold off are our children and our collective future, and that the consequences of this catastrophe can be understood only within the larger framework of a politics and market philosophy that views children as commodities and democracy as the enemy. In a democracy, education in any sphere—whether it be the public schools or the larger media—is, or should be, utterly averse to treating young people as individual units of economic potential and as walking commodities. And it is crucial not to "forget" that democracy should not be confused with hypercapitalism, a lesson that seems to be lost on President Barack Obama and his coterie of neoliberal economic advisers. Obama has no trouble in bailing out the banks, but there will be no efforts to bail out kids subjected to a daily onslaught of the very values that caused the worst economic crisis since the Great Depression of the 1930s.

Inevitably, humans must consume to survive. The real enemy is not consumption per se, but a market-driven consumer society fueled by the endless cycle of acquisition, waste, and disposability, which is at the heart of an unchecked and deregulated global capitalism. Under such circumstances, there are few remaining spaces in which to imagine a mode of consumption that rejects the logic of commodification and embraces the principles of sustainability while expanding the reach and possibilities of a substantive democracy. Schor touches on this issue by rightly arguing that the real issue is "what kind of consumers do we want to be?"[21] Or to put the matter more broadly, What kind of society and world do we want to live in? As politics embraces all aspects of children's lives, it is crucial to make clear that the rising tide of free markets has less to do with ensuring democracy and freedom than with spreading a reign of terror around the globe, affecting the most vulnerable populations in the cruelest ways. The politics of commodification and its underlying logic of waste and disposability do irreparable harm to children, but the resulting material, psychological, and spiritual injuries they incur must be understood not merely as a political and economic issue but also as a pedagogical concern.

At the same time, simply criticizing the market, the privatization of public goods, and the commercialization of children, although helpful, is not enough. Stirring denunciations of what a market society does to kids do not go far enough. What is equally necessary is developing public spaces and social movements that help young people develop healthy notions of self, identities, and visions of their future no longer defined—or, to put it more accurately, defiled—by market values and mentalities. In part, this means dismantling those capitalist structures that undermine democratic values, subordinate social needs to profit margins, and corrupt the political system with inordinate amounts of power and wealth. The current system in which the ideology of free markets combines with a ruthless economic Darwinism has little to do with the needs of children and a great deal to do with a survival-of-the-fittest view of the world. Under the current regime of neoliberal economics, children lack power and any viable sense of agency and are increasingly viewed as either commodities or disposable beings.

Obama's road to recovery must align itself with a vision of a democracy that is on the side of children, particularly young children in need. It must enable the conditions for youth to learn, to "grow," as John Dewey once insisted, as engaged social actors more alive to their responsibilities to future generations than contemporary adult society has proved itself to be.[22] Such a project requires constructing a politics that refuses to be animated by populist rage so easily misdirected, or by a disdain for the social state, mutuality, reciprocity, and compassion, among other democratic values. In short, this project must reject a society whose essence is currently reflected in the faces of children compelled to confront a future that as yet offers very little hope of happiness or even survival.

Chapter 4
Disney, Casino Capitalism, and the Stealing of Childhood Innocence

↪

The right-wing claim that President Barack Obama is a socialist flies in the face of an interview he gave to John Harwood on CNBC in which he declared, "Look, I am a pro-growth, free-market guy.... I love the market."[1] Unfortunately, his love of the market has not been matched by a thoroughgoing concern for the negative consequence of market-driven values, relations, and practices on young people. He has, of course, been forced to level criticisms at those freewheeling and largely unregulated banking, insurance, and investment industries that occupy commanding heights in the age of casino capitalism. The Bush administration's exuberant embrace of market fundamentalism intensified an economic tsunami and a political crisis that the Obama administration cannot ignore, regardless of Obama's romance with neoliberal capitalism. One suggestion for tempering his embrace of the market is for his administration to think seriously about the impact casino capitalism has on children, especially in terms of the market-driven values and commodified identities it produces. One corporation, despite its purchase on innocence, that provides an exemplary model for such an analysis is the Disney Corporation.

Casino capitalism may be getting a bad rap in the mainstream media, but the values that nourish it are alive and well in the world of Disney.[2] As reported in a front-page article in the *New York Times*,

Disney is at the forefront of finding ways to capitalize on the $50 billion spent worldwide by young boys between the ages of six and fourteen.[3] As part of such efforts, Disney has enlisted the help of educators, anthropologists, and a former researcher with "a background in the casino industry" to study all aspects of the culture and intimate lives of young boys and to do so in a way that allows Disney to produce "emotional hooks" that lure young boys into the wonderful world of corporate Disney in order to turn them into enthusiastic consumers.[4]

The potential for lucrative profits to be made off the spending habits and economic influence of kids has certainly not been lost on Disney and a number of other multinational corporations, which under the deregulated, privatized, no-holds-barred world of the free market have set out to embed the dynamics of commerce, exchange value, and commercial transactions into every aspect of personal and daily life. If Disney had its way, kids' culture would become not merely a new market for the accumulation of capital but also a petri dish for producing new commodified subjects. As a group, young people are vulnerable to corporate giants such as Disney, which makes every effort "to expand 'inwardly' into the psyche and emotional life of the individual in order to utilize human potential" in the service of a market society.[5] Children's identities have to be actively directed toward the role of consumers, which means that knowledge, information, entertainment, and cultural pedagogy become central in shaping and influencing every waking moment of children's daily lives. Disney, with its legion of media holdings, armies of marketers, and omnipresent advertisers, sets out not just to exploit young boys and other youth for profit; it also actually constructs them as commodities—promoting the concept of childhood as a salable commodity.

What is particularly disturbing in this scenario is that Disney and a growing number of marketers and advertisers now work with child psychologists and other experts who study young people in order to better understand children's culture so as to develop marketing methods that are more camouflaged, seductive, and successful. For example, Disney's recent attempts to "figure out the boys' entertainment market" includes the services of Kelly Pena, described as "the kid whisperer," who in an attempt to understand what makes young boys tick uses her anthropological skills to convince young boys and their parents to allow her to look into kids' closets, go shopping with young boys, and pay them $75 to be interviewed. Pena, with no irony intended, prides herself on the fact that "children ... open up to her."[6] Several psychologists, especially Allen D. Kanner, have publicly criticized such disingenuous practices.[7]

Wrapping itself up in the discourse of innocence and family-oriented amusement in order to camouflage the mechanisms and deployment of corporate power, Disney relentlessly uses its various entertainment platforms, which cut across all forms of traditional and new media, in the search for younger customers and in the incessant bombarding of young people with the pedagogy of commerce.[8] As my coauthor, Grace Pollock, and I explore in detail in *The Mouse That Roared: Disney and the End of Innocence*,[9] children under the tutelage of Disney and other megacorporations are no longer simply a captive audience to traditional forms of media, such as television, film, and print. In recent years, they have become even more enthralled by new media, such as mobile phones, MP3 players, the Internet, computers, and other forms of electronic culture that now seem to provide the latest products at the speed of light. Kids can download enormous amounts of media in seconds and carry around such information, images, and videos in a device the size of a thin cigarette lighter. Moreover, "[media] technologies themselves are morphing and merging, forming an ever-expanding presence throughout our daily environment."[10] Mobile phones alone have grown "to include video game platforms, e-mail devices, digital cameras, and Internet connections," making it easier for marketers and advertisers to reach young people.[11] Kids of all ages now find themselves in what the Berkeley Media Studies Group and the Center for Digital Democracy call "a new 'marketing ecosystem' that encompasses cell phones, mobile music devices, broadband video, instant messaging, video games, and virtual three-dimensional worlds," all of which provide the knowledge and information that young people use to navigate consumer society.[12]

Disney, along with its researchers, marketing departments, and purveyors of commerce, largely controls and services this massive virtual entertainment complex, spending vast amounts of time trying to understand the needs, desires, tastes, preferences, social relations, and networks that define youth as a potential market. Disney's recent attempt to corner the young male market through the use of sophisticated research models, ethnographic tools, and the expertise of academics indicates the degree to which the language of the market has disengaged itself from either moral considerations or the social good. Disney claims this kind of intensive research pays off in lucrative dividends and reinforces the Disney motto that in order to be a successful company, "you have to start with the kids themselves."[13] One example of this type of marketing can be seen in Disney's plan to reboot its 340 stores in the United States and Europe. The new stores will no longer simply stack endless rows of Disney merchandise; they will also become high-tech entertainment centers focusing on interactive technology. As reported in the *New York Times*, "The goal is to make children clamor to visit the stores and stay longer, perhaps bolstering sales as a result."[14] Of course, under the guise of entertainment Disney will expand its $30 billion in global sales for 2008 as well as use its interactive technology to seduce, influence, and produce another generation of young people who will believe that such technologies are simply about shopping and consuming. Dressing up Disney stores as entertainment centers indicates how far the Disney Corporation will go to colonize the minds and empty the bank accounts of children and their parents.

Children are increasingly exposed to a marketing and advertising pedagogical machinery eager and ready to transform them into full-fledged members of consumer society. And the amount of time they spend in this commercial world defined by Disney and a few other corporations is as breathtaking as it is disturbing. For instance, "it has been estimated that the typical child sees about 40,000 ads a year on TV alone," and that by the time they enter the fourth grade, they have "memorized 300–400 brands."[15] In 2005, the Kaiser Family Foundation reported that young people are "exposed to the equivalent of 8½ hours a day of media content ... [and that] the typical 8–18 year-old lives in a home with an average of 3.6 CD or tape players, 3.5 TVs, 3.3 radios, 2.0 VCRs/DVD players, 2.1 video game consoles, and 1.5 computers."[16] In the synoptic world of ads and marketing practices, the project of commercializing and commodifying children is ubiquitous and can be found wherever a previously noncommodified space existed. Hence, it comes as no surprise to find ads, logos, and other products of the marketing juggernaut pasted on school walls, public buildings, and public transportation systems, in textbooks and public washrooms, and even on baseball diamonds.

Given Disney's powerful role in monopolizing all modes of communication, especially those that are media driven, the company exercises a highly disproportionate concentration of control over the means of producing, circulating, and exchanging information, especially to kids. By spreading ideology all over the globe through film, television, satellite broadcasting technologies, the Internet, posters, magazines, billboards, newspapers, videos, and other media forms and technologies, Disney has transformed culture into a pivotal educational force. Through this insidious form of public pedagogy, Disney commercializes and infantilizes most of what it touches, while further shutting down those public spaces where kids can learn noncommodified values. Pixie-dust magic may appeal to the world of fantasy, but it offers no language for defining vital social institutions as a public good, links all dreams to the logic of the market, and harnesses the imagination to forces of unfettered consumerism. Whether talking about the United States or other parts of the globe, we can argue that for the first time in human history centralized commercially driven conglomerates hold sway over the stories and narratives that shape children's lives. Unfortunately, this rather sublime education—increasingly derived from unethical modes of research—is absorbed by kids and adults as entertainment and too often escapes any criticism or self-reflection.

The disconnect between market values and ethical considerations is on full display in Disney's almost boastful use of research to mine the inner lives and experiences of young children. That such an admission receives uncritical, front-page coverage in the *New York Times* is a testament to how commercial values have numbed the public's ability to recognize the danger such values often present to children. Questioning the meaning, legacy, and ideology of the Disney empire is part of a larger challenge to the emergence of free-market fundamentalism as both an economic model and a form of public pedagogy that disavows public life and any notion of a democratic future for young people. Getting beyond Disney means, in part, theorizing children as a social investment and democracy as a process and a promise, rather than a fantasy world in which pixie dust and mass entertainment cover up the swindle of fulfillment and joy that Disney offers in its endless appeal to consumerism.

As citizenship becomes increasingly privatized and youth more and more are educated to become consuming subjects rather than civic-minded and critical citizens, it becomes all the more imperative for people everywhere to develop a critical language in which notions of the public good, public issues, and public life become central to overcoming the privatizing and depoliticizing language of the market. Disney, like many corporations, trades in sound bytes. The result is that the choices, exclusions, and values that inform its narratives about joy, pleasure, living, and survival in a global world are often difficult to discern. Disney needs to be addressed within a widening circle of awareness, so that we can place the history, meaning, and influence of the Disney empire outside of enforced horizons and confinements that often shut down critique and critical engagement with Disney's commercial carpet bombing of children.

All of us who participate in the Disneyfication of culture need to excavate the silences, memories, and exclusions that challenge the identities offered to young people by Disney under the name of innocence, nationalism, and entertainment. As one of the most influential corporations in the world, Disney does more than provide entertainment; it also shapes in very powerful ways how young people understand themselves, relate to others, and experience the larger society. We can easily see a certain tragedy in the fact that because of a lack of resources, kids disappear literally in foster care institutions, teachers are overwhelmed in overcrowded classrooms, and state services are drained of funds and cannot provide basic food and shelter to the growing numbers of kids who now inhabit rapidly emerging tent cities. Yet corporations such as Disney have ample funds to hire a battalion of highly educated and specialized experts to infiltrate the most intimate spaces of children and family life—all the better to colonize the fears, aspirations, and future of young people and to commodify the netherworld of childhood. Disney's commodification of childhood is neither innocent nor simply entertaining, and the values it produces as it attempts to commandeer children's desires and hopes may offer us one of the most important clues about the nature and destructive forces behind the current economic and financial crisis. But do not expect the Obama administration to soon launch a congressional hearing on this issue.

Chapter 5
Ten Years After Columbine
The Deepening Tragedy of Youth

For young people, it just keeps getting worse. Ten years after the Columbine tragedy, the debate over school safety has clearly shown that educators, parents, politicians, and the mainstream media have created the conditions in which young people have increasingly become the victims of adult mistreatment, indifference, neglect, even violence. The tragic shootings at Columbine High School on April 20, 1999, seem to fix in time and space an image of children as violent, as a threat to public safety, and as increasingly in need of surveillance, policing, and containment. How children experience, resist, challenge, and mediate the complex culture, politics, and social spaces that mark their everyday lives do not seem to warrant the attention such issues deserve, especially in light of the ongoing assaults on minority youth of color and class that have taken place following the Columbine killing spree. Rather than giving rise to a concern for young people, Columbine helped to put into place the development of a youth control complex in which crime became the fundamental axis through which kids' lives are both defined and monitored, while the militarization of schools became the order of the day.

One major effect of the Columbine tragedy can be seen in the increasingly popular practice of organizing schools through disciplinary practices that closely resemble the culture of prisons.[1]

For instance, many public schools, traditionally viewed as nurturing, youth-friendly spaces dedicated to protecting and educating children, have become one of the most punitive institutions young people now face—on a daily basis. Educating for informed citizenship, work, and the public good has been replaced with models of schooling in which students are viewed narrowly either as threats or perpetrators of violence, on the one hand, or as infantilized potential victims of crime (on the Internet, at school, and in other youth spheres) who must endure modes of governing that are demeaning and repressive, on the other. Jonathan Simon captures this transformation of schools from a public good to a security risk in the following comment:

> Today, in the United States, it is crime that dominates the symbolic passageway to school and citizenship. And behind this surface, the pathways of knowledge and power within the school are increasingly being shaped by crime as the model problem, and tools of criminal justice as the dominant technologies. Through the introduction of police, probation officers, prosecutors, and a host of private security professionals into the schools, new forms of expertise now openly compete with pedagogic knowledge and authority for shaping routines and rituals of schools.... At its core, the implicit fallacy dominating many school policy debates today consists of a gross conflation of virtually all the vulnerabilities of children and youth into variations on the theme of crime. This may work to raise the salience of education on the public agenda, but at the cost to students of an education embedded with themes of "accountability," "zero tolerance," and "norm shaping."[2]

As *New York Times* op-ed writer Bob Herbert points out, "School officials and the criminal justice system are criminalizing children and teenagers all over the country, arresting them and throwing them in jail for behavior that in years past would have never have led to the intervention of law enforcement."[3] Young people are being ushered "into the bowels of police precincts and jail cells" for minor offenses, which Herbert argues "is a problem that has gotten out of control.... Especially as zero-tolerance policies proliferate, children are being treated like criminals."[4] Sociologist Randall Beger writes that the new security culture in schools comes with an emphasis on "barbed-wire security fences, banned book bags and pagers ... 'lock down drills' and 'SWAT team' rehearsals."[5] As the logic of the market and "the crime complex" frame a number of social actions in schools, students are subjected to a growing security apparatus in which youth are increasingly treated as criminals and in which a culture of fear, surveillance, and social control that undermines schools as sites of critical learning and spaces of safety prevails.[6]

Once seen as an invaluable public good and laboratory for critical learning and engaged citizenship, public schools in the aftermath of Columbine have been increasingly viewed as sites of potential violence and redefined as containment centers—when not simply warehousing poor youth of color who are often considered utterly disposable. Consequently, students have been redefined through the optic of crime as populations to be managed and controlled primarily by security forces. In accordance with this perception of students as potential criminals and the school as a site of disorder and delinquency, schools across the country since the 1980s, but especially in light of the Columbine and the Virginia Tech massacres, have implemented zero tolerance policies that involve the automatic imposition of severe penalties for first offenses of a wide range of undesirable, but often harmless, behaviors.[7] Based on the assumption that schools are rife with crime and fueled by the emergence of a number of state and federal laws, mandatory sentencing legislation, and the popular "three strikes and you're out" policy, many educators first invoked zero tolerance rules against kids who brought firearms to schools.

In the aftermath of Columbine, exacerbated by a number of high-profile school shootings in last decade and an increase in the climate of fear, the assumption that schools were dealing with a new breed of student—violent, amoral, and apathetic—began to take hold in the public imagination. Moreover, as school safety became a top educational priority, zero tolerance policies were broadened; they now include a range of behavioral infractions from possessing drugs or weapons to threatening other students—all broadly conceived. Under zero tolerance policies, forms of punishments that were once applied to adults are now applied to first graders. The punitive nature of such policies is on display in a number of cases in which students have had to face harsh penalties that defy human compassion and reason. For example, an eight-year-old boy in the first grade at a Miami Elementary School took a table knife to his school, using it to rob a classmate of $1 in lunch money. School officials claimed he was facing "possible expulsion and charges of armed robbery."[8] In another instance that took place in December 2004, "Porsche, a fourth-grade student at a Philadelphia, PA, elementary school, was yanked out of class, handcuffed, taken to the police station and held for eight hours for bringing a pair of 8-inch scissors to school. She had been using the scissors to work on a school project at home. School district officials acknowledged that the young girl was not using the scissors as a weapon or threatening anyone with them, but scissors qualified as a potential weapon under state law."[9] It gets worse. Adopting a rigidly authoritarian zero tolerance school discipline policy, Chicago Public Schools signaled both bad faith and terrible judgment on the part of educators implementing these practices in the following incident: "In February 2003, a 7-year-old boy was cuffed, shackled, and forced to lie face down for more than an hour while being restrained by a security officer at Parker Community Academy on the Southwest Side. Neither the principal nor the assistant principal came to the aid of the first grader, who was so traumatized by the event he was not able to return to school."[10]

Traditionally, students who violated school rules and the rights of others were sent to the principal, guidance counselor, or another teacher. Corrective discipline in most cases was a matter of judgment and deliberation generally handled within the school by the appropriate administrator or teacher. Under such circumstances, young people could defend themselves, the context of their rule violation was explored (including underlying issues, such as problems at home, that may have triggered the behavior in the first place), and the discipline they received was suited to the nature of the offense. Today, as school districts link up with law enforcement agencies and private security agencies, young people find themselves not only being expelled or suspended in record rates but also being "subject to citations or arrests and referrals to juvenile or criminal courts."[11] Students who break even minor rules, such as pouring a glass of milk on another student or engaging in a school yard fight, have been removed from the normal school population, handed over to armed police, arrested, handcuffed, shoved into patrol cars, taken to jail, fingerprinted, and subjected to the harsh dictates of the juvenile and criminal justice systems. As Bernadine Dohrn points out: "Today, behaviors that were once punished or sanctioned by the school vice-principal, family members, a neighbor, or a coach are more likely to lead to an adolescent being arrested, referred to juvenile or criminal court, formally adjudicated, incarcerated in a detention center, waived or transferred to adult criminal court for trial, sentenced under mandatory sentencing guidelines, and incarcerated with adults."[12]

The horror that the Columbine tragedy legitimately produced, when mediated through a culture of fear fueled in large part through the war on terror, worked against, rather than in the interests of, kids, especially poor youth of color.[13] This legacy is obvious today in the way in which educators and policymakers think about children. What we have seen in the last ten years is a shift in discourse and policies from one of hope to punishment, a shift most evident in the effects of zero tolerance policies, which criminalize student behavior in ways that take an incalculable toll on their lives and their future. For example, between 2000 and 2004 Denver Public Schools experienced a 71 percent increase in the number of student referrals to law enforcement, many for nonviolent behaviors. The Chicago school system in 2003 had more than eight thousand students arrested, often for trivial infractions such as pushing, being late, and using spitballs. As part of a human waste management system, zero tolerance policies have been responsible for suspending and expelling black students in record high numbers. For instance, "in 2000, Blacks were 17 percent of public school enrollment nationwide and 34 percent of suspensions."[14]

And when poor black youth are not being suspended under the merger of school security and law and order policies, they are increasingly at risk of falling into the school-to-prison pipeline. As the Advancement Project points out, the racial disparities in school suspensions, expulsions, and arrests feed and mirror similar disparities in the juvenile and criminal justice systems: "In 2002, Black youths made up 16% of the juvenile population but were 43% of juvenile arrests, while White youths were 78% of the juvenile population but 55% of juvenile arrests. Further, in 2008, minority youths accounted for 39% of the U.S. juvenile population but 60% of the youths in juvenile facilities." Because higher rates of suspensions and expulsions are likely to lead to higher rates of juvenile incarceration, "Black and Latino youths are disproportionately represented among young people held in juvenile prisons."[15]

Given that so many young people are being pushed out of school, it is not surprising that the incarceration rates for poor minority youth are being fed by this dangerous trend. For instance, a recent study from Northeastern University stated that "on any given day, about one in every 10 young male high school dropouts is in jail or juvenile detention, compared with one in 35 young male high school graduates.... The picture is even bleaker for African-Americans, with nearly one in four young black male dropouts incarcerated or otherwise institutionalized on an average day.... That compares with about one in 14 young, male, white, Asian or Hispanic dropouts."[16]

The city of Chicago, which has a large black student population, implemented a take-no-prisoners approach in its use of zero tolerance policies, and the racially skewed consequences are visible in grim statistics that reveal that "every day, on average, more than 266 suspensions are doled out ... during the school year."[17] Moreover, the number of expulsions has "mushroomed from 32 in 1995 to 3000 in the school year 2003–2004," most affecting poor black youth.[18]

In the aftermath of Columbine, a culture of fear, crime, and repression has come to dominate American public schools, just as the culture of schooling is reconfigured through the allocation of resources used primarily to hire more police, security staff, and technologies of control and surveillance. In some cases, schools such as the Palm Beach County system have established their own police departments. Saturating schools with police and security personnel and creating militarized models of schooling have created a host of problems for schools, teachers, and students—not to mention that such policies tap into financial resources otherwise used for actually enhancing learning. In many cases, the police and security guards assigned to schools are not properly trained to deal with students and often use their authority in ways that extend far beyond what is either reasonable or legal.

Rather than using Columbine for a national dialogue on the declining state and welfare of young people and what it might mean to make their lives more secure, the U.S. government expanded its use of domestic terrorism, and young people and schools became a prime target in that ongoing war. Since Columbine, student rights have been undercut by federal policies and judicial decisions. Free speech and privacy rights are increasingly undercut as schools reduce students to the status of potential criminals. One example of the war on terror tactics used domestically and directly affecting schools and the civil rights of students can be seen in the use of the roving metal detector program in which the police arrive at a school unannounced and submit all students to metal detector scans. In *Criminalizing the Classroom*, Elora Mukherjee describes some of the disruptions caused by the program in New York City: "As soon as it was implemented, the program began to cause chaos and lost instructional time at targeted schools, each morning transforming an ordinary city school into a massive police encampment with dozens of police vehicles, as many as sixty SSAs [school security agents] and NYPD [New York Police Department] officers, and long lines of students waiting to pass through the detectors to get to class."[19]

Under such circumstances, schools begin to take on the obscene and violent contours of maximum security prisons: unannounced locker searches, armed police patrolling the corridors, mandatory drug testing, and the ever-present phalanx of lockdown security devices such as metal detectors, X-ray machines, surveillance cameras, and other technologies of fear and control. School drug policies have become so draconian that in a recent case an assistant principal in a Safford, Arizona, school, suspecting that an eighth-grade student had brought prescription grade ibuprofen to school, had the thirteen-year-old girl pulled out of a math class so that an administrative aide and school nurse could conduct a strip search on her. The girl later dropped out of the school, claiming that she felt humiliated and pointing out that after they had "stripped her to her underwear, [they] 'asked me to pull out my bra and move it from side to side. . . . They made me open my legs and pull out my underwear.'"[20] In this context, student rights become meaningless. Appreciated less for their capacity to be educated than for the threat they pose to adults, students are now treated as if they were inmates, often humiliated, detained, searched, and, in some cases, arrested. Beger is right in suggesting that the new "security culture in public schools [has] turned them into 'learning prisons' where the students unwittingly become 'guinea pigs' to test the latest security devices."[21]

Poor black and Latino male youth are particularly at risk from punitive modes of control as they are the primary object of racist stereotypes and of a range of disciplinary policies that criminalize their behavior.[22] Such youth, increasingly viewed as burdensome and dispensable, now bear the brunt of these assaults by being expelled from schools, tried in the criminal justice system as adults, and arrested and jailed at rates that far exceed those of their white counterparts.[23] Although black children make up only 15 percent of the juvenile population in the United States, they account for 46 percent of those put behind bars and 52 percent of those whose cases end up in adult criminal courts. Shockingly, in the land of the free and the home of the brave, a "jail or detention cell after a child or youth gets into trouble is the only universally guaranteed child policy in America."[24]

Public debate has consistently ignored the most pressing questions to be raised post-Columbine, preferring the superfluous and colorfully carnevalesque accusations against a host of alleged villains, from working mothers to rock icons, the Internet, and video gaming. As David Sirota points out, why are we "surprised that Columbine-like shootings are still happening, or even that our national discussion about violence hasn't yet matured past gun control and video games?"[25] Why is it that there is almost no connection being made between Columbine-like shootings and the values and practices of an economy that operates from a winner-take-all ethos, produces massive inequality in wages and wealth, disinvests in schools and health care, destroys the welfare state, supports torture as state policy, rules society through a culture of fear and insecurity, and turns violence into a commodified spectacle. Most importantly, what is it about the nature of American society that in the face of such a tragedy produces policies and practices that further punish, rather than aid, young people? Given the horrible suffering experienced by young people at Columbine High School, how was it possible for politicians, school officials, and law enforcement to react in ways that vilify future generations by viewing them as a threat to society rather than asking about larger economic, political, and social forces in the fabric of American life that subject so many young people to various forms of violence, abuse, and hatred?

Sadly, what we have learned in the wake of the Columbine tragedy is that children have sunk to our lowest national priority, most evident in the social policies that have shifted from one of social investment to a politics of containment and criminalization.[26] The aftermath of the Columbine tragedy does not simply reflect the loss of social vision, the ongoing privatization and corporatization of public space, and the inevitable erosion of democratic life that results. It also suggests the degree to which children have been "othered" across a wide range of ideological positions, deemed unworthy of serious analysis as an oppressed group—posited no longer as *at risk* but as *the risk* to democratic public life. Fear, indifference, and demonization share an unholy alliance in the willful refusal to foreground the increasing precariousness—materially, economically, socially—of children's lives, especially when one in four children is on food stamps and the American economy appears broken and dysfunctional. Media panics that incessantly and falsely suggest that schools are more violent and students more dangerous undermine the urgent political task of focusing on the role that young people can play in shaping a future that will not be simply a repeat of the present, in which children increasingly count less as valuable resources than as a financial drain and pervasive danger to adult society. Maybe the time has come to stop simply replaying the heart-pounding video footage that is tragically reduced to spectacle in the absence of any thoughtful critique. Bob Herbert is right in insisting that "we have an obligation and an opportunity at this special moment in history to do [the right thing] for America's kids. It's a special moment because we've seen so clearly the many things that have gone haywire in the society, and while it may not be easy to articulate, we have a sense of what needs to be done."[27]

Surely, the one thing that can be done ten years after Columbine is to ask ourselves about the failure of American society to take responsibility for its children and about what it might mean to protect and nourish young people rather than treat them as a generation of suspects.

Chapter 6
Child Beauty Pageants
A Scene from the "Other America"

⊸

Mark Shultz's play *The Gingerbread House* operates from the absurd and repulsive assumption that when kids start to become a burden, one option is to treat them as a commodity and simply sell them. In this case, Stacy and Brian, a young married couple, want to start their lives over, free of the endless time, money, and responsibilities that are part of rearing their two young children. As Brian puts it: "We can start our lives again.... We can have it back. All of it."[1] To act on their quest for personal happiness, they decide to traffic their children for the right price to an Albanian couple, freeing themselves to indulge their private aims, joys, desires, and goals. Although Shultz is clearly making a critical statement about the selfish market-driven values that shape our highly individualized and self-seeking commodified age, he has hit upon a repellent conceit that finds everyday expression in the dreadful emergence and popularity of child beauty pageants.

These pageants gain legitimacy within the context of what might be called the "myth of innocence," in which children are often portrayed as inhabiting a world that is untainted, magical, and utterly protected from the harshness of adult life. Innocence in this scenario not only erases the complexities of childhood and the range of experiences different children encounter, but also offers an excuse for adults to evade responsibility for how children are firmly connected to and shaped by social, economic, and cultural institutions run largely by adults. Innocence in this instance makes children invisible except as projections of adult fantasies—fantasies that allow adults to believe that children do not suffer from adult greed, recklessness, and perversions of will and spirit, and that adults are, in the final analysis, unaccountable.[2] Childhood innocence is also, as Daniel Thomas Cook points out, "something of a privilege, a bourgeois privilege," one that is not only "a scarce resource" for many children, but also a construct that hides the web of subordination to adults that many kids cannot wait to escape from.[3]

The child beauty pageant is an exemplary site for examining critically how the discourse of innocence mystifies the appropriation of children's bodies in a society that increasingly sexualizes and commodifies them. Not only do child beauty pageants function as a pedagogical site where children learn about pleasure, desire, and the roles they might assume in an adult society, but these pageants also rationalize and uphold commercial and ideological values within the larger society that play an important role in marketing children as objects of pleasure, desire, and sexuality. Rather than viewing child beauty pageants as rituals of innocence, we must reconsider the role they play as part of a broader cultural practice in which children are reified and objectified.

This is not meant to suggest that all child beauty pageants engage in a form of child abuse. Pageants vary in both the way they are constructed and how they interact with local and national audiences. Moreover, their outcomes are variable and contingent. But as sites of representation, identity formation, consumption, and regulation, these events and the dominant and assigned meanings attached to them have to be understood in terms of how they align with other cultural sites engaged in offering mostly young girls regressive notions of desire, femininity, sexuality, beauty, and self-esteem.

Sometimes there are flash points in a culture that signal that children are in danger. This seems to have been the case during the blitz of media coverage following the brutal murder at home of six-year-old JonBenet Ramsey on December 26, 1996, in Colorado. On one level, JonBenet's case attracted national attention because it fed into the frenzy and moral panic Americans were experiencing over the threat of child abuse—fueled by horrific crimes such as the kidnap and murder of Polly Klaas in California. Similarly, the case resonated with the highly charged public campaigns by various legislators and citizen groups calling for the death penalty for sex offenders such as Jesse Timmendequas, the child molester who killed seven-year-old Megan Kanka.

On another level, the Ramsey case opened to public scrutiny another high-profile example of a child succeeding at the make-believe game of becoming an adult, but in terms that made visible a dark and seamy element in the culture—one that seemed to belie the assumption that the voyeuristic fascination with the sexualized child was confined to the margins of society, inhabited largely by freaks, pedophiles, and psychopaths. The endless replay of images of JonBenet and other young children strutting and preening on-stage and the perceived sexualization both intrigued and shocked the American public. What the JonBenet Ramsey case made visible across the wide landscape of the culture was the recognition that images of six-year-olds cosmetically transformed into sultry, Lolita-like waifs were difficult to watch. Such images struck the heart of a culture beset by a deep disturbance in its alleged respect for children and decency. Whereas the blame for the often violent consequences associated with this eroticized costuming has been usually placed on young women, the JonBenet Ramsey affair made it difficult to blame kids for this type of objectification and com-modification.

For many, the images of JonBenet dressed up like a twenty-five-year-old and moving suggestively across the stage amounted to nothing less than kiddie porn. Frank Rich wrote a courageous piece in the *New York Times* in which he argued that the "strange world of kids' pageantry is not a 'subculture'—it's our culture. But as long as we call it a subculture, it can remain a problem for somebody else."[4] Richard Goldstein followed up Rich's insights with a three-part series in the *Village Voice* in which he argued that the marketing of the sexual child has a long history in the United States and that the JonBenet case "brings to the surface both our horror at how effectively a child can be constructed as a sexual being and our guilt at the pleasure we take in such a sight."[5] For Goldstein, the JonBenet case challenged the American public to confront the actual nature of child abuse, which is all too often a part of family life and further legitimated in the hateful practices of a culture willing to capitalize on children as an all too valuable source for the production of pleasure, profits, and commodification. After the JonBenet Ramsey case, it became more difficult to portray child beauty pageants as American as apple pie, embraced uncritically as simply good, clean, family entertainment and defended for their civic value to the community. Even Hollywood took aim at this myth with the Oscar-winning film *Little Miss Sunshine*, which deftly satirized parents more than willing to dress up children as young as four years old like Barbie dolls, more than willing to provide them with bleached and lacquered hair, fake eyelashes, flamboyant costumes, and garish jewelry—"painted and pompadoured to look like mini-hookers" while teaching them to suggestively bump and grind their way to winning a plastic tiara and, if lucky, some prize money.[6]

For a short time, it seemed that the American public finally recognized that these glitzy child beauty pageants were both shocking and exploitative and in some cases symptomatic of something very wrong with the broadening influence of corporate power and the ever-growing commercialization of children. Even though the popularity of child beauty pageants took a nosedive after the JonBenet Ramsey affair, these pageants have nevertheless withstood the satire of an Oscar-winning film and have increasingly gained in popularity over the last decade. More than five thousand child beauty pageants are held in the United States each year, representing a $5 billion industry and a source of rich profits for makeup experts, pageant coaches, and corporate sponsors of everything from beauty products to child fashion magazines. And as Rich points out, "Today the merchandising of children as sexual commodities is ubiquitous and big business—not just in beauty contests for toddlers … but everywhere—from the increased garishness of Barbie displays at the local mall to the use of Sally Mann-esque child models in home-furnishing magazines."[7] Moreover, the costs of these pageants are often prohibitive, including hundreds of dollars in entrance fees, thousand-dollar dresses, and thousands more spent for hotel rooms, travel, and, in some cases, professional training. As such, child beauty pageants represent places where the rituals of small-town America combine with the ideology of mass consumer culture.

Unfortunately, the ghost of JonBenet, with its disparaging foregrounding of children as commodities, reduced to sexualized ornaments in fake tans, capped teeth, and over-the-top makeup, has returned with a vengeance with a slew of shows such as *Little Miss Perfect*, *Little Beauties*, and the wildly popular reality-based docudrama *Toddlers & Tiaras*, which is being shown with no irony intended on the Learning Channel. *Toddlers & Tiaras* takes its audiences backstage at child beauty pageants from all over the country, offering up to viewers a spectacle of what kids as young as a few months old have to go through as they and their moms (and some dads) prepare to compete in the pageants. The first episode highlights three girls who are two, six, and nine years old. We follow each of the three families from South Carolina to Austin, Texas, as they coach, cajole, and prepare their kids for the ordeal of becoming a reigning pint-sized beauty queen. The images of these kids dressed up like little adults, with the moms insisting that they be spray tanned, adorned with fake nails and eyelashes, and wearing more makeup on their faces than the late Tammy Faye Bakker once used, are harder to watch than even the cheesy dance routines in which they learn to swing their hips and flip their hair back in a shameful highly eroticized manner. Watching a two-year-old parade around the stage in a Velcro rip-away outfit in stripperlike fashion induces more than repulsion: It also raises questions about the limits of subjecting kids to such pornographic practices and the distorted values these pageants provide for these children.

The entertainment value of shows such as *Toddlers & Tiaras* seems to be measured in how high their freak quotient can go. Young children dressed up in hideous fashions barely suitable for thirty-year-olds are unsettling and act as fodder for reality television voyeurism. Similarly, the parents of these kids supply much of the disturbing entertainment. One mom who is putting her daughter, Rebecca, a six-year-old, through her prepageant tanning insists that the tanning is necessary to hide any imperfections. Providing cosmetic corrections for kids who range in age from toddlers to twelve-year-olds, in spite of the damage that doing so inflicts on children, seems to attract large viewing audiences. Another self-proclaimed super-pageant dad named David makes all of his two-year-old daughter's pageant costumes and also serves as her makeup artist. He readily admits on national television that when he and his wife found out they were having a girl, they started signing her up for pageants, which, oddly enough, indicates that she started competing when she was in the womb. In another episode, a mother tells her four-year-old daughter as she is putting false eyelashes on her in preparation for the pageant competition, "You have a receding hairline." One mother of two little boys, ages two and three, glibly proclaims on one episode that "I always wanted to have girls, so I'm turning my boys into girls by putting them into pageants and modeling."

When asked why they do this to their children, most parents fall back upon the tired cliché that it promotes self-respect, as if defining children largely by what they lack and celebrating utterly regressive sexist standards of aesthetic perfection promote self-esteem. Some parents often respond to criticisms of child abuse by claiming that their kids are doing exactly what they want to do and that they enjoy being in the pageants. This argument appears strained when parents enter into pageants children who are as young as eight months old, or when parents decide that their four-year-old child needs a talent agent to ensure that she makes the right connections outside of the beauty pageants.

In both of these responses, little is heard from either the children subjected to such practices or prestigious organizations such as the American Psychological Association Task Force on the Sexualization of Girls, which issued a report indicating a strong connection between young girls who have to endure a premature emphasis on sex and appearance and "three of the most common mental health problems of girls and women: eating disorders, low self-esteem and depression."[8] Other child psychologists insist that the intense competition at pageants coupled with the nomadic lifestyle of traveling from one hotel to another when school is not in session makes it difficult for young children to make friends, putting them at risk for developing a number of problems in their social interactions with other children. Moreover, some child specialists argue that it is as developmentally inappropriate to "teach a six year-old to pose like a twenty-year-old model as it is to allow her to drive [and] drink alcohol."[9]

Of course, there is also the stress of competition and the danger of undermining a child's self-confidence, especially when she loses, if the message she receives is that how she looks is the most important aspect of who she is. Renowned psychologist David Elkind reminds us that parents used to be concerned with the ethical behavior of kids. A few decades ago, when kids got home from school, their parents asked them if they had been good. Now, because of the new economic realities of downsizing and major economic recession, parents are fearful that their kids will be losers.[10] *Toddlers & Tiaras* models a type of economic Darwinism that is at the heart of much of reality TV in which the greatest fear that parents have is that their kids will join the ranks of the losers. The question kids get when they come home in the new millennium is no longer "Have you been good?" but "Did you win?" One pageant director tells viewers that "they're all here to win and it'll be a fight to the finish, I promise." Clearly, this model of market-driven competition, which celebrates the notion that life is largely reduced to a "war of all against all," is what provides part of the motivation, if not legitimation, for parents to teach their kids how to perform booty-shaking dance routines in order to get the edge needed to win. Another criticism worth mentioning is that the money spent on child pageants by parents, up to $10,000 per child a year in some cases, could be invested in more productive ways for kids, not the least of which could be a savings plan established to help children alleviate the cost of a college education.

Rather than being an aberration in American society, child beauty pageants are symptomatic of the tragic disconnect between those public values essential to democracy and the well-being of children and the market-driven commercial values that turn everything, even young kids, into a commodity. Most disturbing about such pageants is what they tell us about what we have become as a society, how ready we are to sell our kids on the beauty block, and how much in politics and everyday life we are willing to disconnect who we are and how we live, work, and engage public life from ethical considerations. Child beauty pageants are just one reminder of how in the last thirty years we have factored out of both politics and everyday life issues of morality, social responsibility, and the importance of the common good.[11]

In the run-up to the 2008 election, John Edwards reminded us that there were two Americas, divided by wealth and poverty and growing forms of inequality. This model might be useful for talking about the two Americas for children, one for which the Obama family serves as the contemporary exemplar—a family that refuses to commodify its own children, a stable, caring, functioning family headed by loving parents who are invested in their children's lives while providing for them models of intellectual and moral integrity. To be sure, the Obamas have the material wealth and extended family support necessary to sustain such commitment—conditions not all working parents are fortunate enough to secure. But it is understood that childhood is a special estate that must be carefully protected as part of socially investing in children's future.

The other America is the at times glitzy, often gaudy, and, in the case of most child beauty pageants, outright obscene world of rampant commodification and sexualization. In this world, innocence is less a thing to be protected than a pretext for all forms of exploitation by adult hands—from multinational corporations whose quest for profit is packaged under the mantel of innocence and purity to the often seedy netherworld of child beauty pageants, a world in which children have no rights, no say, and no adult advocates for their well-being and security. Too many children are trapped in this world of exploitation, and even though pageants provide one shocking glimpse of this often ignored world, it far exceeds the limited world of pageants and plastic tiaras and points to a society that has lost its ability to both question itself and protect its most vulnerable and precious asset—its children.

III
RACE

Chapter 7
Youth and the Myth of a Postracial Society
Under Barack Obama

‹›

With the election of Barack Obama, many have argued that the social state will be renewed in the spirit and legacy of the New Deal and the punishing racial state and its vast complex of disciplinary institutions will, if not come to an end, at least be significantly reformed.[1] From this perspective, Obama's presidency not only represents a postracial victory but also signals a new space of postracial harmony. In assessing the Obama victory, *Time* magazine columnist Joe Klein wrote, "It is a place where the primacy of racial identity—and this includes the old Jesse Jackson version of black racial identity—has been replaced by the celebration of pluralism, of cross-racial synergy."[2] Conservative commentator George Will suggested that Obama was just another "liberal on a leash" whose election win would "bring down the curtain on the long running and intensely boring melodrama 'Forever Selma,' starring Jesse Jackson and Al Sharpton."[3]

Obama won the 2008 election because he was able to mobilize 95 percent of African American voters, more than 65 percent of Latino voters, and a large proportion of young voters under the age of thirty. At the same time, what is generally ignored in the exuberance of this assessment is that the majority of white Americans voted for the John McCain–Sarah Palin ticket. What is also forgotten is the racism that permeated the McCain-Palin campaign, the racial furor expressed over Reverend Jeremiah Wright, and the rampant rise in white supremacist hate groups just before and after Obama's election. Of course, there are also the more obvious forms of domestic institutional racism ranging from the racial gap in income and wealth to an apartheid-based prison system.

Even though "postracial" may mean less overt racism, the idea that we have moved into a postracial period in American history is not merely premature—it is an act of willful denial and ignorance. Paul Ortiz puts it well in his comments on the myth of postracialism:

> The idea that we've moved to a post-racial period in American social history is undermined by an avalanche of recent events. Hurricane Katrina. The U.S. Supreme Court's dismantling of *Brown v. Board of Education* and the resegregation of American schools. The Clash of Civilizations thesis that promotes the idea of a War against Islam. The backlash facing immigrant workers. A grotesque prison industrial complex. [Moreover,] ... while Americans were being robbed blind and primed for yet another bailout of the banks and investment sectors, they were treated to new evidence from Fox News and poverty experts that the great moral threats facing the nation were greedy union workers, black single mothers, Latino gang bangers and illegal immigrants.[4]

Missing from the exuberant claims that Americans are now living in a postracial society is the historical legacy of a neoconservative revolution, officially launched in 1980 with the election of Ronald Reagan, and its ensuing racialist attacks on welfare "queens"; Bill Clinton's cheerful compliance in signing bills that expanded the punishing industries; and George W. Bush's "willingness to make punishment his preferred response to social problems."[5] In the last thirty years, we have witnessed the emergence of policies that have amplified the power of the racial state and expanded its mechanisms of punishment and mass incarceration, the consequences of which are deeply racist—even as the state and its legal apparatuses insist on their own race neutrality.

The politics of racism has hardly disappeared from the landscape of American culture and the institutions that support it. Poor minority kids now find themselves on a fast track extending from school to juvenile courts to prison. And the number of poor and minority kids, now aptly called the "recession generation" by Dr. Irwin Redlener, president of New York City's Children's Health Fund, has increased from 13 million before the economic meltdown to more than 17 million by the end of 2010. Their ranks include the 17 percent of children who lack health care, the one in four kids who is on food stamps, and the more than 1 million children who are homeless in the richest country in the world.[6] And who are these kids? These are the kids marginalized by race and class who are largely seen either as a drain on the economy or as obstacles in the way of market freedoms, free trade, consumerism, and the whitewashed fantasies of a cleansed, Disneyfied social order. These are kids who not only have to fend for themselves in the face of life's tragedies but are also supposed to do it without being seen by the dominant society. Excommunicated from the sphere of human concern, they have been rendered invisible, utterly disposable, and heir to that legacy of social homelessness that allegedly no longer existed in color-blind America. Many of them, if not actually homeless, live in dilapidated housing, attend schools that are underfunded and falling apart, receive food stamps, and eat mostly junk food when they can get it. They are the major targets of gun violence, often lacking the decent health care they need if they find themselves in a hospital emergency room.

These are the kids who experience daily, whether on the street or in school, draconian discipline policies that endlessly criminalize every aspect of their behavior and increasingly banish them from the very institutions such as schools that remain their last chance for getting a fair shake in life. It gets worse. For instance, a full 60 percent of black high school dropouts, by the time they reach their midthirties, will be prisoners or ex-cons; the dropout rate is as high as 65 percent in some cities.[7] This apartheid-based system of incarceration bodes especially ill for young black males. According to Paul Street, "It is worth noting that half of the nation's black male high-school dropouts will be incarcerated—moving, often enough, from quasi-carceral lock-down high schools to the real 'lock down' thing—at some point in their lives. These dropouts are over represented among the one in three African American males aged sixteen- to twenty-years old who are under one form of supervision by the U.S. criminal justice system: parole, probation, jail, or prison."[8]

As the toll in human suffering increases daily, Obama and his Wall Street advisers bail out the banks and the rich just as crucial social services for children are being cut back, unemployment is soaring into record numbers, and more and more youth of color are disappearing into an abysmal pit of poverty, despair, and hopelessness. Raised in a blood-drenched culture of violence mediated by an economic Darwinism that harbors a rabid disdain for the common good, poor minority kids appear to be completely off the radar of public concern and government compassion. And Obama, for all of his soaring poetic imagery of unity and justice, falls flat on his face by allowing his secretary of education, Arne Duncan, to offer up reform policies that amount to nothing more than another version of Bush's No Child Left Behind, with its antiunion ideology and obsessive investment in measurement and accountability schemes that strip any talk of educational reform of any viability while turning schools into nothing more than testing factories—policies that disproportionately punish brown and black youth. These racially exclusionary set of policies and institutions have become especially cruel since the beginning of the neoconservative revolution in the 1980s and are not poised to disappear soon under the presidency of Barack Obama—in fact, given the current economic crisis, they may even get worse.

In short, the discourse of the postracial state ignores how political and economic institutions, with their circuits of repression and disposability and their technologies of punishment, connect and condemn the fate of many impoverished youth of color in the inner cities to persisting structures of racism that "serve to keep [these youth] in a state of inferiority and oppression."[9] Not surprisingly under such circumstances, individual suffering no longer registers as a social concern, and all notions of injustice are assumed to be the outcome of personal failings or deficits. Signs of the pathologizing of both marginalized youth and the crucial safety nets that have provided them some hope of justice in the past can be found everywhere, from the racist screeds coming out of right-wing talk radio to the mainstream media that seem to believe that the culture of black and brown youth is synonymous with the culture of crime. Poverty is now imagined to be a problem of individual character. Racism is now understood as merely an act of individual discrimination (if not discretion). And homelessness is reduced to a choice made by lazy people. Unfortunately, missing from the discourse of those who are arguing for the kind of progressive change the Obama administration should deliver is any mention of the race-based crises facing youth and the terrible toll these crises have taken on generations of poor, black, and brown kids.

Bringing these crises to the forefront of the political and social agenda is crucial, particularly because Obama, in a number of speeches prior to assuming the presidency, refused to adopt the demonizing rhetoric often used by politicians when talking about youth. Instead, he pointedly called upon the American people to reclaim young people as an important symbol of the future and of democracy itself: "Come together and say, 'Not this time.' This time we want to talk about the crumbling schools that are stealing the future of black children and white children and Asian children and Hispanic children and Native American children. This time we want to reject the cynicism that tells us that these kids can't learn; that those kids who don't look like us are somebody else's problem. The children of America are not those kids, they are our kids."[10]

But if Barack Obama's call to address the crucial problems facing young people in this country is to be taken seriously, the political, economic, and institutional conditions that both legitimate and sustain a shameful attack on poor minority youth have to be made visible, open to challenge, and transformed. This can happen only when we refuse the race-based somnambulance and social amnesia that coincide with the pretense of a postracial politics and society, especially when the matter concerns young people of color. To reclaim poor minority youth as part of a democratic vision and a crucial symbol of the future requires more than hope and a civics lesson: It necessitates transforming the workings of racist power arrangements both in and out of the government, along with the market-driven institutions and values that have enabled the rise of a predatory corporate state and a punishing apparatus that have produced a polity that governs through the logic of finance capital, consumerism, crime, disposability, and a growing imprisonment binge.

The marriage of economic Darwinism and the racialized punishing state is on full display not merely in the rising rate of incarceration for black and brown people in the United States but also in places such as East Carroll Parish in Louisiana, where inmates provide cheap or free labor at barbecues, funerals, service stations, and a host of other sites. According to Adam Nossiter: "The men of orange are everywhere," and people living in this Louisiana county "say they could not get by without their inmates, who make up more than 10 percent of its population and most of its labor force. They are dirt-cheap, sometimes free, always compliant, ever-ready and disposable.... You just call up the sheriff, and presto, inmates are headed your way. 'They bring me warm bodies, 10 warm bodies in the morning,' said Grady Brown, owner of the Panola Pepper Corporation. 'They do anything you ask them to do.'... 'You call them up, they drop them off, and they pick them up in the afternoon,' said Paul Chapple, owner of a service station."[11] Nossiter claims that the system is jokingly referred to by many people who use it as "rent a convict" and is, to say the least, an "odd vestige of the abusive convict-lease system that began in the South around Reconstruction."[12] This is not merely an eccentric snapshot of small-town racism; it is also an image of what kind of future many poor minority youth will inhabit.

Treating prisoners as commodities to be bought and sold like expendable goods suggests the degree to which the punishing state has divested itself of any moral responsibility with regard to those human beings who in the logic of free-market fundamentalism are considered either as commodities or as waste products. This is true especially of young people. At the same time, as racism has been relegated to an anachronistic vestige of the past, especially in light of Barack Obama's election to the presidency, the workings of the punishing state are whitewashed and removed from the racialized violence of the governing-through-crime complex. Consequently, the American public becomes increasingly indifferent to the ways in which neoliberal rationality—with its practices of market deregulation, privatization, the hollowing out of the social state, and the disparaging of the public good—wages a devastating assault on African American and Latino communities, young people, and, increasingly, immigrants and other people of color who are relegated to the borders of American normalcy and patriotism. The punishing state not only produces vast amounts of inequality, suffering, and racism; it also propagates collective amnesia, cynicism, and moral indifference.

Under this insufferable climate of increased repression and unabated exploitation, young people and communities of color become the new casualties in an ongoing war against justice, freedom, citizenship, and democracy. Even though Obama speaks eloquently about the need to develop public policies that stress social investment rather than adding to the coffers of the rich, he has not produced such policies, especially in education, through which poor and minority youth will no longer be viewed as either criminals or disposable beings. Instead of testing schemes, young people need structurally sound schools, smaller class sizes, high-quality teachers, social programs that address the conditions that disable students from learning, and a Marshall Plan committed to providing youth, especially poor and minority youth, with free education, health care, full employment, and tangible signs that the government is willing to invest as much time, money, and resources in their future as it has invested so freely in the military-industrial complex and its expanding discourse of militarism. How much longer can a nation ignore those youth who lack the resources and opportunities that were available, in a partial and incomplete way, to previous generations? And what does it mean when a nation becomes frozen ethically and imaginatively in providing its youth with a future of hope and opportunity?

Chapter 8
Disposable Youth in a Suspect Society
A Challenge for the Obama Administration

‑❧‑

Although there is little question that the United States—with its burgeoning police state, its infamous status as the world leader in jailing its own citizens, and its history of foreign and domestic "torture factories"[1]—has moved into lockdown (and lockout) mode both at home and abroad, it is a mistake to assume that the Bush administration is solely responsible for transforming the United States to the degree that it has now become unrecognizable to itself as a democratic nation. Such claims risk reducing the serious social ills now plaguing the United States to the reactionary policies of the Bush regime—a move that allows for complacency in light of the potentially inflated hopes raised by Barack Obama's successful bid for the presidency. What the United States has become in the last decade suggests less a rupture than an intensification of a number of already existing political, economic, and social forces that since the late 1970s have unleashed the repressive antidemocratic tendencies lurking beneath the damaged heritage of democratic ideals.

What marks the present state of American "democracy" is the uniquely bipolar nature of the degenerative assault on the body politic, which combines elements of unprecedented greed and fanatical capitalism with a new kind of politics more ruthless and savage in its willingness to abandon—even vilify—those individuals and groups now rendered disposable within the "new geographies of exclusion and landscapes of wealth" that mark the neoliberal new world order.[2] Nowhere is this assault more evident than in what might be called the "war on youth," a war that not only attempts to erase the democratic legacies of the past, but also disavows any commitment to the future.

Any discourse about the future has to begin with the issue of youth because young people embody the projected dreams, desires, and commitment of a society's obligations to the future. In many respects, youth register symbolically the importance of modernity's claim to progress; they also affirm the importance of the liberal democratic tradition of the social contract in which adult responsibility is mediated through a willingness to fight for the rights of children, enact reforms that invest in their future, and provide the educational conditions necessary for them to make use of the freedoms they have while learning how to be critical citizens. Within such a modernist project, democracy is linked to the well-being of youth, while the status of how a society imagines democracy and its future is contingent on how that society views its responsibility toward future generations. But the category of youth does more than affirm modernity's social contract, rooted in a conception of the future in which adult commitment and intergenerational solidarity are articulated as a vital public service; this category also affirms those representations, images, vocabularies, values, and social relations central to a politics capable of both defending vital institutions as a public good and contributing to the quality of public life.

Yet as the twenty-first century unfolds, it is not at all clear that the American public and government believe any longer in youth, the future, or the social contract, even in its minimalist version. Since the 1980s, the prevailing market-inspired discourse has argued that there is no such thing as society, and, indeed, following that nefarious pronouncement, institutions committed to public welfare, especially for young people, have been disappearing ever since. Those of us who believe, against the prevailing common sense, that the ultimate test of morality resides in what a society does for its children cannot help but acknowledge that if we take this standard seriously, American society has deeply failed its children and its commitment to democracy.

At stake here is not merely how American culture is redefining the meaning of youth, but also how it constructs children in relation to a future devoid of the moral and political obligations of citizenship, social responsibility, and democracy. Caught up in an age of increasing despair, uncertainty, and a quagmire of a global financial collapse, youth no longer appear to inspire adults to reaffirm their commitment to a public discourse that envisions a future in which human suffering is diminished while the general welfare of society is increased. Constructed primarily within the language of the market and the increasingly conservative politics of a corporate-dominated media culture, contemporary youth appear unable to constitute themselves through a defining generational referent that gives them a sense of distinctiveness and vision, as did the generation of youth in the 1960s. The relations between youth and adults have always been marked by strained generational and ideological struggles, but the new economic and social conditions that youth face today, along with a callous indifference to their spiritual and material needs, suggest a qualitatively different attitude on the part of many adults toward American youth—one that indicates that the young have become our lowest national priority. Put bluntly, American society at present exudes a deep-rooted hostility and a chilling indifference toward youth, reinforcing the dismal conditions that young people are increasingly living under.

The hard currency of human suffering that affects children is evident in some astounding statistics (some of which are mentioned in other parts of this book) that suggest a profound moral and political contradiction at the heart of our culture. For example, the rate of child poverty is currently at 17.4 percent, boosting the number of poor children to 13.3 million. In addition, about one in three severely poor people are under age seventeen. Moreover, children make up 26 percent of the total population but constitute an astounding 39 percent of the poor.[3] Just as alarming as this is the fact that 9.4 million children in America lack health insurance and millions lack affordable child care and decent early childhood education. Sadly, the United States ranks first in billionaires and defense expenditures and yet ranks an appalling twenty-fifth in infant mortality. As we might expect, behind these grave statistics lies a series of decisions that favor economically those already advantaged at the expense of the young. Savage cuts to education, nutritional assistance for impoverished mothers, veterans' medical care, and basic scientific research are often cynically administered to help fund tax cuts for the already inordinately rich.

This inversion of the government's responsibility to protect public goods from private threats further reveals itself in the privatization of social problems and the vilification of those who fail to thrive in this vastly iniquitous social order. Too many youth within this degraded economic, political, and cultural geography occupy a "dead zone" in which the spectacle of commodification exists alongside the imposing threat of massive debt, bankruptcy, the prison-industrial complex, and the elimination of basic civil liberties. Indeed, we have an entire generation of unskilled and displaced youth who have been expelled from shrinking markets, blue-collar jobs, and the limited political power granted to the middle-class consumer.

Rather than investing in the public good and solving social problems, the state now punishes those who are caught in the downward spiral of its economic policies. Punishment, incarceration, and surveillance represent the new face of governance. Consequently, the implied contract between the social state and its citizens has been broken, and social guarantees for youth, as well as civic obligations to the future, have vanished from the public agenda. Within this utterly privatizing market discourse, alcoholism, homelessness, poverty, joblessness, and illiteracy are not viewed as social issues but rather as individual problems—that is, such problems are viewed as the result of a character flaw or a personal failing.

As the Alliance for Excellent Education points out, "Over a million of the students who enter ninth grade each fall fail to graduate with their peers four years later. [Moreover,] about seven thousand students drop out every day.... Of the 1.2 million kids who fail to graduate, more than half are from minority groups."[4] Poor black youth are especially disadvantaged. Not only do a mere 42 percent who enter high school actually graduate, but they also are increasingly jobless in an economy that does not need their labor. For instance, recent figures indicate that more than 19.3 million young people between the ages of sixteen and twenty-four are unemployed.[5] Marked as a surplus and disposable population, "black American males inhabit a universe in which joblessness is frequently the norm [and] over the past few years, the percentage of black male high school graduates in their 20s who were jobless has ranged from well over a third to roughly 50 percent.... For dropouts, the rates of joblessness are staggering. For black males who left high school without a diploma, the real jobless rate at various times over the past few years has ranged from 59 percent to a breathtaking 72 percent."[6] For many poor youth of color, punishment and fear have replaced compassion and social responsibility as the most important modalities mediating the relationship of youth to the larger social order. For instance, a "black boy born in 2001 has a 1 in 3 chance of going to prison in his lifetime.... A Latino boy born in 2001 has a 1 in 6 chance of going to prison in his lifetime [and] although they represent just 39 percent of the U.S. juvenile population, minority youth represent 60 percent of committed youth."[7]

Youth within the last two decades are increasingly represented in the media as a source of trouble rather than as a resource for investing in the future and are increasingly treated as either a disposable population, cannon fodder for barbaric wars abroad, or the source of most of society's problems. As Lawrence Grossberg points out: "It has become common to think of kids as a threat to the existing social order and for kids to be blamed for the problems they experience. We slide from kids in trouble, kids have problems, and kids are threatened, to kids as trouble, kids as problems, and kids as threatening."[8] With youth, particularly those of color, increasingly associated in the media and by dominant politicians with a rising crime wave, what is really at stake in this discourse is a punishment wave, one that reveals a society that does not know how to address those social problems that undercut any viable sense of agency, possibility, and future for many young people. Even though crime continues to decline among youth in the United States, the popular media still represent young people as violent and threatening. When youth are addressed in more complex terms, they are still disparaged as self-indulgent and irresponsible. Then again, in a society in which politicians and the marketplace can imagine youth only as consumers, commodities, or billboards to sell sexuality, beauty products, music, athletic gear, clothes, and a host of other products, it is not surprising that young people can be so easily misrepresented.

Both the problems that young people face and the sites they inhabit are increasingly criminalized. Under the reign of ruthless neoliberal politics, with its hyped-up social Darwinism and theater of cruelty, the popular demonization of the young now justifies responses to youth that were unthinkable twenty years ago, including criminalization and imprisonment, prescription of psychotropic drugs, psychiatric confinement, and zero tolerance policies that model schools after prisons. School has become a model for a punishing society in which children who violate a rule as minor as a dress code or slightly act out in class can be handcuffed, booked, and put in a jail cell. Such was the case in Florida when the police handcuffed and arrested six-year-old Desré Watson, who was taken from her kindergarten school to the Highlander County jail, where she was fingerprinted, photographed for a mug shot, and charged with a felony and two misdemeanors. Her crime? She had thrown a tantrum in her kindergarten class.[9] Given this shocking treatment of a mere child, perhaps it is not surprising that the United States was the only country that voted against a 2007 UN resolution calling for the abolition of life imprisonment without the possibility of parole for children under the age of sixteen.[10] Moreover, the United States is currently the only nation that locks up child offenders for life. A report issued in 2007 by the Equal Justice Initiative claims that "there are 73 Americans serving [life] sentences for crimes they committed at 13 or 14."[11]

The Bush administration not only waged a war against youth, especially poor youth of color; it also offered no apologies for doing so because it was too arrogant and ruthless to imagine any resistance. For many young people, the future looks bleak, filled with the promise of low-paying, low-skilled jobs; the collapse of the welfare state; and, for those who are persons of color and poor, the threat of unemployment or incarceration. Youth have disappeared from the concerns of many adults and certainly from the policies that have been hatched in Washington during the last twenty years. In his acceptance speech, Barack Obama raised the issue of what kind of country young people would inherit if they lived to see the next century. The question provides an opening for taking the Obama administration seriously with regard to its commitment to young people. Young people need access to decent schools with more teachers; they need universal health care; they need food, decent housing, job training programs, and guaranteed employment. In other words, we need social movements that take seriously the challenge of dismantling the punishing state and reviving the social state so as to be able to provide young people not with incarceration and contempt, but with dignity and those economic, political, and social conditions that ensure they have a decent future. Surely, this is an issue that the Obama administration should be pushed to recognize and address. Dietrich Bonhoeffer, a great Protestant theologian, believed that the ultimate test of morality resided in what a society did for its children. If we take this standard seriously, American society has deeply failed its children and its commitment to democracy.

The politics and culture of neoliberalism rest on the denial of youth as a marker of the future and of the social responsibility entailed by an acceptance of this principle. In other words, the current crisis of American democracy can be measured in part by the fact that too many young people are poor, lack decent housing and health care, and attend decrepit schools filled with overworked and underpaid teachers. These youth, by all standards, deserve more in a country that has historically prided itself on its level of democracy, liberty, and alleged equality for all citizens. We live in a historic moment of both crisis and possibility, one that presents educators, parents, artists, and others with the opportunity to take up the challenge of reimagining civic engagement and social transformation, but these activities have a chance of succeeding only if we also defend and create those social, economic, and cultural conditions that enable the current generation of young people to nurture thoughtfulness, critical agency, compassion, and democracy itself.

After a year in office, the Obama administration has done little to improve the lives of children suffering under the weight of one of the worst economic crises in American history. As much-needed funds are diverted from a jobs-creation program for young people and the rebuilding of American public schools to two unwinnable and wasteful wars in Iraq and Afghanistan, it is all the more imperative for the American people to exhibit the moral outrage and collective action necessary to reverse such dreadful and empty priorities. Nothing less is at stake than the future of young people and the fate of democracy.

Chapter 9
Locked Out and Locked Up
Youth Missing in Action from Obama's Stimulus Plan

⊸

Already imperiled before the recent economic meltdown, the quality of life for many young people appears even more fragile in the United States in this time of political, economic, and social crisis. A great deal has been written critically about both the conditions that enabled the free market to operate without accountability in the interests of the rich and how it has produced a theater of cruelty that has created enormous suffering for millions of hardworking, decent human beings. Yet at the same time, there is a thunderous silence on the part of many critics and academics regarding the ongoing insecurity and injustice experienced by young people in this country, which has been intensified in recent years as a result of the state's increasing resort to repression and punitive social policies. The current concerns about poverty, homelessness, economic injustice, and galloping unemployment rates and Barack Obama's plan to rectify them almost completely ignore the effects of these problems on young people in the United States, especially poor whites and youth of color.

Increasingly, children seem to have no standing in the public sphere as citizens and as such are denied any sense of entitlement and agency. Children have fewer rights than almost any other group and fewer institutions protecting these rights. Consequently, their voices and needs are almost completely absent from the debates, policies, and legislative practices that are constructed in terms of their needs. This is not to suggest that adults do not care about youth, but most of those concerns are framed within the realm of the private sphere of the family and can be seen most clearly in the moral panics mobilized around drugs, truancy, and school shootings. The response to such events, tellingly, is more "get tough on crime policy," never an analysis of the systemic failure to provide safety and security for children through improved social provisions. In public life, children seem absent from any discourse about the future and the responsibilities this implies for adult society. Rather, children appear as objects, defined through the debasing language of advertising and consumerism. If not being represented as a symbol of fashion or hailed as a hot niche, youth are often portrayed as a problem, a danger to adult society, or, even worse, something irrelevant to the future.

This merging of the neoliberal state, in which kids appear as commodities or as sources of profits, with the punishing state, which harkens back to the old days of racial apartheid in its ongoing rush to incarcerate, was made quite visible in a recent shocking account of two judges in Pennsylvania who took bribes as part of a scheme to fill up privately run juvenile detention centers with as many youth as possible, regardless of how minor the infractions they had committed. One victim, Hillary Transue, appeared before one of the "kickback" judges for "building a spoof *MySpace* page mocking the assistant principal at her high school."[1] A top student who had never been in trouble, she anticipated a stern lecture from the judge for her impropriety. Instead, he sentenced her "to three months at a juvenile detention center on a charge of harassment." It has been estimated that the two judges, Mark A. Ciavarella Jr. and Michael T. Conahan, "made more than $2.6 million in kickbacks to send teenagers to two privately run youth detention centers" and that more than five thousand juveniles have gone to jail since the "scheme started in 2003. Many of them were first time offenders and some remain in detention."[2]

Although this incident received some mainstream news coverage, most of the response focused less on the suffering endured by the young victims than on the breach of professional ethics committed by the two judges. None of the coverage treated the incident as either a symptom of the war being waged against youth marginalized by class and race or an issue that the Obama administration should give top priority in reversing. In fact, just as there was almost no public outcry over a market-driven scheme to incarcerate youth to fill the pockets of corrupt judges, there was very little public anger over the millions slashed from the economic stimulus plan that would have directly benefited kids by investing in schools, Head Start, and other youth-oriented programs. It seems that the real failure of postpartisan politics is its willingness to sacrifice young people in the interests of winning political votes.

Portraying poor minority youth as a danger and a threat to society no longer requires allusions to biological inferiority: The invocation of cultural difference is enough to racialize and demonize "difference without explicitly marking it" in the postracial Obama era.[3] This disparaging view of young people has promulgated the rise of a punishing (in)security industry whose discourses, technologies, and practices have become visible across a wide range of spaces and institutions, extending from schools to shopping malls to the juvenile criminal justice system.[4] Of course, as shocking as the story is about judges taking kickbacks for jailing young people, it pales next to an apartheid system of racialized justice that is incarcerating youth in record numbers and increasingly trying them as adults. As Loïc Wacquant points out, as more and more young people marginalized by race and class are being placed under the jurisdiction of the criminal justice system and treated as adult offenders, they are subject to three modes of exclusion that disrupt their families, fragment their communities, and close down opportunities for them to function in the larger society:

[They] are denied access to valued *cultural capital*: just as university credentials are becoming prerequisite for employment in the (semi-) protected sector of the labour market, inmates have been expelled from higher education by being made ineligible for Pell Grants, starting with drug offenders in 1988, continuing with convicts sentenced to death or lifelong imprisonment without the possibility of parole in 1992, and ending with all remaining state and federal prisoners in 1994. Prisoners are systematically excluded from *social redistribution* and public aid in an age when work insecurity makes access to such programs more vital than ever for those dwelling in the lower regions of social space. Laws deny welfare payments, veterans' benefits and food stamps to anyone in detention for more than 60 days. The Work Opportunity and Personality Responsibility Act of 1996 further banishes most ex-convicts from Medicaid, public housing, Section 8 vouchers and related forms of assistance. Convicts are banned from *political participation* via "criminal disenfranchisement" practiced on a scale and with a vigor unimagined in any other country. All but four members of the Union deny the vote to mentally competent adults held in detention facilities; 39 states forbid convicts placed on probation from exercising political rights and 32 states also interdict parolees. In 14 states, ex-felons are barred from voting even when they are no longer under criminal justice supervision—for life in ten of these states. The result is that nearly 4 million Americans have temporarily or permanently lost the ability to cast a ballot, including 1.47 million who are not behind bars and another 1.39 million who served their sentence in full.[5]

As the protocols of governance become indistinguishable from military operations and crime control missions, youth are more and more losing the protections, rights, security, or compassion they deserve in a viable democracy. The model of policing that now governs all kinds of social behaviors constructs a narrow range of meaning through which young people define themselves. Moreover, this rhetoric and the practice of policing, surveillance, and punishment have little to do with the project of social investment and a great deal to do with increasingly powerful modes of regulation, pacification, and control—together making up a "youth control complex" whose prominence in American society points to a state of affairs in which democracy has lost its claim and the claiming of democracy goes unheard. Rather than dream of a future bright with visions of possibility, young people, especially youth marginalized by race and color, face a coming-of-age crisis marked by mass incarceration and criminalization, one that is likely to be intensified in the midst of the global financial, housing, and credit crises spawned by neoliberal capitalism.

As Alex Koroknay-Palicz argues, "Powerful national forces such as the media, politicians and the medical community perpetuate the idea of youth as an inferior class of people responsible for society's ills and deserving of harsh penalties."[6] Whereas such negative and demeaning views have had disastrous consequences for all young people, who live under the reign of a punishing society and the deep structural racism of the criminal justice system, the situation for a growing number of young people and youth of color is getting much worse. The suffering and deprivation experienced by millions of children in the United States in 2008—and bound to become worse in the midst of the current economic meltdown—testify to a state of emergency and a burgeoning crisis regarding the health and welfare of many children, but also bear witness to, and indeed indict, a model of market sovereignty and a mode of punitive governance that have failed both children and the promise of a substantive democracy. The Children's Defense Fund in its 2007 annual report offers a range of statistics that provide a despairing glimpse of the current crisis facing too many children in America. What are we to make of a society marked by the following conditions?

- Almost 13 million children in America live in poverty—5.5 million in extreme poverty.
- 4.2 million children under the age of five live in poverty.
- 35.3 percent of Black children, 28.0 percent of Latino children, and 10.8 percent of White, non-Latino children live in poverty.
- There are 9.4 million uninsured children in America.
- Latino children are three times as likely and Black children are 70 percent more likely to be uninsured than White children.
- Only 11 percent of Black, 15 percent of Latino, and 41 percent of White 8th-graders perform at grade level in math.
- Each year 800,000 children spend time in foster care.
- On any given night, 200,000 children are homeless—1 out of every 4 of the homeless population.
- Every 36 seconds a child is abused or neglected, almost 900,000 children each year.
- Black males ages 15–19 are about eight times as likely to be gun homicide victims as White males.
- Although they represent 39 percent of the U.S. juvenile population, minority youth represent 60 percent of committed juveniles.
- A Black boy born in 2001 has a 1 in 3 chance of going to prison in his lifetime; a Latino boy has a 1 in 6 chance.
- Black juveniles are about four times as likely as their White peers to be incarcerated. Black youths are almost five times as likely and Latino youths about twice as likely to be incarcerated as White youths of drug offenses.[7]

As these figures suggest, the notion that children should be treated as a crucial social resource and represent for any healthy society important ethical and political considerations about the quality of public life, the allocation of social provisions, and the role of the state as a guardian of public interests appears to be lost.

Under the reign of the market-driven punishing state, the racialized criminal justice system, and a "financial Katrina" that is crippling the nation, the economic, political, and educational situation for a growing number of poor young people and youth of color has gone from bad to worse. As families are being forced out of their homes because of record-high mortgage foreclosures and many businesses declare bankruptcy, tax revenues are declining and effecting cutbacks in state budgets, thereby further weakening public schools and social services. The results in human suffering are tragic and can be measured in the growing ranks of poor and homeless students, the gutting of state social services, and the sharp drop in employment opportunities for teens and young people in their twenties.[8] Within these grave economic conditions, children disappear, often into bad schools, prisons, foster care, and even graves.

Under the rule of an unchecked market-driven society, the punishing state has no vocabulary for or stake in the future of poor minority youth and increasingly in youth in general. Instead of being viewed as impoverished, minority youth are seen as lazy and shiftless. Instead of society recognizing that many poor minority youth are badly served by failing schools, it labels them as uneducable and pushes them out of schools. Instead of providing minority youth with decent work skills and jobs, society sends them to prison or conscripts them to fight in wars abroad. Instead of being given decent health care and a place to live, they are placed in foster care or pushed into the swelling ranks of the homeless. Instead of addressing the very real dangers that young people face, the punishing society treats them as suspects and disposable populations, subjecting them to disciplinary practices that close down any hope they might have for a decent future.

All of the talk about a postracial society in light of Obama's election is meaningless as long as young people of color are disproportionally criminalized at younger and younger ages, allowed to disappear into the growing ranks of the criminal justice system, and increasingly viewed as a racial threat to society rather than as a crucial social, political, and economic investment. Obama's message of hope and responsibility seems empty unless he addresses the plight of poor white youth and youth of color and the growing youth control complex. The race to incarcerate, especially youth of color, is a holdover and reminder that the legacy of apartheid is still with us and can be found in a society that now supports a crime complex that models schools for poor kids after prisons, puts almost as many police in its schools as it does teachers, and views the juvenile justice system as a crucial element in shaping the future of young people.

Chapter 10
Judge Sonia Sotomayor and the New Racism
Getting Beyond the Politics of Denial

◦⊖◦

With the election of Barack Obama to the presidency, many liberals now suggest that the United States has become a postracial society, whereas many conservatives have taken the opposite position, specifically prompted by the nomination of Judge Sonia Sotomayor to the Supreme Court, that racism is alive and well in the American republic.[1] According to many right-wing pundits and politicians extending from Rush Limbaugh to Tucker Carlson, Judge Sotomayor is a "racist" and a "bigot" because of a largely decontextualized thirty-two-word quotation abstracted from a speech she gave in 2001 in which she stated, "I would hope that a wise Latina woman with the richness of her experiences would more often than not reach a better conclusion than a white male who hasn't lived that life."[2] Newt Gingrich ignored the broader context in which the quotation appeared, insisting that Sotomayor's statement was symptomatic of a new type of racism. He exclaimed in Twitter-like fashion, "Imagine a judicial nominee said 'my experience as a white man makes me better than a Latina woman'—new racism is no better than old racism."[3] All of this saber-rattling rhetoric about the emergence of a new kind of racism suggests rather ironically that whites, rather than people of color, are the real victims of personal and institutional racism and points to a kind of historical amnesia that rewrites the meaning of racism and indicates a long-standing fear among many conservatives that diversity, rather the bigotry, is the real threat to democracy.

What the ongoing attack on Judge Sotomayor suggests is that the public morality of American life and social policy regarding matters of racial justice is increasingly subject to a politics of denial. Denial in this case is not merely about the failure of public memory or the refusal to know; this denial is an active ongoing attempt on the part of many conservatives to rewrite the discourse of race so as to deny its valence as a force for discrimination and exclusion, either by translating it as a threat to American culture, specifically white men, or relegating it to the language of the private sphere. The idea of race and the conditions of racism have real political effects, and eliding them only makes those effects harder to recognize.

And yet recognizing how language is used to name, organize, order, and categorize matters of race not only has academic value, but also provides a location from which to engage difference and the relationships between the self and the other and between the public and the private. In addition, the language of race is important because it strongly affects political and policy agendas. We only have to think about the effects of Charles Murray's book *Losing Ground*, which played a crucial role in undermining American welfare policies in the 1980s.[4] But language is more than a mode of communication or a symbolic practice that produces real effects; it is also a site of contestation and struggle.

The charge that Judge Sotomayor is a racist suggests something about the changing vocabulary of race and racial injustice that has to be both critically understood and politically engaged. In fact, there *is* something called a new racism, and it has been brilliantly explored by a number of writers, including David Theo Goldberg, Elizabeth Ansell, Howard Winant, and Manning Marable, though they do not use the term in the same way as conservatives do. Unlike the old racism, which defined racial difference in terms of fixed biological categories organized hierarchically, the new racism operates in various guises, proclaiming, among other things, race neutrality; asserting culture as a marker of racial difference; or marking race as a private matter. Unlike crude racism, with its biological referents and pseudoscientific legitimations buttressing its appeal to white racial superiority, the new racism cynically recodes itself within the vocabulary of the civil rights movement, invoking the language of Martin Luther King Jr. to argue that individuals should be judged by the "content of their character" and not by the color of their skin.

What is crucial about the new racism is that critics should respond to it with an updated analysis of how racist practices work through the changing nature of language and other modes of representation. One of the most sanitized and yet pervasive forms of the new racism is evident in the language of color-blindness and the ideology of privatization. This approach argues that racial conflict and discrimination are things of the past and that race has no bearing on an individual's or a group's location or standing in contemporary American society. Color-blindness does not deny the existence of race; it nullifies the claim that race is responsible for alleged injustices that reproduce group inequalities, privilege whites, and negatively affect economic mobility, the possession of social resources, and the acquisition of political power. Put differently, inherent in the logic of color-blindness is the central assumption that race has no valence as a marker of identity or power when factored into the social vocabulary of everyday life and the capacity for exercising individual and social agency. In an era "free" of racism, race becomes a matter of personal taste, lifestyle, or heritage but has nothing to do with politics, legal rights, educational access, or economic opportunities.

Missing here is any talk about "racially fashioned policing and the prison industrial complex, homelessness, substandard schools and housing, foster care for children marred by indifference, inadequate oversight and resources, the poverty draft into an immoral war, and 'shoot-to-kill' edicts for (black) survivors of New Orleans's substandard levees designed by the Army Corps of Engineers."[5] Moreover, as politics becomes more racialized, the discourse about race becomes more privatized. Veiled by a denial of how racial histories accrue political, economic, and cultural weight to the social power of whiteness, color-blindness and the privatization of racism delete the relationship between racial differences and power and in doing so reinforce whiteness as the arbiter of value for judging difference.[6] But color-blindness does more than privilege the hidden power of whiteness. When politics is reduced to individual preferences or prejudice, judgments become difficult because there is no language for translating private issues into public concerns.

For advocates of color-blindness, race as a political signifier is conveniently denied, relegated to the historical past, or defined merely as an individual prejudice or simply a matter of individualized choices, allowing many conservatives to ignore racism as a corrosive force for expanding the dynamics of ideological and structural inequality throughout society.[7] Color-blindness is a convenient ideology for enabling whites to ignore the degree to which race is tangled up with asymmetrical relations of power, functioning

as a potent force for patterns of exclusion and discrimination including, but not limited to, housing, mortgage loans, health care,
schools, and the criminal justice system. This is the issue missing
from the current debate about the new racism being put forth by
Gingrich and others.

If one effect of color-blindness is to deny racial hierarchies, another is to offer whites the beliefs that America is now a level playing
field and that the success that whites enjoy relative to minorities of
color is largely due to individual determination, a strong work ethic,
high moral values, and a sound investment in education. Not only
does color-blindness offer up a highly racialized (though paraded
as race-transcendent) and privatized notion of agency, but it also
provides an ideological space free of guilt, self-reflection, and political responsibility, despite the fact that blacks have a disadvantage
in almost all areas of social life: housing, jobs, education, income
levels, mortgage lending, and basic everyday services.[8]

In a society marked by profound racial and class inequalities, it
is difficult to accept that character and merit—as color-blindness
advocates would have us believe—are the prime determinants for
social and economic mobility and a decent standard of living. The
relegation of racism and its effects in the larger society to the realm
of private beliefs, values, and behavior does little to explain a range
of overwhelming realities—such as soaring black unemployment,
the stepped-up resegregation of American schools, and the growing militarization and lockdown status of public education through
the widespread use of zero tolerance policies whose most egregious
effects are on poor minority youth.[9] Nor does the privatization of
racism explain why African American males live on average six
years less than their white counterparts.

It is worth noting that nothing challenges the myth that America
has become a color-blind postracist nation more than the racializa-
tion of the criminal justice system since the late 1980s. As sociologist
Loïc Wacquant has observed, the expansion of the prison-industrial
complex represents a "de facto policy of 'carceral affirmative action' towards African Americans."[10] This is borne out by the fact
that while American prisons house more than 2.3 million inmates,
"roughly half of them are black even though African-Americans
make up less than 13 percent of the nation's population.... According to the Justice Policy Institute there are now more black men
behind bars than in college in the United States. One in ten of the
world's prisoners is an African-American male."[11]

As one of the most powerful ideological and institutional factors
for deciding how identities are categorized and power, material

privileges, and resources are distributed, race represents an essential political category for examining the relationship between justice and a democratic society. What the Sotomayor debate suggests is that far from being relegated to the past, racism in its various forms can be resurrected to attack minorities of color and to appropriate victim status by whites who suggest that people of color are the "real" racists. How else can we explain Rush Limbaugh's charge that Judge Sonia Sotomayor is a racist, Newt Gingrich's charge that she is a "Latina woman racist," or Karl Rove's charge that she is "not necessarily" smart, thereby resurrecting elements of genetic racism.[12]

Rather than simply defend Sotomayor against such racist charges, progressives and others may be wise to take the debate about racism a step further and engage in a real dialogue about the historical antecedents of the new racism and how it functions in American society, particularly as it seeks to suggest that the main victims of racism in its various rhetorical and institutional guises are white men. Angry nonsensical cries of racism dominate the conservative mainstream media. When President Obama stated at a news conference that the Cambridge Police Department acted stupidly in arresting and shackling Professor Henry Louis Gates Jr., a preeminent African American scholar, in his own home, Glenn Beck on Fox News labeled Obama a racist, "with a deep-seated hatred for white people."[13]

Frank Rich, commenting on Beck's racism, wondered aloud in a *New York Times* op-ed piece if Obama's hatred of white people included his own mother. Rich went on to connect Beck's racism to the rise of the "birther" movement, which is intent on positioning Obama as the undeserving "other" by claiming that he does not have a proper birth certificate and hence is not really an American citizen.[14] Rich then quotes CNN host Lou Dobbs's support of this discredited and racist movement, while reminding us that Dobbs's previous cause was "trying to link immigrants, especially Hispanics, to civic havoc."[15] Rich goes on to argue rightly that "the escalating white fear of newly empowered ethnic groups and blacks is a naked replay of more than a century ago, when large waves of immigration and the northern migration of emancipated blacks, coupled with a tumultuous modernization of the American work force, unleashed a similar storm of racial and nativist panic."[16] Surely, this is the reason that six out of seven Republicans on the Senate Judiciary Committee refused to approve Sotomayor's nomination to the Supreme Court.

Like Frank Rich, Bob Herbert has responded to the attacks on Judge Sotomayor by arguing:

Here's the thing. Suddenly these hideously pompous and self-righteous white males of the right are all concerned about racism. They're so concerned that they're fully capable of finding it in places where it doesn't for a moment exist. Not just finding it, but being outraged by it to the point of apoplexy. Oh, they tell us, this racism is a bad thing! Are we supposed to not notice that these are the tribunes of a party that rose to power on the filthy waves of racial demagoguery.... Where were the howls of outrage at this strategy that was articulated by Lee Atwater as follows: "By 1968, you can't say 'nigger'—that hurts you. Backfires. So you say stuff like forced busing, states' rights, and all that stuff."[17]

Herbert is only partly right on this issue. The right-wing attack on Sotomayor is about more than "the howling of a fading species." It is about how racism takes on different forms in different historical contexts, making clear the need for it to be constantly challenged critically and politically. Of course, Herbert is correct in suggesting that the conservative appropriation of the new racism is not just disingenuous but hypocritical, and that even a minor lesson in history reveals the bigotry behind the strategy. But he is remiss in not suggesting that we actually take up the discourse of the new racism and do it in ways that give it real meaning and substance so it can be easily recognized and politically challenged in terms not set by conservatives. The teachable moment in this instance is that racism is alive and well in America and that it must be made visible in both its history and its current institutional and ideological manifestations. Conservatives belittle people of color who occupy positions of power, dismiss people of color when they are the victims of state violence by either invoking the discourse of personal moral failings or simply calling them angry, and then console themselves by claiming they are the real victims of racism. That this argument has any credence at all tells us just how far we have yet to go if we are going to talk seriously or expect our political leaders to talk seriously about a predatory society marked by racial violence, inequality, injustice, and ethical blindness.

Chapter 11
Children of the Recession

Remembering *Manchild in the Promised Land*

◆

If Reno was in a bad mood—if he didn't have any money and he wasn't high—he'd say, "Man, Sonny, they ain't got no kids in Harlem. I ain't never seen any. I've seen some real small people actin' like kids, but they don't have any kids in Harlem, because nobody has time for a childhood. Man, do you ever remember bein' a kid? Not me. Shit, kids are happy, kids laugh, kids are secure. They ain't scared-a nothin'. You ever been a kid, Sonny? Damn, you lucky. I ain't never been a kid, man. I don't ever remember bein' happy and not scared. I don't know what happened, man, but I think I missed out on that childhood thing, because I don't ever recall bein' a kid.[1]

—Claude Brown

When Claude Brown published *Manchild in the Promised Land* in 1965, he wrote about the doomed lives of his friends, families, and neighborhood acquaintances. The book is mostly remembered as a brilliantly devastating portrait of Harlem under siege, ravaged and broken by drugs, poverty, unemployment, crime, and police brutality. But what Brown really made visible was that the raw violence and dead-end existence that plagued so many young people in Harlem stole not only their future but also their childhood. In the midst of the social collapse and psychological trauma wrought by the systemic fusion of racism and class exploitation, children in Harlem were held hostage to forces that robbed them of the innocence that comes with childhood and forced them to take on the risks and burdens of daily survival that older generations were unable to shield them from.

At the heart of Brown's narrative, written in the midst of the civil rights struggle in the 1960s, is a "manchild," a metaphor that indicts a society that is waging war on those children who are black and poor and have been forced to grow up too quickly. The hybridized concept of manchild marked a space in which innocence was lost and childhood stolen. Harlem was a well-contained, internal colony, and its street life provided the conditions and the very necessity for insurrection. But the many forms of rebellion young people expressed—from the public and progressive to the interiorized and self-destructive—came with a price, which Brown revealed near the end of the book: "It seemed as though most of the cats that we'd come up with just hadn't made it. Almost everybody was dead or in jail."[2]

Childhood stolen became less a plea for self-help—that short-sighted and mendacious appeal that would define the reactionary reform efforts of the 1980s and 1990s—than a clarion call for condemning a social order that denied children a future. Even though Brown approached everyday life in Harlem more as a poet than as a political revolutionary, he embedded politics in every sentence in the book—not a politics marked by demagoguery, hatred, and orthodoxy, but one that made visible the damage done by a social system characterized by massive inequalities and a rigid racial divide. *Manchild* created the image of a society without children to raise questions about the future of a country that turned its back on its most vulnerable population. Like the great critical theorist C. Wright Mills, Brown's lasting contribution was to reconfigure the boundaries between public issues and private sufferings. For Brown, racism was about power and oppression and could not be separated from broader social, economic, and political considerations. Rather than denying systemic, structural conditions as in the discourse of individual pathology or self-help, Brown insisted that social forces had to be factored into any understanding of group suffering and individual despair. Brown explored the suffering of the young in Harlem, but he did so by refusing to utterly privatize it, to dramatize and spectacularize private life over public dysfunction, or to separate individual hopes, desires, and agency from the realm of politics and public life.

Nearly fifty years later, Brown's metaphor of the manchild is more relevant today than when he wrote the book, and "the promised land" is more mythic than ever as his revelation about the sorry plight of poor and minority children takes on a more expansive meaning in light of the current economic meltdown. The suffering and hardships many children face in the United States have been greatly amplified by the economic crisis, and in some cases the effects and consequences of that suffering have been captured in images, interviews, and television programs that have born witness to what has become the shame of the nation. For example, *CBS Nightly News with Katie Couric* ran a probing and poignant series called "Children of the Recession," which foregrounds the suffering and despair faced by so many millions of young kids today. Many of these images portray kids who through no fault of their own (or their parents for that matter) are homeless and lack food, health care, adequate shelter, clothing, even spaces to play. They are forced to inhabit a rough world where childhood is nonexistent, crushed under the heavy material and existential burdens they are forced to bear.

Current statistics paint a bleak picture for the nation's young people. One and a half million are unemployed, which marks a seventeen-year high, and 12.5 million are without food. A number of unsettling reports indicate that the number of children living in poverty will rise to "nearly 17 million by the end of the year [2009]."[3] In what amounts to a national disgrace, one out of every five children lives in poverty, and nearly 9 million lack any health insurance. School districts across the nation have identified and enrolled more than 800,000 homeless children.[4] Their numbers are growing at an exponential rate as one out of every fifty kids is now living in a crowded room at a motel like the Budget Inn, in a seedy welfare hotel, in an emergency shelter, or with relatives, or they simply exist on the streets with their parents.[5]

What is unique about these kids is not just the severity of deprivations they experience daily, but how they have been forced to view the world and redefine the nature of their own childhood within borders of hopelessness and despair. Unlike Brown's narrative, there is no sense of a bright future lying just beyond highly policed, ghettoized spaces. An entire generation of youth will not have access to the jobs, the material comforts, or the security available to previous generations. These children are a new generation of manchildren who think, act, and talk like adults; worry about their families, which may be headed by a single parent or two parents out of work and searching for jobs; wonder how they are going to get the money to buy food and what it will take to pay for a doctor in case of illness. These children are no longer confined to so-called ghettoes. As the burgeoning landscape of poverty and despair increasingly finds expression in our cities, suburbs, and rural areas, these children make their presence felt—too many to ignore or hide away in the usually contained and invisible spaces of disposability. They constitute a new and more unsettling scene of suffering, one that reveals vast inequalities in our economic landscape and voices a future that has no purchase on the hope that characterizes a vibrant democracy. And their voices must be heard, and their stories must be made public.

In one episode of "Children of the Recession," a twelve-year-old, Michael Rotundo, living in motel room with his parents, complains that he cannot think straight in school and is failing. His mind is filled not with the demands of homework, sports, girls, or friends, but with grave concerns about his parents not having enough money to pay rent or put a down payment on a house. His voice is eerily precocious as he tells the interviewer that he dreams about having a normal kid's life, but is not hopeful. When asked what he does when he is hungry, another child states, with a sadness no child should experience, "I just cry." In another episode, a young boy says the unthinkable for any child. He says that his life is ruined and that all he now thinks about is death because he doesn't see any way out of the circumstances he and his family find themselves in. And thirteen-year-old Lewis Roman tells an interviewer he wants to get a job to help his mother, and when asked how he copes with being hungry, he says he hides it from people because he does not want them to know. His only recourse from gnawing hunger is to try falling asleep.

Millions of children in the richest country in the world now find themselves suffering social, physical, intellectual, and developmental problems that thus far go unacknowledged by the Obama administration as it bails out the automotive industries, banks, and other financial institutions. What kind of country have we become that we cannot protect our children or offer them even the most basic requirements to survive? What does it mean to witness this type of suffering among so many children and not do anything about it—our attentions quickly diverted to view the spectacle and moral indifference that define so much of the world of celebrity entertainment or the bombastic, even demagogic, editorialists and talk show hosts who bookend the evening news? How do we reconcile all of the pious talk by the Obama administration about renewed democracy, truth, and justice as the essence of what America is all about when so many of our children are suffering, plagued by psychological and physical problems that are entirely unnecessary in country that can spend $534 billion on a military budget, "account for roughly half of the world's military expenditures,"[6] and spend trillions more on wars abroad, but cannot liberate its children from the pain of homelessness, poverty, sickness, and a mounting inability to simply be just kids.

Children should not be reduced to statistics, commodities, or disposable populations; they represent a window into the failure of the United States to take seriously the crisis enveloping youth and to uphold its end of a social contract that should guarantee them a decent future. It may be tempting to ignore these children, to look away, to blame them for their plight, or to allow a generation of manchildren to develop because of our political indifference and lack of social responsibility. But they will not go away, and as their ranks swell, the Obama administration will lose its moral and political credibility, and we will all become contaminated by a level of suffering and hardship that only gets worse.

Of course, we need more than the mobilizing influence of shame, moral outrage, and social responsibility. We need more than a president who speaks movingly about children but does little to address the urgency of the immediate crisis. We need more than the sloganized language of "change" and "hope." We need action that goes well beyond philanthropy and individual charity and transforms government in the interests of both children's and democracy's future.

Clearly, the issue at stake here is not a onetime bailout or temporary fix but real structural reforms. At the very least, as Dorothy Roberts argues, this suggests fighting for a child welfare system that would reduce "family poverty by increasing the minimum wage," and mobilizing for legislation that would institute "a guaranteed income, provide high-quality subsidized child care, preschool education, and paid parental leaves for all families."[7] Young people need a federally funded jobs-creation program and wage subsidy that would provide year-round employment for out-of-school youth and summer jobs that target in-school low-income youth. Public education and higher education, increasingly shaped by corporate and instrumental values, must be reclaimed as democratic public spheres committed to teaching young people about how to govern rather than merely be governed. Incarceration should be the last, not the first, resort for dealing with our children. Any viable notion of educational reform must include equitable funding schemes for schools, reinforced by the recognition that the problems facing public schools cannot be solved with corporate solutions or with law enforcement strategies. We need to get the police out of public schools, greatly reduce spending for prisons and military expenditures, and hire more teachers, support staff, and community people in order to eliminate the school-to-prison pipeline.

To make life livable for young people and others, basic supports must be put in place, such as a system of national health insurance that covers everybody and provisions for affordable housing. At the very least, we need guaranteed health care for young people, and we need to lower the age of eligibility for Medicare to fifty-five to keep poor families from going bankrupt. And, of course, none of this will take place unless the institutions, social relations, and values that legitimate and reproduce current levels of inequality, power, and human suffering are dismantled. The widening gap between the rich and the poor has to be addressed if young people are to have a viable future. And that requires pervasive structural reforms that constitute a real shift in power and politics away from a market-driven system that views too many children as disposable. We need to reimagine what liberty, equality, and freedom might mean as truly democratic values and practices. Have we so lost our moral and political bearings that we cannot raise our voices in protest, forge social movements, and promote direct action that makes children the center of our politics and a call for democratic renewal? I hope not.

When Claude Brown wrote *Manchild in the Promised Land* in 1965, he recognized clearly that the future and the morality of any society are intimately connected to how it treats its children, and that such an insight should motivate a politics informed by the courage of conviction and moved by a public consciousness of compassion and justice.

IV

DEMOCRACY

Chapter 12
Beyond Bailouts
Education After Neoliberalism
coauthored with Susan Searls Giroux

✑

As the financial meltdown reaches historic proportions, free-market fundamentalism, or neoliberalism as it is called in some quarters, is losing both its claim to legitimacy and its claims on democracy. Once upon a time a perceived bastion of liberal democracy, the social state is being recalled from exile after a decades-long conservative campaign against the alleged abuses of "big government"— the neoliberal euphemism for a form of governance that assumed a measure of responsibility for the education, health, and general welfare of its citizens. Not only have the starving and drowning efforts of the right been revealed in all their malicious cruelty, there is also some public support for the notion that government might begin to have a Cinderella moment. It is about to become "cool," as President Charming Barack Obama famously put it.

The idea has enchanted many. Economist and recent Nobel laureate Paul Krugman has argued that the correct response to the current credit and financial crises is to "greatly expand the role of government to rescue an ailing economy," with the proviso that all new government programs must be devoid of even a hint of corruption.[1] Bob Herbert has called for more government regulation to offset the dark cloud of impoverishment that resulted from the last thirty years of deregulation, privatization, and tax breaks for the wealthiest Americans.[2] And there are others, sophisticated thinkers all, such as Dean Baker, David Korten, Naomi Klein, and Joseph E. Stiglitz, who have traced the roots of the current financial crisis to the adaptation of neoliberal economic policy, which fostered a grim alignment among the state, corporate capital, and transnational corporations. Even *New York Times* op-ed writer Thomas Friedman has found a way to live comfortably with the idea. He wants to retool the country's educational mainframe, teaching young people to be more creative in their efforts to build "the most productivity-enhancing infrastructure"—even as his stated goal unhappily recapitulates the neoliberal fantasy that unchecked growth cures all social ills.[3] And a contrite Alan Greenspan, erstwhile disciple of free-market fundamentalist Ayn Rand, admitted before a congressional committee that he may have made a mistake in assuming "that enlightened self-interest alone would prevent bankers, mortgage brokers, investment bankers and others from gaming the system for their own personal financial benefit."[4]

With the exception of Greenspan and Friedman, all of these economists and intellectuals have rejected a market fundamentalism that dismantled the historically guaranteed social provisions provided—however partially and imperfectly—by the welfare state; defined consumerism and profit making as the essence of democratic citizenship; and equated freedom with the unrestricted ability of markets to govern economic relations free of government regulation. In doing so, these thinkers have repudiated the neoliberal dystopian vision that there are no alternatives to a market-driven society, discrediting the inviolability and inevitability of economic law. And they have condemned a market rationality that advanced private interests as it sold off public goods and services and sought to invest only in corporate and private sectors as it starved those social spheres dedicated to serving the public good. The neoliberal mantra "There Is No Alternative" has been replaced by a new, equally insistent, and increasingly pervasive call for reform and regulation.[5] With the evils of a neoliberal "voodoo" economics exposed at long last, we can look forward to the dawn of a new democratic age.

Unfortunately, what so many writers and scholars, including President Obama in his tepid criticisms of the market, have taken for granted in their criticisms of neoliberalism and their calls for immediate economic reform is the presupposition that we have on hand and in stock generations of young people and adults who have somehow been schooled for the last several decades in an entirely different set of values and cultural attitudes, who do not equate the virtue of reason with an ethically truncated instrumental rationality, who know alternative sets of social relations that are irreducible to the roles of buyer and seller, and who are intellectually prepared *and* morally committed to the staggering challenges that comprehensive reform requires. This is where the fairy-tale ending to an era of obscene injustice careens headlong into reality.

Missing from the road maps that lead us back out of Alice's rabbit hole, back out of a distorted world where reason and moral judgments do not apply, is the necessity of understanding the success of neoliberalism as a pervasive political and educational force, a pedagogy and a mode of governance that couple "forms of knowledge, strategies of power and technologies of self."[6] Neoliberalism not only transformed economic agendas throughout the overdeveloped world; it also transformed politics, restructured social relations, and produced an array of reality narratives (not unlike reality TV) and disciplinary measures that normalized its perverted view of citizenship, the state, and the supremacy of market relations. In the concerted effort to reverse course, we must take account of the profound emotional appeal, not to mention ideological hold, of neoliberalism on the American public. The success of a market ideology that has produced shocking levels of inequality and impoverishment and a market morality that has spawned rapacious greed and corruption should raise fundamental questions. How did market rule prove capable of enlisting in such a compelling way the consent of the vast majority of Americans, who cast themselves, no less, in the role of the "moral majority"? The refusal of such an analysis, framed nonetheless as a response by many theorists (including many leftists), typically explains that working people "do not, under normal circumstances, care deeply about anything beyond the size of their paychecks."[7] But this is too quick an explanation and far too inadequate. We argue that matters of popular consciousness, public sentiment, and individual and social agency are far too important as part of a larger political and educational struggle not be taken seriously by those who advocate the long and difficult project of democratic reform.

Tragically, few intellectuals providing critical commentary on the financial and credit crises offer any insights regarding how the educational force of the culture actually works pedagogically to reproduce neoliberal ideology, values, identifications, and consent. How exactly is it possible to imagine a more just, more equitable transformation in government and economics without a simultaneous transformation in culture, consciousness, social identities, and values? We are not implying that a vulgar economism is at work in such commentaries in our new and sophisticated information age, but there is a tendency to undertheorize the important relationship between the production of neoliberal economics and popular consent, cultural politics, and pedagogy. In this undertheorizing, the primacy of the force and influence of formal and informal educational sites, or the apparatuses of what we call public pedagogy, which have mediated the ever-shifting and dynamic modes of "common sense" for the past several decades, remains invisible and therefore unchecked.

Yet the formation of this common sense, which nonetheless served to legitimate the institutional arrangements of a rapacious capitalism, shifting class formations, and color-blinding racial logics, has emerged alongside a number of significant and unsettling cultural transformations, namely, the now much-discussed culture of fear; the hyperindividualization and isolation of expanding consumer society; the ideology of privatization and the dissolution of social totality (and with it, visions of the good society); and the creation of the punishing state organized around the criminalization of social problems.[8] Indeed, none of these discussions captures the fate of those populations—refugees, jobless youth, the poor, immigrants, black and Latino communities—who came to exemplify all that was allegedly wrong with the social safety nets that produced pathological forms of dependency and who were often the unwitting targets of the war on crime and the war on terror as they played out on the domestic front. These, moreover, are populations increasingly rendered disposable not only because they exist outside any productive notion of what it means to be a citizen-consumer but also because of a decades-long racist campaign that invented cultural deficits and deficiencies raising the specter of contagion and threat.

The questions we need to be asking ourselves must extend beyond how we proceed with competent and effective economic reform. Just as there is a neoliberal logic that extends beyond the economic, we must also consider at a deeper level how we dismantle the culture of fear, how we learn to think beyond the narrow dictates of instrumental rationalities, how we decriminalize certain identities, how we depathologize the concept of dependency and recognize it as our common fate, how we reclaim the public good—how we reconstitute, in short, a viable and sustainable democratic society.

Does it not seem odd, for example, that we bemoan the lack of a culture of service among young college graduates and at the same time seek to improve an educational system by implementing school policy that financially rewards students for scholastic achievement? Is it not a bit naïve to assume that such policy can end in any other way than a "pay to play" mentality? We must surely reform our financial institutions and our economic philosophies more generally, but so, too, must we reform those institutions, professional competencies, and social identities altered by decades of neoliberal rule. And that will prove a most challenging endeavor. It will require that universities, news media, hospitals and clinics, schools, and other institutions return critical and reflexive decisionmaking capacities to professors, journalists, doctors, nurses, teachers, and others. This task demands both a restructuring of power relations and a reaffirmation of those values and experiences central to a democracy. Not only must power be shared among faculty, administrators, and young people in a host of professions, but it also needs to be rooted in a formative democratic culture that supports such changes. The bottom line must not determine curricula or shape research agendas; it must not drive the news media, determine a course of medical treatment, or fix the outcome of clinical trials. Once-trusted relations between doctors and patients, teachers and students, parents and children will no longer suffer the flattening out of their respective roles to that of buyer and seller.

In spite of the crucial connection between various modes of domination and pedagogy, there is little input from progressive social theorists of what it might mean to theorize how education as a form of cultural politics actually constructs particular modes of address, identification, affective investments, and social relations that produce consent and complicity with the ethos and practice of neoliberalism. Hence, even though the current economic crisis has called into question the economic viability of neoliberal values and policies, it often does so by implying that neoliberal rationality can be explained through an economic optic alone and consequently gives the relationship of politics, culture, and education scant analysis. Any viable challenge to the culture of neoliberalism as well the current economic crisis it has generated must address not merely the diffuse operations of power throughout civil society and the globe, but also what it means to engage those diverse educational sites producing and legitimating neoliberal common sense, whether they be newspapers, advertising, the Internet, television, or more recent spheres developed as part of the new information revolution. In addition, we must examine what role public intellectuals, think tanks, the media, and universities actually play pedagogically in constructing and legitimating neoliberal worldviews and how the latter works pedagogically in producing neoliberal subjects and securing consent.

Politics is not simply about the production and protection of economic formations; it is also about the production of individuals, desires, identifications, values, and modes of understanding for inhabiting the ideological and institutional forms that make up a social order. At the very least, any attempt to understand the current crisis and what it would mean to produce a new kind of subject willing to invest in and struggle for a democratic society needs to raise another set of questions in addition to those currently posed. What educational challenges would have to be addressed in overcoming the deeply felt view in American culture that criticism is destructive, or for that matter a deeply rooted anti-intellectualism reinforced daily through various forms of public pedagogical address made available by talk radio and the infotainment sectors? How might we engage pedagogical practices that open up a culture of questioning and enable people to resist and reject neoliberal assumptions that decouple private woes from public considerations, reduce citizenship to consumerism, and make free-market ideology commensurate with democracy? What are the implications of theorizing education, pedagogy, and the practice of learning as essential to social change, and where might such interventions take place? How might it be possible to theorize the pedagogical importance of the new media and the new modes of political literacy and cultural production they employ, or to analyze the circuits of power, translation, and distribution that make up neoliberalism's vast pedagogical apparatus—extending from radio and screen culture to the Internet and newspapers? At stake here are recognizing the importance of the media as a site of public pedagogy and breaking the monopoly of information that is a central pillar of neoliberal common sense. These are only some of the questions that would be central to any viable recognition of what it would mean to theorize education as a condition that enables both critique—understood as more than the struggle against incomprehension—and social responsibility as the foundation for forms of intervention that are oppositional and empowering. To imagine a simpler solution is to be sold on a fairy tale.

Chapter 13
Educating Obama
A Task for Critical Pedagogy

⁓

The first year of Barack Obama's presidency was one of great uncertainty, a time when the conventional wisdom and old assumptions of free-market fundamentalism were thoroughly discredited. At the same time, a new hope was taking shape, fueled by the need to reaffirm the democratic legacy of social, political, and personal rights through a reaffirmation of a discourse of governance and responsible politics and their connection to democracy and the imperatives of the public good. And yet the optimism that accompanied Barack Obama's election has gradually given way among many progressives to either a deep sense of despair in light of his increasing political shift to the center or a doom-and-gloom cynicism in the face of economic crisis.[1] The financial crisis increasingly appears overwhelming and impossible to contain, given how deeply embedded it is in the underlying political and economic power structures that emerged in the conservative counterrevolution beginning with the election of Ronald Reagan in 1980. Moreover, Obama's reforms, particularly his economic, foreign, and education policies, offer no alternative vision about how to change the underlying values and institutions that shape these important sectors of society. Hence, the financial bailout is led by many people who produced the financial crisis, and the reforms for education largely echo the same old corporate endorsement of vouchers, privatization, pay for performance, high-stakes testing, union busting, and deployment of poor white kids and youth of color to military schools. Unfortunately, Obama has continued the Bush policy of making war and empire building permanent features of American society.

What is even more disturbing is that the sustained neoliberal attack on the social state and its disinvestment in those political, social, and economic spheres vital to the development of healthy and critically informed citizenry have worked quite successfully in tandem with a new and vicious rationality—produced in countless sites, such as the media and higher education—that constructs adults and young people according to the dictates, values, and needs of a market fundamentalism. All aspects of life are now measured according to the calculations of a philosophy that construes profit making as the essence of democracy and consuming as the only operable form of citizenship.[2] Government in this case operates not only within the parameters of a corporate state but also within the principles of a ruthless market whose spectacle of cruelty can no longer hide behind an appeal to self-interest, freedom, and, least of all, democracy.

But simply criticizing the market, the privatization of public goods, the politics of deregulation, and the commercialization of everyday life, although helpful, is not enough. Stirring denunciations of what a neoliberal society does to public institutions, identities, and social relations fall short of the real need to develop a language that moves beyond both the politics of Obama's so-called postpartisan notion of hope and a growing cynicism that registers not merely the depth of the current economic and political crisis but also the defeatist assumption that power operates exclusively in the service of domination, tyranny, and violence. Jacques Rancière rightly criticizes this cynical stance with his insistence that "the critique of the market today has become a morose reassessment that, contrary to its stated aims, serves to forestall the emancipation of minds and practices. And it ends up sounding not dissimilar to reactionary discourse. These critics of the market call for subversion only to declare it impossible and to abandon all hope for emancipation."[3] Rancière cannot imagine a mode of criticism or a politics that shuts down resistance, play, and hope—nor should we as teachers, parents, and young people.

At stake here is the need for a new politics of resistance and hope, one that mounts a collective challenge to a ruthless market fundamentalism that for the last thirty years has spearheaded the accumulation of capital and wealth at all costs, the commodification of young people, and the usurpation of democratic modes of sovereignty. At the center of this struggle is a market sovereignty that has replaced the state as the principal regulatory force in developing economies of inequality and power and gained legitimacy and strength through modes of education, persuasion, and consent that rely on the force of new media technologies, corporate values, commodified social relations, and a calculating rationality, all of which have to be challenged and transformed. Any politics capable of disabling the sovereignty of the market must clarify in political and pedagogical terms a vision, project, discourse, and set of strategic practices necessary to confront a neoliberal order that views democracy as the enemy and flawed consumers as expendable. Free-market fundamentalism as a form of casino capitalism has played a major role in creating not only massive human suffering, a financial Katrina, and millions of displaced lives but also a weakened social state and a failing democracy made all the more ominous by the dumbing down of public discourse and the emptying out of critical public spheres.

Democracy is not about the sovereignty of the market, nor is it a form of state governance based largely on fear, manipulation, deceit, and ongoing production of state violence. Any attempt at challenging neoliberal sovereignty and the national (in)security state must recognize the need for a politics in which matters of education, power, and governance are mutually determined. Such a challenge rests, in part, on a politics that takes seriously the need to understand how the institutions of economic Darwinism emerged and recently came unglued as well as how and why modes of governing that embody the grand ideologies of a deflated Gilded Age appealed to so many Americans. Frank Rich is right in alerting us to the importance of analyzing how a bankrupt neoliberalism has given us a "debt-ridden national binge of greed and irresponsibility [partly through] mass forms of conspicuous consumption and entertainment."[4] Implicit in Rich's argument is the need to rethink the discourse of crisis, complicating its underlying causes by raising questions about the role of media and other educational institutions in celebrating and legitimating the pernicious and corrupting values of a rabid market-driven society eager and determined to highjack social responsibility, noncommodified public spheres, and meaningful citizenship, while treating with scorn any discourse of compassion, mutual worth, and ethical responsibility.

Clearly, one challenge the current crisis offers anyone concerned about the fate of democracy is the need for a thorough understanding of how this legacy of market-driven fundamentalism can be comprehended in terms of its power in shaping subjects, citizens, institutions, culture, values, and particular kinds of actions. For instance, how is it that the same old values and market-driven fundamentalism used to support tax cuts for the rich, eliminate the social state, and discredit any commitment to the public good are being mobilized once again by Republicans to thwart Obama's stimulus package without provoking a massive public outcry among either the mainstream media, academics, or the general public? Or, even worse, where is the moral outrage among so many Americans who are suffering from the consequences of a thirty-year tyranny of neoliberal policies aimed at waging a war on the welfare state, science, dissent, the environment, workers, young people, and all aspects of the public good?

Democratic politics and the struggles informed by such a politics cannot come about without putting into place these spaces, spheres, and modes of education that enable people to realize that in a real democracy power has to be responsive to the needs, hopes, and desires of its citizens and other inhabitants around the globe. Democracy is not simply about people wanting to improve their lives; it is also more importantly about their willingness to struggle to protect their right to self-determination and self-government in the interest of the common good. Under the reign of free-market fundamentalism, market relations expanded their control over public space and increasingly defined people as either consuming subjects or commodities, thereby effectively limiting their opportunity to learn how to develop their full range of intellectual and emotional capacities to be critical citizens. Sheldon Wolin has rightly argued that if "democracy is about participating in self-government, its first requirement is a supportive culture of complex beliefs, values, and practices to nurture equality, cooperation, and freedom."[5] The militarized corporate state and the sovereign market reduce the materiality of democracy to either an overcrowded prison or a shopping mall, both of which are more fitting for a society vulnerable to the winds of totalitarianism. The fundamental institutional and educational conditions that connect social, political, and personal rights to a viable notion of agency now face a moment of crisis as severe as the current economic crisis.

As education turns to training in the public schools and as higher education willingly models itself as a business venture or welcome recipient of Pentagon largesse, corporate culture reigns unchallenged as the most powerful pedagogical force in the country, while "democracy becomes dangerously empty."[6] Unfortunately, Obama seems less than inspiring when it comes to mobilizing a new politics that makes public and higher education central to the struggle for democracy.[7] A visionary politics needs to be willing to enlist and actively mobilize artists, intellectuals, academics, parents, young people, workers, and others in the struggle for a public able and willing to confront through multiple levels of resistance the institutions, policies, and values of an ever-expanding military-industrial-academic complex. Obama's call to put money into rebuilding the infrastructures of schools is to be applauded, but it is largely canceled out by his adherence to an educational policy that views schools less as an investment than as an extension of the market, to be largely driven by the corporate values and accountability schemes that the Bush administration supported. Obama's educational policies need to be pushed in a very different direction, one that is able to recognize the value of critical education for reasons Zygmunt Bauman illuminates with razorlike precision:

> Adverse odds may be overwhelming, and yet democratic (or, as Cornelius Castoriadis would say, an autonomous) society knows of no substitute for education and self-education as a means to influence the turn of events that can be squared with its own nature, while that nature cannot be preserved for long without "critical pedagogy"—education sharpening its critical edge, "making society feel guilty" and "stirring things up" through stirring human consciences. The fates of freedom, of democracy that makes it possible while being made possible by it, and of education that breeds dissatisfaction with the level of both freedom and democracy achieved thus far, are inextricably connected and not to be detached from one another. One may view that intimate connection as another specimen of a vicious circle—but it is within that circle that human hopes and the chances of humanity are inscribed, and can be nowhere else.[8]

Making education central to any viable notion of politics as well as making the political more pedagogical suggests that intellectuals, artists, community workers, parents, and others need to connect with diverse groups of people in those public and virtual sites and spheres that enable new modes of dialogue to take place and work to move beyond such exchanges to the much more difficult task of building organized and sustainable social movements. Although it is true that anyone who takes politics seriously needs to take into consideration the profound transformations that have taken place in the public sphere, especially those enabled by new technologies, and how such changes can be used to develop new modes of public pedagogy in which young people are provided with the skills, knowledge, interests, and desire to govern themselves, it is simply wrong to suggest that real change happens only online.[9] Building a more just, ecologically sustainable, and democratic future, or as

Jacques Derrida puts it, the promise of "a democracy to come,"[10] demands a politics in which the new technologies are important but only insofar as they are used in the context of bringing people together, reclaiming those public spheres where people can meet, talk, and plan collective actions. We must learn to resist all technologies that reinforce the sense of excessive individualism and privatization at the heart of the neoliberal worldview. We need more than bailouts; we need a politics that reinvents the concept of the social while providing a language of critique and hope forged not in isolation but in collective struggle that takes social responsibility, commitment, and justice seriously.

We live at a time when social bonds are crumbling and institutions that provide collective help are disappearing. Reclaiming these social bonds and the protections of the social state means, in part, developing a new mode of politics and education in which a critically educated public is as central to this struggle as the future of the democratic society it once symbolized. At the heart of this struggle for both young people and adults is the pressing problem of organizing and energizing a vibrant cultural politics to counter the conditions of political apathy, distrust, and social disengagement so pervasive under the politics of neoliberalism. For this we need a new vocabulary that, in part, demands taking back formal education and diverse modes of public pedagogy for democratic purposes, while also refashioning social movements and modes of collective resistance that are democratic in nature and global in reach. Culture in this instance is not merely a resource but also an instrument of political power.

What must be emphasized in this vision of a democracy to come is that there is no room for a politics animated by a rationality that is about maximizing profit and constructing a society detached from the burden of mutual responsibility—that is, a society whose essence is captured in the faces of children confronting the terror of a future with little hope of survival. Economic crises do more than throw people out of jobs; they also open up an opportunity for social movements and political demands that serve to educate those in power and push them in a very different direction. This is a moment in which education becomes the foundation for collective change and for a rewriting of the social contract, an expansion of the meaning of social responsibility, and a renewed struggle to take democracy back from the dark times that have inched us so close to an unimaginable authoritarianism.

Chapter 14
Beyond the Audacity of Hope
The Promise of an Educated Citizenry

～⊖

A number of progressive pundits argued that with the election of Barack Obama to the presidency, intelligence and hope would once again be embraced as well as promoted as essential elements of American culture. At work in this discourse is a qualified endorsement of Obama's emphasis on hope, an emphasis that is audacious in its reach and courageous in its ability to see beyond the wretched cynicism and inflated self-interest that accompanied the embrace of an unchecked and unprincipled market fundamentalism celebrated with great fervor since the Reagan revolution of the 1980s. But the country needs more than a notion of hope that is audacious; it needs a conception of educated hope, one that is both bold in its vision and keen in its understanding that only by supporting those institutions that provide the conditions for an educated and critically informed citizenry can reform actually work in the interest of sustaining a substantive democracy, in which hope becomes a precondition for politics itself.

Educated hope begins in opposition to a long legacy of privatization and corporatization that has shaped the public imagination, especially with respect to public and higher education. Oddly enough, Obama seems to miss this point. He is a strong advocate for education that is engaged, critical, and on the side of public service, yet he reduces the goal of higher education to providing a competitive workforce, while supporting some of the most reductionistic and instrumental elements of educational reform. What are we to make of Obama's call for educational reform in the public school system that celebrates intelligence and public service while endorsing the mind-deadening methods of drill-and-skill testing schemes and pay-for-performance objectives?

These approaches are not about schooling; they are about training and punishment. They deaden the spirit of curiosity and hijack any claim to critical pedagogical practices. In fact, they are methods that have been used as part of the right-wing war on public schooling that has been going on since the Reagan era and particularly in the eight years under George W. Bush. What is one to make of the "audacity of hope" in Obama's appointment of Arne Duncan—who is well known for supporting bankrupt accountability schemes, charter schools, and military academies for those kids viewed as disposable—to secretary of education? Similarly, where is the audacity of hope when it comes to rescuing higher education from the creeping hand of corporatization and militarization that now structures the governance and research initiatives in so many these schools?

In opposition to the corporatizing of education, parents, teachers, intellectuals, and young people need to define and reclaim public and higher education as resources vital to the democratic and civic life of the nation. At the heart of such a task is the challenge for academics, cultural workers, and labor organizers to join together and oppose the transformation of public and higher education into a consumer-oriented corporation more concerned about accounting than accountability.[1] As Zygmunt Bauman reminds us, schools are one of the few public spaces left where students can learn the "skills for citizen participation and effective political action."[2] Without these institutions, there can be no "citizenship" either. Defending public and higher education as a vital public sphere is necessary for developing and nourish the proper balance between democratic public spheres and commercial power, between identities founded on democratic principles and identities steeped in forms of competitive, self-interested individualism that celebrate selfishness, profit making, and greed.

This view suggests that public and higher education be defended through intellectual work that self-consciously recalls the tension between the democratic imperatives or possibilities of public institutions and the everyday realization of these imperatives within a society dominated by market principles. If formal education is to remain a site of critical thinking, collective work, and social struggle, public intellectuals and progressive social forces need to expand its meaning and purpose. That is, they need to define public and higher education as resources vital to the moral life of the nation, open to working people and communities whose resources, knowledge, and skills have often been viewed as marginal. The goal here is to redefine knowledge and skills to more broadly reconstruct a tradition that links critical thought to collective action, human agency to social responsibility, and knowledge and power to a profound impatience with a status quo founded upon deep inequalities and injustices.

There is more at stake here than recognizing the limits and social costs of an unchecked free-market fundamentalism that reduces all relationships to the exchange of goods and money. There is also the responsibility on the part of critical intellectuals and other activists to rethink the nature of the public. For instance, it may be argued that schools are being accused of failing by Obama and a slew of liberal and conservative commentators not because they are inefficient, but precisely because they are public and have the potential to function as democratic public spheres. All the more reason for educators, parents, and young people to address and embrace new forms of social citizenship and civic education that have a purchase on people's everyday lives and struggles. In light of the profound crisis of spirit, vision, and economics now facing the nation, I believe that academics and others bear an enormous responsibility in opposing Obama's courtship with neoliberal values by bringing democratic political culture back to life. Part of this challenge involves creating new locations of struggle, vocabularies, and subject positions that allow people in a wide variety of public spheres to become more than they are now, to question what it is they have become within existing institutional and social formations, and "to give some thought to their experiences so that they can transform their relations of subordination and oppression."[3]

In part, this necessity to reclaim democratic schooling, values, and culture suggests that educators, parents, young people, and others should take Obama's notion of hope seriously by resisting his administration's use of neoliberal values to shape any discourse about educational reform. At the same time, the defense of education as a democratic public sphere should extend further to push the Obama administration to provide the financial and ideological support for giving all students regardless of race, ethnicity, or class position access to a quality education that does not carry the burden of lifelong debt. Of course, in the first instance Obama and his administration must recognize that education is more than a financial investment; education is also an investment in educating future generations in what it means to take seriously their own sense of civic courage and agency and the need to struggle for a democracy that is never finished and always has to be on guard in not allowing itself to degenerate into a new form of authoritarianism.

Obama is right in wanting to revitalize the language of civic education as part of a broader discourse of hope, but this discourse must extend to the conditions that make political agency and critical citizenship possible in a global world. Militant utopian thinking in this context suggests that any viable notion of the political must address the primacy of pedagogy as part of a broader attempt to revitalize the conditions for individual and social agency, while simultaneously addressing the most basic problems facing the prospects for social justice and global democracy. Educators need a new vocabulary for linking hope, social citizenship, and education to the demands of substantive democracy. I am suggesting that educators and others need a new vocabulary for connecting how we read critically to how we engage in movements for social change.

I also believe that simply invoking the relationship between theory and practice, critique and social action, will not do. Any attempt to give new life to a substantive democratic politics must address how people learn to be political agents and what kind of educational work is necessary within what kind of public spaces to enable people to use their full intellectual resources. Such an attempt must provide a profound critique of existing institutions and struggle to create, as Stuart Hall puts it, "what would be a good life or a better kind of life for the majority of people."[4] As educators, writers, parents, and workers, we are required to understand more fully why the tools we used in the past feel awkward in the present, often failing to respond to problems now facing the United States and other parts of the globe. More specifically, we face the challenge posed by the failure of existing critical discourses to bridge the gap between how society represents itself and how and why individuals fail to understand and critically engage such representations in order to intervene in the oppressive social relationships these representations often legitimate.

Obama's notion of hope at least signals something crucial about the bankruptcy of the old political languages and the need for a new vocabulary and vision for clarifying our intellectual, ethical, and political projects, especially as they work to reabsorb questions of agency, ethics, and meaning back into politics and public life. But this is not the language of postpartisanship and consensus; it is the language of civic responsibility, engaged citizenship, power, and social justice. Along these lines, Sheldon Wolin argues that we need to rethink the notion of loss and how it influences the possibility for opening up democratic public life. Wolin points to the need for progressives, theorists, and critical educators to resurrect and raise questions about "what survives of the defeated, the indigestible, the unassimilated, the 'cross grained,' the 'not wholly obsolete.'"[5] He argues that "something is missing" in an age of manufactured politics and pseudopublics catering almost exclusively to desires and drives produced by the commercial hysteria of the market.

What is missing are a language, a movement, and a vision that refuse to equate democracy with consumerism, market relations, and privatization. In the absence of such a language and the social formations and public spheres that make it operative, politics becomes narcissistic and caters to the mood of widespread pessimism and the cathartic allure of the spectacle. Instead of the "audacity of hope," maybe we need a language that embraces a militant utopianism, while constantly being attentive to those forces that seek to turn such hope into a new slogan or punish and dismiss those who dare look beyond the horizon of the given. Educated hope, in this instance, is the precondition for individual and social struggle, the ongoing practice of critical education in a wide variety of sites, and the mark of courage on the part of intellectuals in and out of the academy who use the resources of theory to address pressing social problems.

But hope is also a referent for civic courage and its ability to mediate the memory of loss and the experience of injustice as part of a broader attempt to open up new locations of struggle, contest the workings of oppressive power, and undermine various forms of domination. At its best, hope translates civic courage into political practice, one that often begins when a person's life can no longer be taken for granted. In doing so, educated hope makes concrete the possibility for transforming politics into an ethical space and a public activity that confront the flow of everyday experience and the weight of social suffering with the force of individual and collective resistance and the unending project of democratic social transformation. Educated hope involves struggle, assumes a boldness that sees beyond the discourse of consensus, and takes seriously a view of education that reclaims learning as part of an engaged and practical politics that is inextricably linked to the quality of moral and political life of the wider society. There is more at stake here than the semantics of hope. There is the question of whether a democracy can survive without an educated citizenry.

Chapter 15
The Iranian Uprisings and the Challenge of the New Media
Rethinking the Politics of Representation

⟡

The new communications technology and the diverse social networking sites associated with it are generally represented in the dominant media in terms that are utterly depoliticizing and privatizing and are reduced thereby to personal tools and entertainment devices that allegedly enamour young people all over the world.[1] Little is said about the prevalent technological and market-driven rationalities that guide the dominant uses of the electronically based media or how the diverse screen cultures that enable it—such as Facebook, Twitter, and other social networking platforms—either enhance or limit matters of agency, ethics, knowledge, and social responsibility.[2] Herbert Marcuse's concern about how instrumental rationality has undermined technology's emancipatory possibilities, reducing it to a tool for domination, is generally ignored, except by a few critical scholars whose work is too often missing from larger public debates about the new media.[3] For instance, Zygmunt Bauman warns how screen culture and its virtual networking sites undermine democratic notions of the social while promoting a culture of privatization, a culture more akin to the dictates of neoliberalism than to democracy. He writes: "We talk compulsively about networks and try obsessively to conjure them (or at least their phantoms) out of 'speed dating,' personal ads and magic incantations of 'messaging' because we painfully miss the safety nets which the true networks of kinship, friends and brothers-in-fate used to provide matter-of-factly, with or without our efforts. Mobile-telephone directories stand for the missing community and are hoped to deputize for the missing intimacy; they are expected to carry a load of expectations they lack the strength to lift, let alone to hold."[4]

Even though Bauman indeed captures the transformation of North American consumer culture through the new digital media, other sites have also emerged that defy, even as they are made possible by, neoliberal logic and technological domination. Perhaps most significantly, the democratic protests in Iran about alleged electoral fraud in the reelection of President Mahmoud Ahmadinejad on June 12, 2009, have rekindled questions about the relations between the new media and the terms on which politics operates, including the new media's potential to revitalize the public sphere and its construction of social practices and modes of communication that cannot be defined exclusively within the power relations of the nation-state. As the uprisings in Iran illustrated, new electronic technologies and the popular social networking sites they have produced have transformed both the landscape of media production and reception and the ability of state power to define the borders and boundaries of what constitutes the very nature of political engagement. Indeed, politics itself has been increasingly redefined by a screen culture and newly emergent public spaces of education and resistance embraced by students and other young people.[5] For example, nearly 75 percent of Iranians now own cell phones.[6] Screen culture and its attendant electronic technologies have created a return to a politics in which many young people in Iran are forcefully asserting their power to act and express both criticisms and support of Mir Hussein Moussavi, the primary opposition candidate seeking to be the president of the Islamic Republic of Iran, and are willing to risk their lives in the face of attacks by thugs and state-sponsored vigilante groups.

Texts and images calling for "death to the dictator" circulate in a wild zone of representation on the Internet, on YouTube, and among Facebook and Twitter users, giving rise to a chorus of dissent and collective resistance that places many young people in danger and at the forefront of developing political uprisings. Reports have emerged in the press and other media outlets about a number of protesters being attacked or killed by government forces, especially as the government launched an assault on the demonstrators in the aftermath of the insistence by Iran's supreme leader, Ayatollah

Ali Khamenei, that there "would be 'bloodshed,' if street protests continued over the disputed presidential election."[7] In the face of massive arrests by the police and threats of execution from some government officials, public protest continued to be visible in the world media—though, as Nazila Fathi reported in the *New York Times* on June 18, 2009, the Iranian government worked "on many fronts to shield the outside world's view of the unrest, banning coverage of the demonstrations, arresting journalists, threatening bloggers and trying to block Web sites like Facebook and Twitter, which have become vital outlets for information about the rising confrontation here."[8]

It is impossible to comprehend the political nature of the ongoing protests in Iran (and more recently in Moldova) without recognizing the centrality of the new visual media and new modes of social networking. New image-based media devices—camcorders, cellular camera phones, satellite television, digital recorders, and laptop computers, to name a few—have enacted a structural transformation of everyday life by fusing sophisticated electronic technologies with a ubiquitous screen culture. These devices have also revolutionized the relationship between the moment of an event and its public display by making events accessible almost instantly to a global audience. The Internet, YouTube, Twitter, and Facebook have reconstituted, especially among young people, how social relationships are constructed and how communication is produced, mediated, and received. These sites have also ushered in a new regime of visual imagery in which screen culture creates spectacular events just as much as it records them. Under such circumstances, state power becomes more porous and less controlled, leading governments of countries such as Iran to accuse the United States and Canada of producing "deviant news sites."[9] But such charges remain impotent when compared with the impact of images uploaded on YouTube of a young man bleeding to death as a result of an assault by Iranian government forces, his white shirt stained with blood and bystanders holding his hand while he died.[10] The Internet and the new media outlets in this context provide new public sites of visibility for an unprecedented look into the workings of state-sponsored violence, civil unrest, and a politics of massive resistance that simply cannot be controlled by traditional forces of repression.

The pedagogical force of culture is now writ large within circuits of global transmission that defy the military power of the state, while simultaneously provoking the state's reliance on physical force and military power to control its own citizens. In Iran, the state-sponsored war against democracy, with its requisite pedagogy of fear dominating every conceivable media outlet, creates the conditions for transforming a fundamentalist theocratic state into a more dangerous, overtly militaristic authoritarian regime. Meanwhile, insurgents use digital video cameras to defy official power, cell phones to recruit members to battle occupying forces, and Twitter messages to challenge the doctrines of fear, militarism, and censorship. The endless flashing of screen culture confronts those inside and outside of Iran with the reality of state-sponsored violence and corruption as well as with the spread of new social cartographies of power and resistance among young people as an emerging reality of contemporary politics in Iran. Text messaging, cell phone images, Facebook, Twitter, YouTube, and the Internet have given rise to a reservoir of political energy that posits a new relationship among the new media technologies, politics, and public life—a glimpse of which was also seen in the ways in which young people in the United States mobilized to get out the vote for Barack Obama in the 2008 U.S. presidential election.

These new media technologies and Web sites have proved a powerful force in resisting dominant channels of censorship and militarism. But they have done more in allowing an emerging generation of young people and students in Iran to narrate their political views, convictions, and voices through a screen culture that opposes the one-dimensional cultural apparatuses of certainty, while rewriting the space of politics through new social networking sites and public spheres.

A spectacular flood of images produced by a subversive interconnected web of technologies that opened up a cinematic politics of collective resistance and social justice overrode Iran's official narratives of repression, totalitarianism, and orthodoxy—unleashing the wrath of a generation that hungers for a life in which matters of dignity, agency, and hope are aligned with the democratic institutions that make them possible. Death and suffering are now inscribed in an order of politics and power that can no longer hide in the shadows, pretending that there are no cracks in its body politic or suppressing the voices of a younger generation emboldened by courage and dreams of a more democratic future.

In this remarkable historical moment, a sea of courageous young people in Iran led the way in instructing an older generation about a new form of politics in which mass and image-based media have become a distinctly powerful pedagogical force, reconfiguring the very nature of politics, cultural production, engagement, and resistance. Under such circumstances, this young generation of Iranian students, educators, artists, and citizens is developing a new set of theoretical tools and modes of collective resistance in which the educational force of the new media both records and challenges representations of state, police, and militia violence while becoming part of a broader struggle for democracy itself.

The alienation felt by many Iranian young people in an utterly repressive and fundamentalist society is exacerbated within a government- and media-produced culture of fear according to which the terror Iranian youth face at home and abroad cannot be fought without a surrender of their sense of agency and social justice to a militarized state. And yet as the technology of the media expands, so do the sites for critical education, resistance, and collective struggle.

Any critical attempt to engage the courageous uprisings in Iran must also try to understand how the new media and electronic technologies can be used as a tool of insurgency and opposition to state power. State power no longer has a hold on information, at least not in the way it did before the emergence of the new media, with their ability to reconfigure public exchange and social relations while constituting a new sphere of politics. The new media technologies are being used in Iran in ways that redefine the very conditions that make politics possible. Public spaces emerge in which data and technologies are employed to bypass government censors. The public and the private inform each other as personal discontent is translated into broader social issues. Global publics of opposition emerge through electronic circuits of power offering up wider spheres of exchange, dialogue, and resistance—and a broader theoretical conception of the value of cultural politics. For example, protesters from all over the world are producing proxy servers, "making their own computers available to Iranians," and fueling worldwide outrage and protests by uploading on YouTube live videos exposing the "brutality of the regime's crackdown."[11] Demonstrations of solidarity are emerging between the Iranian diaspora and students and other protesters within Iran as information, technological resources, and skills are exchanged through the Internet, cell phones, and other technologies and sites.

While forging a new conception of politics, education, and society, the uprisings in Iran clearly raise significant questions about the new media and its centrality to democracy. Image-based technologies have redefined the relationship among the ethical, the political, and the aesthetic. Although "the proximity [of politics and the new media] is perhaps discomforting to some, ... it is also the condition of any serious intervention" into what it means to connect cultural politics to matters of political and social responsibility.[12]

The rise of the new media and the conditions that have produced it do not sound the death knell of democracy as some have argued, but rather demand that we "begin to rethink democracy from within these conditions."[13] The brave Iranian youth provided the world with a lesson in how the rest of us might construct a cultural politics based on social relations that enable individuals and social groups to rethink the crucial nature of what it means to make power visible, exhibit civic courage, and assume a measure of social responsibility in a media-saturated global sphere. These youth are working out in real time what it means to address how these new media technologies might foster a democratic cultural politics that challenges religious fundamentalism, state censorship, militarism, and the cult of certainty.

Such a collective project requires a politics that is in the process of being invented, one that has to be attentive to the new realities of power, global social movements, and the promise of a planetary democracy. Both the old and new media and the technologies of screen culture are inextricably implicated in not simply the crisis of information and communication, but also in the crisis of democracy itself. Whatever the outcome, the magnificent and brave uprising by the young people of Iran illustrates that they have legitimated once again a new register of both opposition and politics. What is at stake, in part, is a mode of resistance and educational practice that is redefining in the heat of the battle the ideologies and skills needed to critically understand the new visual and visualizing technologies not only as new modes of communication, but also as weapons in the struggle for expanding and deepening the ideals and possibilities of democratic public life and the supportive cultures vital to democracy's survival.

As these students and young people have demonstrated, it would be a mistake to simply align the new media exclusively with the forces of domination and commercialism—what Allen Feldman calls "total spectrum violence"[14]—as many critics do in the United States. The Iranian uprising, with its recognition of the image as a key force of social power, makes clear that cultural politics is now constituted by a plurality of sites of resistance and social struggle, offering up new ways for young people to conceptualize how the media might be used to create alternative public spheres that enable them to claim their own voices and challenge the dominant forces of oppression. Theorists such as Thomas Keenan, Mark Poster, Douglas Kellner, and Jacques Derrida are right in suggesting that the new electronic technologies and media publics "remove restrictions on the horizon of possible communications" and, in doing so, suggest new possibilities for engaging the new media as a democratic force both for critique and for positive intervention and change.[15]

The ongoing struggle in Iran, if examined closely, provides some resources for rethinking how the political is connected to particular understandings of the social; how distinctive modes of address are used to marshal specific and often dangerous narratives, memories, and histories; and how certain pedagogical practices are employed in mobilizing a range of affective investments around images of trauma, suffering, and collective struggle. The images and messages coming out of Iran demonstrate the courage of this generation of young people and others, while also signifying new possibilities for redefining a global democratic politics. What the dictatorship in Iran is witnessing is not simply generational discontent or the power of networking and communication sites such as Twitter, Facebook, and YouTube, but a much more dangerous lesson in which democracy implies an experience in which power is shared, dialogue is connected to involvement in the public sphere, hope means imagining the unimaginable, and collective action portends the outlines of a new understanding of power, freedom, and democracy.

Unfortunately, hope manifested in this important struggle against a rigid theocratic government received little support from the Obama administration. Hope in this case was sacrificed to the logic of political centrism and expediency—which translates into "Tread carefully and make sure you offend no one." Obama's audacity of hope seems to have little relevance when it comes to those youth who constitute the global others pushing hard against fundamentalism in the interest of democratization.

As the crushing force of the state bears down on the students and other protesters in Iran, pushing their struggles out of the streets and into the shadows of power, it is crucial to grasp both the strengths and the limitations of screen culture in this ongoing political conflict. Those whose voices are removed from the narratives of official power have found new ways to counter such narratives, criticize them, and offer counternarratives in their place. The new media and its social networks point to distinct modes of representation and a more capacious politics for correcting what Nick Couldry calls "current injustices of representation."[16]

Yet critical, if not radical, appropriations of the new media are only a precondition for the more crucial task of organizing diverse publics around political struggles and goals and building long-term organizations and social movements that have the power to challenge dominant regimes through a diverse number of political channels and actions. The new media may be highly novel in their ability to bring mass numbers of people into the streets, but as Angela Davis points out, organizing for the long term is not synonymous with mobilizing demonstrations. As she puts it: "It is difficult to encourage people to think about protracted struggles, protracted movements that require very careful organizing interventions that don't always depend on our capacity to mobilize demonstrations. It seems to be that mobilization had displaced organization, so that in the contemporary moment, when we think about organizing movements, we think about bringing masses of people into the streets."[17]

Let us hope that in the aftermath of the ongoing massive demonstrations in Tehran, we can rethink how the new media technologies of screen culture and electronically mediated social networks can refigure existing modes of communication, and we can rewrite a democratic politics in which social movements can emerge that challenge antidemocratic tendencies in Iran and other countries around the world. The new technologies, with their instant modes of communication, have a purpose, as we have seen in Iran and among various forms of opposition that have emerged in China, Moldova, and Egypt. But what is crucial now is the fostering of relationships to technology that are predicated not only on instant, widely circulated, and uncensored modes of communication but also on the creation of conditions for the development of critical literacies, modes of agency, critical thinking, and other aspects of civic engagement and education that are the precondition for any lasting form of democratic governance and social relations.

Chapter 16
Obama's Tortured Democracy
The Power of Images and the Politics of State Secrecy

↭

Before the thick fog of government censorship stifled electronically mediated videos and pictures of savage state violence and repression in the streets of Tehran, one image became both a rallying point and an iconic symbol of the fierce protest movement challenging the allegedly stolen election of hard-line president Mahmoud Ahmadinejad and the repressive nature of the Islamic Republic founded in 1979. The "Neda video," filmed by two people holding a camera phone, graphically shows in disturbing detail a twenty-six-year-old woman, Neda Agha-Soltan, lying in a pool of blood on a Tehran street, unable to speak as her father bends over her stunned body and pleads with her to hold on. The horror of the scene reveals itself more acutely with the juxtaposed images of a once-vibrant Neda smiling serenely into the camera—as if she were gently seeking the viewer's gaze and asking for justice. She died as a result of being shot in the chest by a plainclothes member of the Basij militia.

The now-deceased victim, whose blood-streaked face is powerfully captured on video, communicates not just the needless suffering and death of an innocent woman, but also the brutality and harsh violence of state-sponsored repression. In spite of the seriousness of the crime and the global indignation it produced, the

Iranian government thus far has refused to launch an investigation of Neda's death and banned any public funerals or memorials. As Glenn Greenwald rightly insists, "Like so many iconic visual images before it—from My Lai, fire hoses and dogs unleashed at civil rights protesters, Abu Ghraib—that single image has done more than the tens of thousands of words to dramatize the violence and underscore the brutality of the state response."[1] The image of Neda's death has kindled a global tsunami of moral outrage, turning her into a coveted icon of collective resistance to state violence and a symbol of struggle for the promise of a future Islamic democracy. Indeed, given the concerted efforts by technophiles the world over, the event crystallized, for a moment, the emerging possibilities of new forms of global citizenship.

The dramatic Neda video reconfigured the ways in which an oppressive government attempted to define the boundaries of the possible and the ways in which new spaces and modes of criticism came to exist nonetheless, no longer contained by official hierarchies of power and control. The image of Neda's death ruptured the circuit of dominant power and official knowledge that made antidemocratic policies acceptable, producing an outpouring of public anger while providing evidence of a state-supported atrocity and government repression that revealed and challenged the carefully managed way in which the Iranian government framed its perception of itself and its attempts to educate the wider society. For a moment, social and state power were made accountable in novel ways, held up to critical scrutiny, and challenged with a massive discharge of anguish and protests among students, intellectuals, and a variety of other groups. The Neda video has now became an inseparable part of a historic legacy of images that have served to modify the nature of politics and government abuse by making power visible and loosening the coordinates of government-sanctioned ways of seeing and knowing. Or as French philosopher Jacques Rancière puts it in a different context, the video functions "to modify the visible, the ways of experiencing and perceiving the tolerable as intolerable."[2]

The political importance of the power of the image to reveal government abuse and unleash public outrage was almost lost on members of the American media establishment when President Barack Obama was asked by CNN's Suzanne Malveaux about his reaction to the Neda video. Obama responded by calling the image "heartbreaking," adding that "anybody who sees it knows that there's something fundamentally unjust about that." He then offered some support, however oblique, to those protesting Iran's contested election by quoting Dr. Martin Luther King Jr.: "The arc of the moral universe is long, but it bends toward justice."[3]

Fortunately, Helen Thomas, one of the more courageous reporters covering the White House, refused to accept his answer as a humble expression of grief and queried him about how he might reconcile his positive statements about the Neda video and images of Iranians protesting in the streets of Tehran with his concerted attempts to block the release of photos of detainees abused and tortured abroad by the United States. Obama responded by suggesting that Thomas's question was out of line—in actuality, she was focusing on a contradiction that seems to connect Obama more to the forces of government suppression and censorship than to those sympathetic to the ideals of freedom and government transparency. As Randy Cohen wrote in the *New York Times*, "We should not rebuke Iran for lack of openness and then resist it ourselves."[4] Glenn Greenwald further heightened the contradiction by asking, "How is it possible for Obama to pay dramatic tribute to the 'heartbreaking' impact of that Neda video in bringing to light the injustices of the Iranian government's conduct while simultaneously suppressing images that do the same with regard to our own government's conduct?"[5]

Obama publicly acknowledged the suffering of this young girl but refused to acknowledge or respond to the suffering and pain of those countless detainees tortured by U.S. military and intelligence forces. In Obama's contradictory logic, the life of Neda Agha-Soltan is eminently grievable, whereas the lives of those who have survived horrible abuses at the hands of U.S. government employees, some of whom have most certainly committed war crimes, are not. At the same time, Obama's invocation of the state secrecy privilege in refusing to release images of torture and abuse represents an attempt on the part of his administration to ratify what kinds of government actions can be made visible and open to debate and what practices should be hidden from public purview, even if the government is guilty of war crimes.

State secrecy operating in the service of abuse has more in common with dictatorships reminiscent of Augusto Pinochet's Chile, with its infamous torture chambers and willingness to "disappear" all those considered enemies of the state, than it does with a vibrant and open democracy. Such secrecy shuts down public debate, makes the policies of governments invisible, and implies that state power should not be held accountable. But this secrecy does more: It sanctions criminal behavior, undermines the need for public dialogue, contaminates moral values, and furthers a culture of violence and cruelty by suggesting that those who criminally promote torture, break the law, and engage in human rights violations should not be held responsible for their actions.

Obama and his defenders argue that releasing the inflammatory torture photos would reflect badly on the United States, increasing anti-American sentiment around the world and putting the lives of American troops in jeopardy. According to Obama: "The publication of these photos would not add any additional benefit to our understanding of what was carried out in the past by a small number of individuals.... In fact, the most direct consequence of releasing them, I believe, would be to further inflame anti-American opinion and to put our troops in danger."[6] In this view, the legal framework for ensuring government transparency should be abandoned in order to protect American idealism against what might be perceived as the sordid reality of U.S. foreign policy. The utter weakness of this position has been cogently exposed by Greenwald:

> Think about what Obama's rationale would justify. Obama's claim—that release of the photographs "would be to further inflame anti-American opinion and to put our troops in greater danger"—means we should conceal or even outright lie about all the bad things we do that might reflect poorly on us. For instance, if an Obama bombing raid slaughters civilians in Afghanistan (as has happened several times already), then, by this reasoning, we ought to lie about what happened and conceal the evidence depicting what was done—as the Bush administration did—because release of such evidence "would be to further inflame anti-American opinion and to put our troops in greater danger."[7]

Indeed, according to this logic, the best way to deal with criminal behavior on the part of the American government is to suppress any evidence that it happened. This position shields executive wrongdoing on the part of the Bush administration, the CIA, and the national intelligence agencies, and it also empties history of any critical meaning and ethical substance. How would history be written according to this logic? To promote a sanitized view of history, would it be reasonable to eliminate images from textbooks and public view that record atrocities such as lynchings of African Americans? When acts of state torture of people of color take place in prisons, should we disavow such criminal acts on the grounds that they would discredit America's image in the world? Would it be deemed patriotic to prevent young people from being able to see, or study for that matter, any disturbing image that might put into focus police brutality, the violence of the racial state, or orchestrated government terror often directed against poor whites and minorities of race and class who are often considered disposable? Should we rewrite the narrative of U.S. policies and politics so as to cleanse it of human suffering in order to promote a cheerful Disney-like image of American society, while simultaneously disclaiming any responsibility toward the other?

In spite of Obama's support of the state secrets privilege, the task of history is not to bury dangerous memories but to draw out the darkness embedded in the recesses of the past, to make clear that the cover of secrecy and silence will not protect those who violate the law, and to reject a notion of national amnesia that sanctions illegality in the name of progress. But this is more than the task of history: It is also an obligation of democratic leadership and governance. What we need are public disclosure and a mode of government transparency that reveal that the United States has a long history of torture that extends from the genocide of Native Americans to slavery to the killing of twenty-one thousand Vietnamese under the aegis of the CIA's infamous Phoenix Program. The purpose of this history is not to induce shame but to recognize that such crimes were legitimated by a set of political conditions and institutionalized policies that must be excised from American domestic and foreign policies if we want a future that does not simply repeat the past.

Obama's claim that the United States no longer practices torture implies that a change in policy should coincide with the erasure of the history in which such crimes were committed, thus invoking the need to move on and to practice government censorship as part of the process. Many commentators have rightly argued that Obama's refusal to release the photos of abuse and torture as well as to prosecute officials who legitimated and practiced such abuses violates the law and the public's right to know and stands in violation of the most basic and elemental precepts of human rights. These commentators are right, but what is often left out of their arguments is that historical awareness is the precondition for arousing a sense of moral and legal responsibility and for understanding how we came to the conditions and forces that led to such horrors in the first place. Put differently, such images and other dangerous forms of memory serve a vital civic and educational value. They create the possibility for rethinking both government policies and how a society views itself—as when the horrific images of torture that emerged from Abu Ghraib powerfully revealed and set in motion a public debate based on the recognition that the "United States had transformed itself from a country that, officially at least, condemned torture to a country that practiced it."[8] But such images, memories, and forms of historical evidence also create the conditions for civic engagement. If the disturbing images from the torture chambers of Abu Ghraib had been suppressed, the public would never have learned about the moral and political abuse sanctioned at the highest levels of government, Bush's secret CIA prisons, or the willingness of government lawyers to provide a legal cover for a range of practices considered torture by the United Nations, the Geneva Conventions, the International Committee of the Red Cross, and other human rights organizations.

By refusing to release photos of those tortured by U.S. forces, Obama sadly continues yet another element of the Bush regime organized around an attempt to regulate the visual field, to mandate what can be seen and modify the landscape of the sensible and visible. And equally importantly, as Judith Butler points out, the Obama administration's application of the state secrecy privilege grants it the power to determine "which lives count as human and as living, and which do not."[9] At a time in history when the American public is overly subject to the quasi militarization of everyday life, endlessly exposed to mass-produced spectacles of commodified and ritualized violence, a culture of cruelty and barbarism becomes deeply entrenched and easily tolerated. More is created in this instance than a moral and affective void—a refusal to recognize and rectify the illegal and morally repugnant violence, abuse, and suffering imposed on those allegedly disposable others. We additionally witness an undoing of the very foundation of any vestige of civilization and justice. The descent into barbarism can take many forms, but one form may be glimpsed when torture appears to be one of the last practices left that allow many Americans to feel alive, to mark what it means to be close to the register of death in a way that reminds them of the ability to feel within a culture that deadens every possibility of life. How else can we explain that 49 percent of the American public "consider torture justified at least some of the time [and] fully 71% refuse to rule it out entirely"?[10]

Clearly, such a culture is in dire need of being condemned, unlearned, and transformed through modes of critical education and public debate if American democracy is to survive as more than a distant and unfulfilled promise. We have lived too long with governments that use power to promote violence, conveniently hidden behind a notion of secrecy and silence that selectively punishes those considered expendable—in prisons, schools, or urban slums. Such secrecy privileges officially sanctioned power and makes a mockery of both citizenship and democracy itself. This practice is especially egregious coming from a U.S. president who campaigned on the need for government transparency and accountability. Government secrecy is the hallmark of authoritarian regimes, not substantive democracies, and critical citizenship does not prosper under policies that reward secrecy and ignorance rather than openness and critical dialogue. Let us hope that educators, religious leaders, young people, parents, concerned citizens, and larger social movements will be alerted to the dangers of state suppression in the United States as well as Iran and mobilize to educate Obama about the appropriate limits of power and the promise of democratic leadership.

V
EDUCATION

Chapter 17
Obama and the Promise of Education

֎

Needless to say, like many Americans, I am both delighted and cautious about Barack Obama's election. Symbolically, this is an unprecedented moment in the fight against the legacy of racism while at the same time offering new possibilities for addressing how racism works in a post-Bush period. Politically, his election signals a halt to the many authoritarian and antidemocratic tendencies operating both domestically and internationally, while offering the possibility for a fresh critique of neoliberal and neoconservative policies and for an opportunity to reclaim and energize the language of the social contract and social democracy. Even though the Bush administration may have been uninterested in critical ideas, debate, and dialogue, it was almost rabid about destroying the economic, political, and educational conditions that make them possible. In the end, the Bush administration was willing to sacrifice almost any remnant of democracy to further the interests of the rich and powerful, especially those interests commanded by corporate power.

The Obama administration will fail badly if it does not connect the current financial and credit crises to the crisis of democracy and its poisonous undoing by commanding market forces. Corporate power, rather than just deregulation, has to be addressed head-on if any of the ensuing reforms undertaken by the Obama administration are going to work. Similarly, the social state has to be resurrected once again against the power and interest of the corporate state, and that battle is not just economic and political but also pedagogical. Obama also needs to dismantle the war economy and reinvest the savings in a massive jobs-creation program that focuses on rebuilding the nation's infrastructure and schools. Billions of dollars should be redirected away from the war machine and invested in shoring up the social state, enabling millions of human beings to have adequate health care, housing, child care, and a quality education. Of course, the last thing we need is to overly romanticize the election of Obama. We do not need lone heroes offering a path to salvation and hope. Obama's victory is not about the gripping story of his personal journey and ultimate victory as a black man; rather, it is about the emergence of a certain moment in history when small differences matter and new possibilities appear for making real claims on the promise of democracy to come.

What this historic event should make clear is the necessity for various progressive and left-oriented groups to get beyond their isolated demands and form a powerful progressive movement that can push Obama to the left rather than allow him to drift to the center and right. Of course, this means that progressives will have to do more than embrace a language of critique. They will also have to engage in a discourse of a hope that is concrete, rooted in real struggles, and capable of forging a new political imagination among a highly conservative and fractured polity. This is an especially important time for educators. *New York Times* columnist Nicholas D. Kristof recently argued that one of the most remarkable things about this election is that Obama is a practicing intellectual and that the era of anti-intellectualism so pervasive under the Bush administration may be coming to an end.[1] Surely, this is a message that resonates with anyone interested in the power of ideas.

But there is more at stake here than an appeal to thoughtfulness, critique, and intelligence. There is also a need to rethink the relationship between education and politics, the production of particular kinds of agents as a condition of civic life, and the ways in which new and diverse sites of education in the new millennium have proliferated into one of the most powerful political spheres in history. One of the most important challenges facing the United States in a post-Bush period is to take seriously the educational force of a culture that is central to constructing a new type of citizen. What is needed are citizens defined less through the hatred and bigotry of racism and the narrow obligations of consumerism than through the values, identities, and social relations of a democratic society.

Chapter 18
Obama's Embrace of the Corporate Model of Education

coauthored with Kenneth Saltman

‹❦›

Since the 1980s, but particularly under the Bush administration, certain elements of the religious right, corporate culture, and the Republican right wing have argued that free public education represents either a massive fraud or a contemptible failure. Far from a genuine call for reform, these attacks largely stem from an attempt to transform schools from a public investment to a private good, answerable not to the demands and values of a democratic society but to the imperatives of the marketplace. As educational historian David Labaree rightly argues, public schools have been under attack in the last few decades "not just because they are deemed ineffective but because they are public."[1]

Right-wing efforts to disinvest in public schools as critical sites of teaching and learning and govern them according to corporate interests is obvious in an emphasis on standardized testing, a use of top-down curricular mandates, an influx of advertising in schools, a use of profit motives to "encourage" student performance, an attack on teacher unions, and modes of pedagogy that stress rote learning and memorization. For the Bush administration, testing became the ultimate accountability measure, belying the complex mechanisms of teaching and learning. The hidden curriculum used testing as a ploy to deskill teachers by reducing them to mere technicians, reduced students from being critical learners to being customers in the marketplace, and underfunded public schools so that they would fail—all steps taken toward justifying the real goal of privatization.

But there is an even darker side to the reforms initiated under the Bush administration and now used in a number of school systems throughout the country. As the logic of the market and "the youth crime complex" frame the field of social relations in schools,[2] students are subjected to three particularly offensive policies, defended by school authorities and politicians under the rubric of school safety. First, students are increasingly subjected to zero tolerance policies that are used primarily to punish, repress, and exclude them. Second, students are increasingly absorbed into a "crime complex" in which security staff, using harsh disciplinary practices, now displace the normative functions teachers once provided both inside and outside of the classroom.[3] Third, more and more schools are breaking down the space between education and juvenile delinquency, substituting penal pedagogies for critical learning, and replacing a school culture that fosters a discourse of possibility with a culture of fear and social control.

Consequently, many youth of color in urban school systems, because of harsh zero tolerance polices, are not just being suspended or expelled from school. They also are being ushered into the dark precincts of juvenile detention centers, adult courts, and prisons. Surely, the dismantling of this corporatized and militarized model of schooling should be a top priority under the Obama administration. Unfortunately, Obama has appointed as his secretary of education someone who actually embodies this utterly punitive, anti-intellectual, corporatized, and test-driven model of schooling.

Barack Obama's selection of Arne Duncan for secretary of education does not bode well either for the political direction of Obama's administration or for the future of public education. Obama's call for change falls flat with this appointment, not only because Duncan largely defines schools within a market-based and penal model of pedagogy, but also because he does not have the slightest understanding of schools as something other than adjuncts of the corporation at best or the prison at worse. The first casualty in this scenario is a language of social and political responsibility capable of defending those vital institutions that expand the rights, public goods, and services central to a meaningful democracy. This is especially true with respect to the issue of public schooling and the ensuing debate over the purpose of education, the role of teachers as critical intellectuals, the politics of the curriculum, and the centrality of pedagogy as a moral and political practice.

Duncan, as CEO of the Chicago Public Schools, presided over the implementation and expansion of an agenda that militarized and corporatized the third largest school system in the nation, one that is about 90 percent poor and nonwhite. Under Duncan, Chicago took the lead in creating public schools run as military academies, vastly expanded draconian student expulsions, instituted sweeping surveillance practices, advocated a growing police presence in the schools, arbitrarily shut down entire schools, and fired entire school staffs. The recent report *Education on Lockdown* claimed that under Duncan's leadership, "Chicago Public Schools (CPS) has become infamous for its harsh zero tolerance policies. Although there is no verified positive impact on safety, these policies have resulted in tens of thousands of student suspensions and an exorbitant number of expulsions."[4]

Duncan also led the Renaissance 2010 plan, which was created in 2004 for Mayor Richard Daley by the Commercial Club of Chicago—an organization representing the largest businesses in the city. The purpose of Renaissance 2010 was to increase the number of high-quality schools that would be subject to new standards of "accountability"—a code word for legitimating more charter schools and high-stakes testing in the guise of hard-nosed empiricism. The Commercial Club hired the corporate consulting firm A. T. Kearney to write Renaissance 2010, which calls for the replacement of public schools with privatized charter schools, contract schools (more charters to circumvent state limits), and "performance" schools. Specifically, the plan targets 15 percent of the city district's alleged underachieving schools in order to dismantle them and open one hundred new experimental schools in areas slated for gentrification. According to the school reform publication *Catalyst*, under Renaissance 2010 the goal is "to close low-performing schools and replace them with smaller, entrepreneurial schools, many of them free from union contracts and some state regulations."[5]

Kearney's Web site is unapologetic about its business-oriented notion of leadership, one that John Dewey thought should be avoided at all costs. It states, "Drawing on our program-management skills and our knowledge of best practices used across industries, we provided a private-sector perspective on how to address many of the complex issues that challenge other large urban education transformations."[6] Thus far, seventy-five new schools have been opened and many of the teachers hired at the "new charter or contract schools … generally cannot join the Chicago Teacher's Union; are on year-to-year contracts; and are often underprepared—which has a detrimental effect on both faculty and students."[7]

Duncan's advocacy of the Renaissance 2010 plan alone should have immediately disqualified him for the Obama appointment. At the heart of this plan is a privatization scheme for creating a "market" in public education by urging public schools to compete against each other for scarce resources and by introducing "choice" initiatives so that parents and students will think of themselves as private consumers of educational services.[8] As a result of his support of the plan, Duncan came under attack by community organizations, parents, education scholars, and students. These diverse critics have denounced it less as a plan designed to improve the quality of schooling than as a scheme for privatization, union busting, and the dismantling of democratically elected local school councils. They also describe it as part of neighborhood gentrification schemes involving the privatization of public housing projects through mixed finance developments.[9] (Tony Rezko, a Barack Obama and Rod Blagojevich campaign supporter, made a fortune from these developments, along with many corporate investors.) Some of the dimensions of public school privatization involve Renaissance schools being run by subcontracted for-profit companies—a shift in school governance from teachers and elected community councils to appointed administrators coming disproportionately from the ranks of business. The plan also establishes corporate control over the selection and model of new schools, giving the business elite and their foundations increasing influence over educational policy. It is no wonder that Duncan had the support of David Brooks, a conservative op-ed writer for the *New York Times*.

One particularly egregious example of Duncan's vision of education can be seen in the conference he organized with the Renaissance Schools Fund. In May 2008, the Renaissance Schools Fund, the financial wing of the Renaissance 2010 plan operating under the auspices of the Commercial Club, held a symposium, "Free to Choose, Free to Succeed: The New Market in Public Education," at the exclusive private club atop the Aon Center. The event was held largely by and for the business sector, school privatization advocates, and others already involved in Renaissance 2010, such as corporate foundations and conservative think tanks. Significantly, no education scholars were invited to participate in the proceedings, although it was heavily attended by fellows from the proprivatization Fordham Foundation and featured speakers from various school choice organizations and the leadership of corporations. Speakers clearly assumed the audience shared their views.

Without irony, Arne Duncan characterized Renaissance 2010's goal of creating the new market in public education as a "movement for social justice." He invoked corporate investment terms to describe reforms explaining that the one hundred new schools would "leverage" influence on the other five hundred schools in Chicago. Redefining schools as stock investments, he said, "I am not a manager of 600 schools. I'm a portfolio manager of 600 schools and I'm trying to improve the portfolio." He claimed that education can end poverty. He explained that having a sense of altruism is important, but that creating good workers is a prime goal of educational reform and that the business sector has to embrace public education. "We're trying to blur the lines between the public and the private," he said. He argued that a primary goal of educational reform is to get the private sector to play a huge role in school change in terms of both money and intellectual capital. He also attacked the Chicago Teachers Union (CTU), positioning it as an obstacle to business-led reform. He also insisted that the CTU opposes charter schools (and hence change itself), even though the CTU runs ten such schools under Renaissance 2010.

Contrary to the representation in the popular press of Duncan as conciliatory to the unions, his statements and those of others at the symposium revealed a deep hostility to teachers unions and a desire to end them. Thus, in Duncan's attempts to close and transform low-performing schools, he not only reinvented them as entrepreneurial schools, but in many cases he also freed "them from union contracts and some state regulations."[10] Duncan effusively praised one speaker, Michael Milkie, the founder of the Nobel Street charter schools, who openly called for the closing and reopening of every school in the district precisely to get rid of the unions. What became clear is that Duncan views Renaissance 2010 as a national blueprint for educational reform, but what is at stake in this vision is the end of schooling as a public good and a return to the discredited and tired neoliberal model of reform that conservatives love to embrace.

In spite of the corporate rhetoric of accountability, efficiency, and excellence, there is to date no evidence that the radical reforms under Duncan's tenure as the CEO of Chicago Public Schools have created any significant improvement. In part, this is because the Chicago Public Schools and the Renaissance Schools Fund report data in obscurantist ways that make traditional comparisons difficult, if not impossible.[11] And, in part, examples of educational claims to school improvement are being made about schools embedded in communities that suffered dislocation and removal through coordinated housing privatization and gentrification policies. The city has decimated public housing in coveted real estate enclaves, thereby dispossessing thousands of residents of their communities. Once the poor are removed, the urban cleansing provided an opportunity for Duncan to open a number of Renaissance Schools, catering to those socioeconomically empowered families whose children would surely improve the city's overall test scores. What are alleged to be school improvements under Renaissance 2010 rests on an increase in the city's overall test scores and other performance measures that parodies the financial shell game corporations used to inflate profit margins—and the prospects for future catastrophes are as inevitable. In the end, all Duncan leaves us with is a Renaissance 2010 model of education that is celebrated as business designed "to save kids" from a failed public system. In fact, this model condemns public schooling, administrators, teachers, and students to a now-outmoded and discredited economic model of reform that can imagine education only as a business, teachers as entrepreneurs, and students as customers.[12]

It is difficult to understand how Barack Obama can reconcile his vision of change with Duncan's history of supporting a corporate vision for school reform and a penchant for extreme zero tolerance policies—both of which are much closer to the retrograde policies hatched in conservative think tanks such as the Heritage Foundation, Cato Institute, Fordham Foundation, and American Enterprise Institute—than to the values of the many millions who voted for the democratic change Obama promised. As is well known, these think tanks share an agenda not for strengthening public schooling but for dismantling it and replacing it with a private market in consumable educational services. At the heart of Duncan's vision of school reform is a corporatized model of education that cancels out the democratic impulses and practices of civil society by either devaluing or absorbing them within the logic of the market or the prison. No longer a space for relating schools to the obligations of public life or social responsibility to the demands of critical and engaged citizenship, schools in this dystopian vision legitimate an all-encompassing horizon for producing market identities, values, and those privatizing and penal pedagogies that both inflate the importance of individualized competition and punish those who do not fit into its logic of pedagogical Darwinism.[13]

In spite of what Duncan argues, the greatest threat to our children does not come from lowered standards, an absence of privatized choice schemes, or a lack of rigid testing measures that offer the aura of accountability. On the contrary, the greatest threat comes from a society that refuses to view children as a social investment, consigns 13 million children to live in poverty, reduces critical learning to massive testing programs, promotes policies that eliminate most crucial health and public services, and defines rugged individualism through the degrading celebration of a gun culture, extreme sports, and the spectacles of violence that permeate corporate-controlled media industries. Students are not at risk because of an absence of market incentives in the schools. Young people are under siege in America because in the absence of funding, equal opportunity, and real accountability, far too many schools have increasingly become institutional breeding grounds for racism, right-wing paramilitary cultures, social intolerance, and sexism.[14]

We live in a society in which a culture of testing, punishment, and intolerance has replaced a culture of social responsibility and compassion. Within such a climate of harsh discipline and disdain for critical teaching and learning, it is easier to subject young people to a culture of faux accountability or put them in jail rather than to provide the education, services, and care they need to face problems of a complex and demanding society.[15] What Duncan and other neoliberal economic advocates refuse to address is what it would mean for a viable educational policy to provide reasonable support services for all students and viable alternatives for the troubled ones. The notion that children should be viewed as a crucial social resource—one that represents for any healthy society important ethical and political considerations about the quality of public life, the allocation of social provisions, and the role of the state as a guardian of public interests—appears to be lost in a society that refuses to invest in its youth as part of a broader commitment to a fully realized democracy. As the social order becomes more privatized and militarized, we increasingly face the problem of losing a generation of young people to a system of increasing intolerance, repression, and moral indifference. It is difficult to understand why Obama would appoint as secretary of education someone who believes in a market-driven model that has not only failed young people but, given the current financial crisis, has also been thoroughly discredited. Unless Duncan is willing to reinvent himself, the national agenda he will develop for education embodies and exacerbates these problems, and as such it will leave a lot more kids behind than it helps.

Chapter 19
Against the Militarized Academy

⟿

Even though there is an ongoing discussion about what shape the military-industrial complex will take under the presidency of Barack Obama, what is often left out of this analysis is the intrusion of the military into higher education. One example of the increasingly intensified and expansive symbiosis between the military-industrial complex and academia was on full display when Secretary of Defense Robert Gates announced the creation of what he called a new "Minerva Consortium" (ironically named after the goddess of wisdom), whose purpose is to fund various universities to "carry out social-sciences research relevant to national security."[1] Gates's desire to turn universities into militarized knowledge factories producing meaning, research, and personnel in the interest of the homeland (in)security state should be of special concern for intellectuals, artists, academics, and others who believe that the university should oppose such interests and alignments. At the very least, the emergence of the Minerva Consortium raises a larger set of concerns about the ongoing militarization of higher education in the United States.

In a post-9/11 world, with its all-embracing war on terror and a culture of fear, the increasing spread of the discourse and values of militarism throughout the social order is intensifying the shift from the promise of a liberal democracy to the reality of a militarized society. Militarization suggests more than simply a militaristic ideal—with its celebration of war as the truest measure of the health of the nation and the soldier-warrior as the most noble expression of the merging of masculinity and unquestioning patriotism. This militarization also suggests an intensification and expansion of the underlying values, practices, ideologies, social relations, and cultural representations associated with military culture.

What appears new about the amplified militarization of the post-9/11 world is that it has become normalized, serving as a powerful educational force that shapes our lives, memories, and daily experiences. As a educational force, military power produces identities, goods, institutions, knowledge, modes of communication, and affective investments—in short, it now bears down on all aspects of social life and the social order. As Michael Geyer points out, what is distinctive about the militarization of the social order is that civil society not only "organizes itself for the production of violence" but also increasingly spurs a gradual erosion of civil liberties.[2] Military power and policies are expanded to address matters of defense and security as well as problems associated with the entire health and social life of the nation, which are now measured by military spending, discipline, and loyalty, as well as hierarchical modes of authority. As citizens increasingly assume the roles of informer, soldier, and consumer willing to enlist in or be conscripted by the totalizing war on terror, we see the very idea of the university as a site of critical thinking, public service, and socially responsible research being usurped by a manic jingoism and a market-driven fundamentalism that enshrine the entrepreneurial spirit and military aggression as means to dominate and control society.

This should not surprise us because, as sociologist William G. Martin indicates, "universities, colleges and schools have been targeted precisely because they are charged with both socializing youth and producing knowledge of peoples and cultures beyond the borders of Anglo-America."[3] But rather than be lulled into complacency by the insidious spread of corporate and military power, we need to be prepared to reclaim institutions such as the university that have historically served as vital democratic spheres protecting and serving the interests of social justice and equality. What I want to suggest is that such a struggle is political *and* pedagogical in nature.

More than 17 million students pass through the hallowed halls of academe, and it is crucial that they be educated in ways that enable them to recognize the creeping militarization and its effects throughout American society, particularly in terms of how these effects threaten "democratic government at home just as they menace the independence and sovereignty of other countries."[4]

But students must also recognize how such antidemocratic forces work in attempting to dismantle the university itself as a place to learn how to think critically and participate in public debate and civic engagement.[5] In part, this means giving students the tools to fight for the demilitarization of knowledge on college campuses—to resist complicity with the production of knowledge, information, and technologies in classrooms and research labs that contributes to militarized goals and purposes.

Even so, there is more at stake than simply educating students to be alert to the dangers of militarization and to the way in which it is redefining the very mission of higher education. In a continuing critique of the threat that the politics of empire presents to democracy at home and abroad, Chalmers Johnson argues that if the United States is not to degenerate into a military dictatorship, in spite of Obama's election, a grassroots movement will have to occupy center stage in opposing militarization, government secrecy, and imperial power, while reclaiming the basic principles of democracy.[6] Such a task may seem daunting, but there is a crucial need for faculty, students, administrators, and concerned citizens to develop alliances for long-term organizations and social movements to resist the growing ties among higher education and the armed forces, intelligence agencies, and war industries—ties that play a crucial role in reproducing militarized knowledge.

Opposing militarization as part of a broader pedagogical strategy in and out of the classroom also raises the question of what kinds of competencies, skills, and knowledge might be crucial to such a task. One possibility is to develop critical educational theories and practices that define the space of learning through the critical consumption of knowledge and through its production for peaceful and socially just ends. In the fight against the biopolitics of militarization, educators need a language of critique, but they also need a language that embraces a sense of hope and collective struggle. This means a concerted effort to expand the space of politics by reclaiming "the public character of spaces, relations, and institutions regarded as private."[7]

We live at a time when matters of life and death are central to political sovereignty. While registering the shift in power toward the large-scale production of death, disposability, and exclusion, a new biopolitics must also point to notions of agency, power, and responsibility that operate in the service of life, democratic struggles, and the expansion of human rights. If higher education is to come to grips with the multilayered pathologies produced by militarization, it will have to rethink not merely the space of the university as a democratic public sphere, but also the global space in which intellectuals, educators, students, artists, labor unions, and other social actors and movements can form transnational alliances to oppose the death-dealing ideology of militarization and its effects on the world—including violence, pollution, massive poverty, racism, the arms trade, growth of privatized armies, civil conflict, child slavery, and the ongoing wars in Iraq and Afghanistan. As the Obama administration implements policy, it is time for educators and students to take a stand and develop global organizations that can be mobilized in the effort to supplant a culture of war with a culture of peace, whose elemental principles must be grounded in relations of economic, political, cultural, and social democracy and the desire to sustain human life.

Chapter 20
Higher Education in Search
of Democracy?

⊸

President Barack Obama's vision of higher education can be glimpsed in his enthusiastic support for passing legislation that would provide billions of dollars to rebuild and revamp community colleges throughout the United States. Even though the financial investment is quite large, the ideology that frames how this money will be spent is far from progressive. In fact, what drives this large investment in higher education is a corporate-based ideology that embraces standardizing the curriculum, supporting top-down management, and reducing community colleges to job training sites. Marc Bousquet rightly argues that central to this view of community colleges is a view of higher education that supports "more standardization! More managerial control! A teacher-proof curriculum! ... and a top-down control of curriculum ... tenured management,"[1] and the reduction of faculty to the status of part-time and temporary workers. Faculty in this view are just another cheap army of reserve labor, a force to eagerly exploit in order to increase the bottom line while disregarding the rights of academic labor and the quality of education that students deserve. There is no talk in this view of higher education about sharing governance between faculty and administrators, educating students as critical citizens rather than as potential employees of Wal-Mart, or affirming faculty as scholars and public intellectuals who have a measure of autonomy and power.

Obama's rhetoric about higher education, although often marked by an appeal to lofty ideals, is really just a slightly modified extension of the neoliberal ideals of the Clinton era and the accountability and punishing logic of the second Bush term. It is almost impossible to recognize anything emancipatory in Obama's notion of educational reform. In what follows, I want to offer an alternative understanding of the purpose of higher education by arguing for the crucial role it plays in educating young people to be knowledgeable, socially responsible, and critically engaged citizens of the world and the equally important role it performs in aligning itself with the deepening and expansion of the imperatives of a substantive democracy.

There is a general consensus among academics around the world that higher education is in a state of crisis. Universities are now facing a growing set of challenges arising from budget cuts, diminishing quality, downsizing of faculty, militarization of research, and revamping of the curriculum to fit the needs of the market.[2] In the United States, many of the problems in higher education can be linked to low funding, domination of universities by market mechanisms, public education's move toward privatization, intrusion of the national security state, massive state deficits, and lack of faculty self-governance, all of which contradict the value of higher education and make a mockery of the very meaning and mission of the university. Universities and colleges have been increasingly abandoned as democratic public spheres dedicated to providing a public service, expanding upon humankind's great intellectual and cultural achievements, and educating future generations to be able to confront the challenges of a global democracy.

The worldwide crisis in higher education has crucial political, social, ethical, and spiritual consequences. At a time when market culture is aggressively colonizing everyday life and social forms increasingly lose their shape or disappear altogether, higher education seems to represent a reassuring permanence, as a slowly changing bulwark in a landscape of rapidly dissolving critical public spheres. But higher education in the United States and elsewhere is increasingly losing its public character and commitment to democracy as it aligns itself with corporate power and military values. Corporate leaders are now hired as university presidents, the shrinking ranks of tenure-line faculty are outsourced to contract labor, students are treated as customers, and learning is increasingly defined in instrumental terms, while critical knowledge is relegated to the dustbins of the impoverished and underfunded liberal arts. As Jennifer Washburn observes:

In the classroom deans and provosts are concerned less with the quality of instruction than with how much money their professors bring in. As universities become commercial entities, the space to perform research that is critical of industry or challenges conventional market ideology—research on environmental pollution, poverty alleviation, occupational health hazards—has gradually diminished, as has the willingness of universities to defend professors whose findings conflict with the interests of their corporate sponsors. Will universities stand up for academic freedom in these situations, or will they bow to commercial pressure out of fear of alienating their donors?[3]

Conscripting the university to serve as corporate power's apprentice, while reducing matters of university governance to an extension of corporate logic and interests, substantially weakens higher education as a democratic public sphere, academics as engaged public intellectuals, and students as critical citizens. Questions regarding how education might enable students to develop a keen sense of prophetic justice, promote the analytic skills necessary to hold power accountable, and provide the spiritual foundation through which they respect the rights of others and, as Bill Moyers puts the matter, "claim their moral and political agency" become increasingly irrelevant in a market-driven and militarized university.[4]

If the commercialization and the militarization of the university continue unabated, then higher education will become yet another institution whose ability to foster critical inquiry, public debate, humane acts of justice, and common deliberation is diminished. The calculating logic of the instrumentalized university does more than diminish the moral and political vision necessary to sustain a vibrant democracy and an engaged notion of social agency; it also undermines the development of public spaces where matters of dissent, public conscience, and social justice are pedagogically valued and offer protection against the growing antidemocratic tendencies that are enveloping much of the United States and many other parts of the world.

Educating young people in the spirit of a critical democracy by providing them with the knowledge, passion, civic capacities, and social responsibility necessary to address the problems facing the nation and the globe also means challenging the existence of rigid disciplinary boundaries, a cult of expertise or highly specialized scholarship unrelated to public life, and antidemocratic ideologies that scoff at the exercise of academic freedom. Such antidemocratic and anti-intellectual tendencies have intensified alongside the contemporary emergence of a number of diverse fundamentalisms, including a market-based neoliberal rationality that exhibits a deep disdain, if not outright contempt, for both democracy and publicly engaged teaching and scholarship. In such circumstances, it is not surprising that higher education in many parts of the world is held hostage to political and economic forces that wish to convert educational institutions into corporate establishments defined by a profit-oriented identity and mission.

American higher education is evermore divided into those institutions educating the elite to rule the world in the twenty-first century and those institutions training students for low-paid positions in the capitalist world economy. It is increasingly apparent that the university in America has become a social institution that fails to address inequality in society and contributes to a growing division between social classes. Instead of being a space of critical dialogue, analysis, and interpretation, the American university is increasingly defined as a space of consumption, where ideas are validated in instrumental terms and valued for their success in attracting outside funding while developing stronger ties to corporate powers. Moreover, as tuition exceeds the budgets of most Americans, quality education at public and private universities becomes a reserve primarily for the children of the rich and powerful.

Prominent educators and theorists such as Hannah Arendt, John Dewey, Cornelius Castoriadis, and C. Wright Mills have longed believed and rightly argued that we should neither allow education to be modeled after the business world nor sit by while corporate power and influence undermine the semiautonomy of higher education by exercising control over its faculty, curricula, and students. All of these public intellectuals share a common vision and project of rethinking what role education might play in providing students with the habits of mind and ways of acting that would enable them to identify and address the most acute challenges and dangers facing a world increasingly dominated by a mode of instrumental and technological thinking that is morally and spiritually bankrupt. All of these theorists offer a notion of the university as a bastion of democratic learning and meaningful social values, a notion that must be defended in discussions about what form will be taken by the relationship among corporations, the war industries, and higher education in the twenty-first century.

Higher education has a responsibility not only to search for the truth regardless of where it may lead, but also to educate students to make authority politically and morally accountable. Universities must strive to expand both academic freedom and the role of the university as a democratic public sphere, even as these are necessarily refashioned at the beginning of the new millennium. Although questions regarding whether the university should serve strictly public, rather than private, interests no longer carry the weight of forceful criticism as they did in the past, such questions are still crucial in addressing the reality of higher education and what it might mean to imagine the university's full participation in public life as the protector and promoter of democratic values, especially at a time when the meaning and purpose of higher education are besieged by a phalanx of narrow economic and political interests.

What needs to be understood is that higher education may be one of the few public spheres left where knowledge, values, and learning offer a glimpse of the promise of education for nurturing critical hope and a substantive democracy.[5] It may be the case that everyday life is increasingly organized around market principles, but confusing democracy with market relations hollows out the legacy of higher education, whose deepest roots are moral, not commercial. In defending young people's ability to access and to learn from educational, rather than corporate, institutions, we must heed the important insight expressed by Federico Mayor, a former director general of UNESCO, who insists that "you cannot expect anything from uneducated citizens except unstable democracy"[6] or, as we are quickly learning, something even worse. As the free circulation of ideas is increasingly replaced by ideas managed by the dominant media, ideas become banal, if not reactionary; intellectuals who engage in dissent are viewed or dismissed as either irrelevant, extremist, or un-American; and complicit public relations intellectuals now dominate the media, all too willing to accept co-option and reap the rewards of venting insults at their alleged opponents. What is lost in these antidemocratic practices are the economic, political, educational, and social conditions that provide a supportive culture for democracy to flourish.

This is, in part, a deeply pedagogical and educational issue that should not be lost on either intellectuals or those concerned about the purpose and meaning of higher education. Democracy places civic demands upon its citizens, and such demands point to the necessity of an education that is broad-based, critical, and supportive of meaningful citizen power, participation in self-governance, and democratic leadership. Only through such a supportive and critical educational culture can students learn how to become individual and social agents, rather than merely disengaged spectators, able not only to think otherwise but also to act upon civic commitments that "necessitate a reordering of basic power arrangements" fundamental to promoting the common good and producing a meaningful democracy.[7]

Retaking the University

Sheldon Wolin, one of the most important political theorists of the last fifty years, has argued that we live at a time when "politics is largely untempered by the political." For Wolin, this means, in part, citizens are no longer "viewed as agents actively involved in the exercise of power and in contributing to the direction of policy."[8] Largely removed from politics, citizens are either transformed into consumers and soldiers or relegated to the dustbin of disposability. Democracy is now managed by corporations, ruling elites, and right-wing fundamentalists. Citizens are largely depoliticized, reduced to shadowy participants in the polity. Matters of power and inequality give way to highly managed media spectacles and work in concert with the corporate logic that power is to be used not for the public good but for private interests. In this context, democratic and state sovereignty is replaced by corporate sovereignty and offers up a notion of "'shareholder democracy' that gives a 'sense of participation' without demands or responsibilities."[9] The power of government is no longer an expression of the collective will of the people. On the contrary, it is the mechanisms of the market economy that now define both politics and the highest ideals of the nation.

This hollowing out of democracy could not happen without the complicity of a loyal intelligentsia or an uninformed public. What is especially disturbing is that higher education, rather than defending the ideals of a strong democracy and the importance of educating an engaged and critical citizenry, has become an ideological bulwark for corporate values, interests, and practices. As Wolin points out: "Through a combination of governmental contracts, corporate foundation funds, joint projects involving university and corporate researchers, and wealthy individual donors, universities (especially so-called research universities), intellectuals, scholars, and researchers have been seamlessly integrated into the system. No books burned, no refugee Einsteins. For the first time in the history of American higher education top professors are made wealthy by the system, commanding salaries and perks that a budding CEO might envy.... The academy has become self-pacifying."[10]

As I have argued elsewhere, it is time to take back the university.[11] It is worth noting that "retaking the university" should not be confused with taking over the university, a more militaristic and overly determined political concept that I want to avoid altogether. Retaking the university is not a call for any one ideology on the political spectrum to take over the university. But it does suggest the need for educators and others to take a stand about the purpose and meaning of higher education and the latter's crucial role in educating students to participate in an inclusive democracy. Retaking the university is an ethical referent and a call to action for educators, parents, students, and others to reject Obama's notion of education as a training center for the needs of the marketplace. This call suggests reclaiming higher education as a democratic public sphere, a place where teaching is not confused with either training, militarism, or propaganda, a safe space where reason, understanding, dialogue, and critical engagement are available to all faculty and students. Higher education accordingly must become a site of ongoing struggle to preserve and extend the conditions in which autonomy of judgment and freedom of action are informed by the democratic imperatives of equality, liberty, and justice.

Higher education has always, though in damaged forms, served as a symbolic and concrete reminder that the struggle for democracy is, in part, an attempt to liberate humanity from blind obedience to authority. Individual agency and social agency gain meaning primarily through the freedoms guaranteed by the public sphere, freedoms in which the autonomy of individuals becomes meaningful only under those conditions that likewise ensure the workings of an autonomous society. What must be acknowledged in light of this intimate relationship between a functioning and strong democracy and higher education is that the principles of the market should not become the organizing structure for either education or social relations. Higher education should neither be run like a business nor simply be sold off to the highest corporate and government bidders.

A campaign must be waged against the corporate view of higher education as merely a training center for future business employees, a franchise for generating profits, a research center for the military, or a space in which corporate culture and education merge to produce literate consumers. Equally important, higher education must divorce itself from those knowledge forms, underlying values, practices, ideologies, social relations, and cultural representations associated with the intensification and expansion of military culture. Higher education has no legitimate or ethical reason for engaging in practices that are organized largely for the production of violence. It is important to reclaim higher education as a site of moral and political practice whose purpose is to introduce students to the great reservoir of diverse intellectual ideas and traditions and to engage those inherited bodies of knowledge through critical dialogue, analysis, and comprehension. At the same time, education is a set of social experiences and an ethical space

155

through which it becomes possible to rethink what Jacques Derrida once called the concepts of the "possible and the impossible" and to enable what Jacques Rancière calls loosening the coordinates of the sensible through a constant reexamination of the boundaries that distinguish the sensible from the subversive.[12]

Both theorists are concerned with how the boundaries of knowledge and everyday life are constructed in ways that seem unquestionable, making it necessary to interrogate commonsense assumptions as well as ask what it means to question such assumptions and to see beyond them. As a political and moral practice, education always presupposes a vision of the future in its introduction to, preparation for, and legitimation of particular forms of social life, demanding answers to the questions of whose future is affected by these forms and for what purposes and to what ends they endure.

The call to retake the university, then, is a reminder that the educational conditions that make democratic identities, values, and politics possible and effective have to be fought for more urgently at a time when democratic public spheres, public goods, and public spaces are under attack by a number of fundamentalisms that share the common dominator of disabling a substantive notion of democratic ethics, agency, and politics. More specifically, I am calling for strategies to reclaim the promise of the university as a bastion of democracy and to struggle against those antidemocratic forces now working to instrumentalize, commodify, and militarize higher education.

In addition, in light of recent attacks on higher education by right-wing groups, media, and think tanks, it is crucial that a new and spirited defense of academic freedom take place. Such groups increasingly threaten the use of critical knowledge, debate, and dialogue in classroom pedagogy, labeling such practices as propagandistic, as if the purpose of teaching should be to reproduce existing knowledges and public opinions, rather than to enter into critical dialogue about them. At stake here is a notion of teaching that refuses simply to serve government power, national interests, and officially sanctioned views of the world. Such efforts at defending academic freedom should take place through the unified attempts of faculty organizations and unions, such as the American Association of University Professors, the American Federation of Teachers, and the National Education Association, and should also include support adjuncts and non–tenure track faculty along with progressive groups, individuals, artists, and intellectuals outside of the university. Central to any defense of academic freedom is the necessity to convince a larger public of how crucial inclusive collaboration is for raising the level of intellectual engagement among faculty and students and for safeguarding the very foundations of a democratic society and the university.

In addition, educators need to create curricula and programs throughout the university that provide students with the humanistic knowledge, technical knowledge, scientific skills, and modes of literacy that enable them to engage and transform when necessary the promise of a global democracy. Education should expand the power of students to be critical agents, to be capable of governing rather than simply be governed, and to imagine the possibilities of a more democratic future. Instead, we are witnessing a dangerous confluence of higher education, the military, and corporate power that degrades "the everyday practice and culture of higher education."[13] The ongoing vocationalization of higher education, the commodification of the curriculum, the increasing connection between the military and universities through joint research projects and Pentagon scholarships, and the transformation of students into consumers have undermined colleges and universities in their efforts to offer students the knowledge and skills they need for learning how to govern as well as for developing the capacities necessary for deliberation, reasoned argumentation, and the obligations of civic responsibility.

For these forces to be challenged by existing and future generations, higher education should provide the modes of critical education and pedagogy that expose students to a genuine intellectual culture, one that is equally pleasurable, stimulating, and empowering. At the very least, higher education should provide students with a broad general education as well as equip them with the habits of critical thought and a passion for social responsibility that enable them to take seriously their participation in public life. What has become clear is that the deeply rooted incursion of corporate values, right-wing ideological politics, and military culture into university life undermines the university's obligation to provide students with an education that allows them to take seriously John Dewey's insistence that "democracy needs to be reborn in each generation, and education is its midwife."[14]

Higher education is increasingly becoming unaffordable for all but the most prosperous students. At best, higher education should be free for all students simply because it is not an entitlement but a right, one that is crucial for a functioning democracy. Hence, the call for strategies to retake higher education also argues for making higher education available to everyone, regardless of wealth and privilege. Higher education has to be democratized and cannot be tuition-driven, a trend that reinforces differential opportunities for students based on their ability to pay. At the very least, student loans must be replaced with a combination of outright financial grants and work-study programs, thus making it possible for all individuals who want to attend higher education, and especially those marginalized by class and race, to be able to do so. Moreover, making higher education free would eliminate the need for those who cannot afford higher education to serve in the military and put their lives in danger "to gain the educational opportunities that arguably would be the right of every citizen in a less shameless democracy."[15]

Reorganized under the force of market principles and modes of leadership, faculty, students, and staff have been removed from the power relations of democratic governance. Such power relations and comparable modes of governance have to be reclaimed if the university is going to fight against the ongoing disciplinary structures collaborating to produce the neoliberal university. As is well known, power relations within universities and colleges today are top-heavy, largely controlled by trustees and administrators and removed from those who actually do the work of the university—namely, the faculty, staff, and students. Power has become centralized largely in the hands of administrators who are close to business, industry, and the national security state. Much-needed reforms include protecting the jobs of full-time faculty, turning adjunct jobs into full-time positions, expanding benefits to part-time workers, and putting more power back into the hands of faculty and students. A weak faculty translates into a faculty without rights or power—one that is governed by fear rather than by shared responsibilities and is susceptible to labor-bashing tactics such as increased workloads, a growing casualization of labor, and a suppression of dissent. Adjunct or part-time educators must be given the opportunity to break the cycle of exploitative labor and, within a short period of time, be moved into tenure-track positions with full benefits and the power to influence governance policies.[16]

Similarly, if the university is to emphasize a discourse of enlightenment, ethics, vision, and democratic politics over a language of militarization, political orthodoxy, and market fundamentalism, higher education must honor its students by providing them with crucial skills and knowledge and by giving them the opportunity to appropriate and exercise a language of critique and possibility as part of a broader effort to connect what they learn in the classroom to the larger world and the promise of an inclusive and substantive democracy. Education is not only about issues of work and economics but also about questions of justice, social freedom, and the capacity for democratic agency, action, and change as well as the related issues of power, exclusion, and citizenship. Education at its best is about enabling students to take seriously questions about how they ought to live their lives, uphold the ideals of a just society, and act upon the promises of a strong democracy. These are educational and political issues and should be addressed as part of a broader concern for renewing the struggle for social justice and democracy.

Educating ourselves means first and foremost that higher education should be embraced, engaged, and struggled over as a place where imagining the unimaginable matters as part of an effort to get students to think otherwise and to act otherwise in the service of taking the promise of democracy seriously. This also means that we need to educate ourselves about the importance of the educational force of the larger culture and how crucial education is for all of us, given that it takes place in so many sites outside of institutional schooling. Recognizing the political nature of pedagogy and making pedagogy central to politics will provide us with new tools and modes of engagement for taking back the university and for reclaiming the connection between education and democracy.

Chapter 21
Obama's Postpartisan Politics and the Crisis of American Education

⊸

The election of Barack Obama represents a milestone both historically and politically. Not only does it symbolize a great accomplish-
ment in challenging (though hardly ending) the persistent legacy
of racism in the United States, but it also signifies an important
repudiation of the "dark times" unleashed by the Bush administration over eight years. Those dark times include, but are not limited
to, forces of corporate corruption, an imperial presidency, an un-
dercutting of civil liberties, a tragic war in Iraq, and a promotion
of a widespread culture of fear and secrecy. In many ways, Obama's
victory has shifted the political ground and opened up a moment
in which moral leadership, public commitment, and social responsibility once again have become central themes in the advancement
of democratic ideals, along with "the idea that government should
take bold action to create equal opportunity for all citizens [and]
doesn't have to explain itself in a defensive mumble."[1]

To what degree this election signals the full embrace of such
progressive commitments or, less promisingly, a reaction to the
old regime remains an open question. As Judith Butler points out
regarding the 2008 election, "We cannot underestimate the force of
dis-identification in this election, a sense of revulsion that George
W. has 'represented' the United States to the rest of the world, a
sense of shame about our practices of torture and illegal detention,

a sense of disgust that we have waged war on false grounds and propagated racist views of Islam, a sense of alarm and horror that the extremes of economic deregulation have led to a global economic crisis."[2]

Regardless of the motives that created the conditions for Obama's ascendancy to the highest office in the land, many Americans feel a great sense of excitement, if not civic renewal, believing that under the Obama administration many of the authoritarian and antidemocratic tendencies operating both domestically and internationally will come to an end. Once again, a collective energy has been mobilized, creating the conditions for a rigorous critique of free-market fundamentalism and neoconservative policies and an opportunity to reclaim the language of the social contract and substantive democracy.

In the aftermath of Obama's election, many progressive economists and intellectuals, such as James Galbraith, Joseph Stiglitz, Dean Baker, Robert Kuttner, William Greider, and Paul Krugman, have rejected neoliberal policy agendas that have systematically reduced public expenditures for social services, while defining consumerism and profit making as the essence of democratic citizenship and equating freedom with the ability of markets to govern economic relations unrestricted by federal regulation. In doing so, these progressives have repudiated the Ronald Reagan–Margaret Thatcher neoliberal dystopian order, celebrated as the "end of history," that dead-ended in a morally devastating neo-Hobbesian "war of all against all"—the inevitable result of the proclaimed inviolability and inevitability of economic law regardless of social cost. And these thinkers have condemned a rationality structured by neoliberal concerns that advanced private interests as it sold off public goods and services and shredded the social safety net protecting millions of disadvantaged Americans. The neoliberal mantra "There Is No Alternative" has lost its legitimacy given the current financial crisis and is increasingly giving way to a call by many critics of free market fundamentalism for more government oversight and regulation of the financial sector. Yet, while the deadly consequences of neoliberal casino capitalism, with its toxic emphasis on deregulation, individual responsibility, and privatization, are on full display, there is no guarantee that the Obama regime will produce reforms that speak to the possibilities of an aspiring democracy. But the promise of such an age hinges not only on the ability of the Obama administration and his supporters to overcome the worst economic crisis since the Great Depression; it also depends on how central the issue of education becomes in providing the knowledge, tools, and skills that can support a political culture invested in progressive change.

As I have mentioned throughout this book, education has to be absolutely basic to this democratizing effort because I cannot imagine the kind of revolutionary change we will need without a significant rethinking of what it means to be educated. What kind of world will become possible and for what kind of citizens? And in whose interests and for what purposes are democracy and citizenship defined? For the last several decades, young people have been schooled in a neoliberal ideology that celebrates an "economic arrangement marked by competition among technologically simple and roughly equal participants, the cutting of government down to size ('... where we can drown it in the bathtub ...' according to Grover Norquist), the privatizing of previously state-owned enterprises, liberalization of trade, the general deregulation of economic life and the glorification of individual self-interest."[3] In this instance, market values trump democratic values, and isolated, cutthroat modes of competition become a model for defining social relations, while self-interest is viewed as far more important than the demands and obligations of social responsibility and civic engagement.

This is a worldview that informs reality television, a ruthless universe in which others exist only to be used or exploited for one's own gain—a world in which dreams are utterly privatized and any vestige of the social registers as part of a war of one against all. This privatized notion of the self and this militarized conception of society have become central to the governing of everyday life as well as the broader sphere of politics. There is more at stake here than a mode of economic rationality; there are also a mode of governance and a particular conception of agency, society, and democracy that are entirely determined by market values and the logic of capital. Central to an understanding of the ideological power of neoliberalism is its role as a form of public pedagogy that circulates from various spheres in the larger culture extending from schools to popular culture. At stake here is the necessity for those who reject the neoliberal call for replacing democracy with a market society to make pedagogy central to any viable understanding of politics in the current historical moment.

The political nature of pedagogy, dissent, and critique can be seen in the efforts of the Bush administration and its conservative acolytes to wage a frontal assault on those intellectuals in higher education, as well as a select group of international scholars who were critical of American domestic and foreign policy. Dissenting international scholars were often denied visas to enter the country, and many critical academics in the United States were often labeled un-American. Under such conditions, dissent was stifled and the very public spheres that made it possible were under attack.[4] In the end, the Bush administration proved willing to weaken or sacrifice through privatization and deregulation the enabling conditions for democratic exchange. This is particularly true in policies that abetted media consolidation and the corporatization of higher education in order to further the interests of the rich and powerful.[5] Less interested in the truth than in expanding its own power, the Bush administration created fake news accounts, paid talk show hosts to endorse official policies, and labeled oppositional positions as unpatriotic.[6] The Obama administration will fail badly if it does not connect the current financial and credit meltdown to the crisis of democracy and education, which have been undermined by market forces for decades.

The last thing we need in pursuit of stronger democratic relations, identities, and institutions is to overly romanticize the highly celebrated image of Obama and his team of "alumni" from "the financial bubble's insiders' club" as lone heroes offering a path to salvation and hope.[7] Within the past year, Obama has moved decidedly to the right, and in doing so, he has extended some of the worst elements of the counterterrorism policies of the Bush administration. He has endorsed the use of military commissions, argued for the use of indefinite detention with no charges for Afghan prisoners, extended the Patriot Act, expanded the war in Afghanistan, and extended Bush's approach to school reform. In light of these conservative policies, Obama's once-inspiring call for hope has largely been reduced to fodder for late-night television comics. I am not suggesting that progressives turn away from the language of hope, but that they turn away from a notion of hope that is as empty as it is disingenuous. Such a challenge suggests embracing a language of critique and a language of hope that mutually inform each other, while engaging in a discourse of hope that is concretely rooted in real struggles and capable of inspiring a new political language and collective vision among a highly conservative and fractured polity.

We are currently, then, watching unfold an especially important time for educators. This is a call for greater thoughtfulness, critique, and intelligence; it is also an appeal to rethink what kind of education matters to a democracy and to restate our commitment to public education and higher education in terms of their value for political culture and democratic public life, in addition to their contributions to economic prosperity. One of the most important challenges facing education in the post-Bush period is to reintroduce educational policies, values, and social practices that help to produce civic identifications and commitments, teach young people how to participate in and shape public life by exercising critical judgment, and provide the pedagogical conditions that enable students to "translate the abstract concept of social citizenship into a practical reality."[8] The government, economic, and social challenges faced by the Obama administration cannot be addressed without a simultaneous transformation in culture, consciousness, social identities, and values. This leads me to the great challenge at the heart of Obama's educational policies, a challenge that needs to be further detailed through analysis of the troubling disjuncture between his stated commitment to education and the values, policies, and vision he is actually putting in place to give his view of education a concrete grounding in political practice.

Educating for What?

In a telling story reported by the national media, Obama in the first month of his presidency decided to get away from the closeted atmosphere of the White House and ventured out to visit an elementary school nearby in the District of Columbia. The scene provided a perfect photo op for the president, signaling his longstanding commitment to education as a centerpiece of his administration's reform efforts. The children themselves became a sign reflecting Obama's audaciousness, his hope, and the democratic future he pledged to restore. What was given only passing comment by mainstream media was that he chose to visit a private charter school rather than bringing much-needed media attention to one of the many public schools in America's capital, including some of the worst in the nation.

It is worth noting that the DC school system, under the leadership of Chancellor Michelle Rhee, has been repeatedly praised by Obama (though he did not enroll his own children in it). Rhee's reform efforts adapt elements of the very business model that mimic those practices that were proved failures after the 2008 financial crisis. Insisting that "detention, remedial classes, summer school, and suspensions to turn around poorly behaved, underachieving middle school students" did not work, Rhee turned to more market-driven options and now offers students "$100 per month to display good behavior," whatever that might mean.[9]

We might think that in light of the ongoing revelations of our deflated second Gilded Age and the now-discredited role that financial incentives played in producing massive corruption and pervasive greed among business executives, Obama might be more cautious, if not critical, before endorsing Rhee's market-oriented educational reforms. Obama's strong condemnation of the irresponsible judgment of those in charge of America's commanding economic institutions should be applauded. At the same time, it is difficult to grasp how such moral denunciations can be reconciled with educational reforms that make financial self-interest, if not outright greed, the cornerstone of a policy clearly aimed at producing empowered consumers rather than engaged critical citizens alert to the very civic responsibilities often promoted in Obama's speeches. Moreover, Rhee has also engaged in tactics adopted by neoliberal school reformers, which include closing dozens of schools, firing more than thirty principals, relying on test-score-driven modes of accountability, undermining teacher security and autonomy, and construing the teachers' union as the major stumbling block of educational reform. Obama's support for Rhee's efforts to boost student achievement in the middle schools, appropriately named "Capital Gains," points to a serious disconnect between Obama's emphasis on education for public service and social responsibility and the neoliberal policies at the heart of the broader reform efforts he supports, which have distressing implications for how education policy will play out—or perhaps *sell out*—during his administration. The puzzling disparity between Obama's call for curbing the excesses of free-market fundamentalism in the realm of economics and his endorsement of the use of market-driven protocols to structure his educational policies needs to be brought to light and challenged if a more democratic political culture is going to take root in the United States.

Obama likes to define himself as a unifier, as someone who is postpartisan, capable of transcending the constraints of hardened orthodoxies and more interested in "what works" rather than in adherence to party-line principles or a set ideology to be implemented.[10] Obama's initial embrace of postpartisanship may have emerged out of a felt need for compromise in the face of multiple crises that demand action, but it says little about what the ethical limits should be regarding what a person is against or is willing to fight for. Moreover, the appeal to what works is meaningless outside of the principles that frame the issues—what works for whom and in whose interest is the policy or practice said to work. In other words, what works is not obvious, nor does it reflect simple matters of efficiency and expediency. As Christopher Hayes points out, "What constitutes 'working' is not self-evident and, indeed, is impossible to detach from some world view and set of principles."[11]

Transcending partisanship appears in the early stages of the Obama presidency to be doing little more than "empowering politicians who take their marching orders from Rush Limbaugh."[12] Making a principle out of consensus, rather than fighting to restore democratic commitments to equality and social justice in the face of those who rigidly inveigh against all social spending as "pork," denounce big government as wasteful, and continue to espouse the virtues of tax cuts, has already taken a toll on Obama's ability to govern with any success.[13]

The Antipolitics of Postpartisanship

Even though Obama's political philosophy is developed around an appeal to unity, compromise, and postpartisanship, many of his policies suggest just the opposite—and this has important implications for education. Obama's postpartisan stance is at odds with his own democratically inspired politics, which he at times appears to disavow. The result is more than ambivalence. The president appears to be caught between two worldviews: one that advocates for justice and equality in the stirring rhetoric of hope and change and another that longs to transcend a politics in which power relations, conflict, and different struggles over education are central. Simon Critchley has argued, correctly I believe, that "Obama's attempt to transcend politics is governed by an anti-political fantasy [that] dreams of a society without power relations, without the agonism that constitutes political life. Against such a position one might assert that justice is always an agon, a conflict, and to refuse this assertion is to consign human beings to wallow in some emotional, fusional balm."[14] What does it mean when the leader of the United States subscribes to the notion that governance works best when politics itself is brought to an end?

In addition, Obama appears quite alone in his desire for postpartisanship, with his call for consensus building being ignored, if not challenged. This is evident in the opposition to Obama's attempts at health care reform, which reveal that Republicans not only have no interest in debate or dialogue but also are willing to lie, misrepresent, and engage in fear and smear tactics to derail his presidency. As economist Paul Krugman writes: "President Obama is now facing the same kind of opposition that President Bill Clinton had to deal with: an enraged right that denies the legitimacy of his presidency, that eagerly seizes on every wild rumor manufactured by the right-wing media complex. This opposition cannot be appeased."[15]

Obama's antipolitical vision runs the risk of failing to curb the historic assaults waged against the social state, health care, and education by the cultural conservatives and market zealots in charge for the last three decades. Obama has spoken firmly about the current financial meltdown as "the final verdict" on what he termed in his presidential campaign a "failed economic policy," but he has filled many senior posts in his administration with people, such as Lawrence Summers, Tim Geithner, and Rahm Emanuel, who played major roles in promoting the same free-market principles that caused the economic meltdown in the first place. These so-called reformed free-market fundamentalists are now in charge of the very regulatory agencies they once helped to deregulate. Oddly enough, in the spirit of postpartisanship, Obama, who initially voted against the Iraq war, has constructed a national security team that does not include one Iraq war opponent.[16] Even though many progressives have pointed to the tension between Obama's critique of the neoliberal economic policies that have prompted the ongoing bailouts and his appointment of free-market advocates to now solve the problem, there is another less visible and more complicated disjunction between Obama's vision of the purpose and meaning of education and his alleged postpartisan approach to policy.

Obama's Educational Vision?

In his many speeches on education, Obama has consistently argued that he wants to get beyond the tired debates over schools that pit Democrats against Republicans. In an address before the United Federation of Teachers in September 2008, he argued that "it's been Democrat versus Republican, vouchers versus the status quo, more money versus more reform. There's partisanship and there's bickering, but there's no understanding that both sides have good ideas that we'll need to implement if we hope to make the changes our children need. And we've fallen further and further behind as a result. If we're going to make a real and lasting difference for our future, we have to be willing to move beyond the old arguments of left and right and take meaningful, practical steps to build an education system worthy of our children and our future."[17]

Obama argued that both positions have "good ideas," but he failed to acknowledge that consensus does not mean much in a situation with fundamentally opposed worldviews about the purpose and meaning of education, curricula content, funding equity, the role of teachers, how students learn, and reliable notions of assessment.

Although finding the common ground among different points of view is not without merit, the most important issue at stake here is what these unique and often contradictory views actually say about the value and importance of education. That is, how do they differ philosophically and politically in addressing the economic, political, cultural, and social challenges that prepare students to learn how to govern rather than be governed, expand their sense of individual and social agency, and connect the fate of each individual to the fate of others, the planet, and democracy itself? The issue that Obama seems to miss in his concern with educational reform is that all educational ideals are not the same. Some are well worth fighting for, and others should be rejected because they are at odds with defining schools as crucial democratic public spheres and because they actually value education less as a public good than as a private right, a right that is deeply and distressingly compatible with viewing schools as a business, education as training, and students as customers.[18]

There is no doubt that Obama is sincerely concerned about the state of public and higher education and that some of his policies focus on issues that conservatives have either ignored or undermined for the last thirty years. He has called for a range of measures that work to improve education: investing in early childhood education; providing tax credits to new teachers willing to work in lower-performing schools in urban and rural areas; putting high-quality teachers in every classroom; increasing Pell grants; providing after-school and summer programs, especially for poor urban youth; making more government funding available for a high-quality education for all young people; increasing student reading, science, and math proficiency; and establishing mentor programs.[19] He has also proposed an ambitious stimulus package in which he calls for the federal government to invest $20 billion in school building renovation and modernization and more than $150 billion in new federal spending for public and higher education.[20]

Unfortunately, moderate Democrats and Republicans in the Senate—the very centrists with whom Obama aligns himself—passed a revised stimulus bill that provides $40 billion less for state aid than the House bill, neither of which will be adequate to cover current or looming school cuts. Also trimmed were dozens of other crucial programs, including $1 billion less for Head Start and $2 billion less for Pell college grants.[21] Krugman, writing in response to these cuts, claims that "all in all, the centrists' insistence on comforting the comfortable while afflicting the afflicted will, if reflected in the final bill, lead to substantially lower employment and substantially more suffering. But how did this happen? I blame President Obama's belief that he can transcend the partisan divide—a belief that warped his economic strategy."[22] I add to Krugman's stinging indictment that Obama's postpartisan politics also threatens to warp his educational strategy.

The larger organizing framework shaping Obama's view of education is fraught with problems. Regarding the purpose and meaning of education, Obama's philosophy does not significantly differ from the views of many conservatives who have been attempting for the last thirty years to undermine public and higher education through an embrace of market-driven rationalities. Obama consistently argues that the relevance of education lies primarily in creating a trained workforce that will enable the United States to compete in a competitive global economy. In a speech to the United Federation of Teachers, he argues that "if we want to keep building the cars of the future here in America, we can't afford to see the number of PhDs in engineering climbing in China, South Korea, and Japan even as it's dropped here in America; we can't afford a future where our high school students rank near the bottom in math and science, and our high school drop-out rate is one of the highest in the industrialized world."[23]

This limited conception of education is present in both Ronald Reagan's A Nation at Risk and George W. Bush's No Child Left Behind (NCLB) policies. No one wants students to rank near the bottom of their class in important subject areas or to drop out of schools in record numbers, but neither should the nature of the support made available to them and the expectations we hold for them be reduced to building better automobiles than the Chinese, Japanese, or South Koreans. Even though mastering work-related knowledge and skills is an important educational task, it is not the only or even the most noble purpose we should assign to education. Providing students with technical mastery and marketable skills is important, but such an approach is too narrow in both the competencies it provides and the vision it offers to young people. At the end of the day, we need much more than that—a generation that can build cars *and* raise questions about the efficacy and sustainability of existing technologies as well as the environmental, political, and cultural consequences of the new technologies they imagine and create. Meaningful and responsible education should be far more encompassing and ambitious in its purpose and goals. At best, public and higher education should be defined as democratic and accessible institutions that provide young people with the skills they need to be autonomous and critically engaged agents involved in the democratic life of their communities, nations, and an emergent global public sphere.

Obama's largely instrumental view of education appears to overlook the legacy of the nation's most prominent educational leaders and philosophers, such as Thomas Jefferson, Horace Mann, John Dewey, W. E. B. Du Bois, Anna Julia Cooper, and Jane Addams, all of whom valued education as a preeminent force for preparing young people to be socially responsible, critically engaged citizens in a democratic society. Reducing the purpose of schooling to the teaching of work-related skills opens the door to a definition of education as a private, rather than public, good; such a view also limits the horizon of what a critical education can be by confusing training with education, while offering only reforms that are both narrowly instrumental and ideologically suspect. In this discourse, citizenship and democracy are often subordinated to market-based notions of choice, hypercompetitiveness, privatization, standardization, and high-stakes testing schemes as the ultimate object and measure of learning. Situating the purpose and meaning of education in a business model both unnecessarily truncates school practices and mistakenly legitimates a number of market-based assumptions. As Stephen Metcalf points out:

> This is a view of schooling advanced by conservatives and a corporate elite who support a testing regime [that] emphasizes minimal competence along a narrow range of skills, with an eye toward satisfying the low end of the labor market. All this sits well with a business community whose first preoccupation is "global competitiveness": a community most comfortable thinking in terms of inputs (dollars spent on public schools) in relation to outputs (test scores). No one disputes that schools must inculcate the skills necessary for economic survival. But does it follow that the theory behind public schooling should be overwhelming economic? One of the reform movement's founding documents is *Reinventing Education: Entrepreneurship in America's Public Schools,* by Lou Gerstner, [former] chairman of IBM. Gerstner describes schoolchildren as human capital, teachers as sellers in a marketplace and the public school system as a monopoly. Predictably, CEOs bring to education reform CEO rhetoric: stringent, intolerant of failure, even punitive—hence the world "sanction," as if some schools had been turning away weapons inspectors.[24]

Obama consistently argues that his view of educational reform is grounded in "new ideas and new reforms based not on ideology but on what works to give our children the best possible chance in life."[25] In actuality, this is a misrepresentation for a number of reasons. Not only does Obama's broader vision of education reflect much of what conservatives have been saying for three decades about schools (viewing them largely in corporate and instrumental terms), but it also echoes a number of educational arguments that have nothing to do with socially ameliorative reforms and would be more accurately labeled as counterreforms because they are designed to narrow or disable the emancipatory possibilities of American schooling. Obama's support of vouchers, charter schools, merit pay for teachers, use of financial incentives to reward students, privatization, limiting of the bargaining power of teacher unions, and high-stakes testing schemes appears incompatible with his postpartisan view of education. Moreover, his philosophy of education betrays an indifference to the dominant role of neoliberal, market-based ideology in shaping current approaches to what works in education. Even more than his supposed neutrality, this lack of vision regarding education undermines his own call for larger economic and political renewal in the interest of social responsibility, justice, and equality. It is difficult to comprehend how this submission to privatization schemes and policies that have noticeably exacerbated the inequalities in schools and the larger society could possibly provide a critical language, pedagogy, and set of values capable of educating existing and future generations of young people to confront an era marked by "profligate consumption, growing poverty and inequality in wealth and income, a crumbling economy, and a widening net of despair about the future."[26] Just as Obama's economic advisory team and his security council include not one progressive or antiwar advocate, Obama's education team is divorced from liberal and progressive perspectives.[27]

Educational Implications and Hope

Obama's postpartisan call "to move beyond the old arguments of left and right and take meaningful, practical steps to build an education system worthy of our children and our future" is in stark conflict with his selection of Arne Duncan, former CEO of the Chicago Public Schools (CPS), as the new secretary of education. There is nothing postpartisan about Duncan's educational philosophy. Duncan has defined himself as a firm supporter of charter schools, school choice, privatization, elimination of teacher tenure, performance pay, and business-style models of accountability.[28] During his Senate confirmation hearing, Duncan argued without irony that central to his vision of education was the need to bridge "the disconnect between the education and business communities,"[29] which reflected an undaunted trust or incredulous indifference to a market-driven model of leadership that has repeatedly failed young people and been thoroughly discredited as a result of the current financial and economic meltdown. While endless daily reports about CEO greed, Gilded Age excess, shameful scandals around bonuses, and outright corporate corruption occur, none of these realities seemed to have penetrated Duncan's unwavering faith in business leadership and his own free-market model of school reform.

Duncan's neoliberal ideology is quite visible in the various connections he has established with the political and business elite in Chicago.[30] It is not surprising that a range of conservatives who have been firm supporters of Bush's educational policies—including Senator Lamar Alexander and David Brooks, a conservative op-ed writer for the *New York Times*—have praised Duncan's appointment as Obama's secretary of education. Conservatives are delighted that Duncan may bring to Washington what one education critic has called a blend of "more standardized testing, closing neighborhood schools, militarization, and the privatization of school management."[31]

Duncan's endorsement of high-stakes testing schemes, a data-driven performance culture, and harsh zero tolerance policies is compatible with his support of the philosophical underpinnings of the punitive and test-driven No Child Left Behind policy, the drawbacks of which, he insists, largely stem from its being underfunded. In contrast, Linda Darling-Hammond, who was passed over by Obama for the position of secretary of education, has challenged NCLB on the grounds that it largely focuses on a number of backward measures: testing children rather than addressing the "profound educational inequalities that plague our nation," employing punitive threats and sanctions against schools to improve student performance, discouraging states from using "forward-looking performance assessment systems," and creating "incentives for schools to rid themselves of students who are not doing well, producing higher scores at the expense of vulnerable students' education."[32]

As head of CPS, Duncan reproduced the worst dimensions of the Bush policy in deskilling teachers, closing underperforming (and radically underfunded) schools, shutting parents out of the policy-making realm, and removing from schools mostly poor students of color who were considered "dead weight."[33] Not only did Duncan support the privatization of public schools, turning them over to private operators "at a rate of about 20 a year,"[34] but he also played a major role in establishing more military academies in Chicago than in any other school system in the nation. According to Andrew Kroll: "Chicago's school system is currently the most militarized in the country, boasting five military academies, nearly three dozen smaller Junior Reserve Officer Training Corps programs within existing high schools, and numerous middle school Junior ROTC programs. More troubling yet, the military academies he's started are nearly all located in low-income, minority neighborhoods. This merging of military training and education naturally raises concerns about whether such academies will be not just education centers, but recruitment centers as well."[35]

Duncan argues that such academies instill leadership and discipline, but when considered alongside a larger culture of surveillance, punishment, repression, and confinement, especially for poor students of color, the pervasive militarization of school spaces and practices begins to look like a system that offers kids two choices: Either join the U.S. Army, or become fodder for an ever-expanding youth control complex that has increasingly become a dumping ground for poor black and brown youth.[36] As more kids experience school as a feeder into the criminal justice system, "crime becomes racialized and race criminalized."[37] According to the Advancement Project, the CPS system has "become infamous for its harsh zero tolerance policies [and] has aggressively ignited a schoolhouse to jailhouse track that is ravaging this generation of youth. For example, in 2003 over 8,000 students were arrested in CPS (an astounding 830, or almost 10%, were arrests of children aged 12 and under). More than 40% of these arrests were for simple assaults or batteries which involve no serious injuries or weapons and are often nothing more than threats or minor fights.... Seventy-seven percent (77%) of the arrests were of Black students even though they constituted only 50% of the student enrollment."[38] Under Duncan's leadership, underperforming schools came to resemble prisons, as illustrated in a growing use of police and security guards in the schools along with a professionalized security apparatus, most evident in the use of metal detectors, surveillance cameras, and other technologies of fear and containment. Transformed into a waste management system, the CPS did less to invest in students marginalized by class and race than to screen them out through excessive rates of suspension and expulsion, rendering them finally a disposable population whose future was left in the hands of juvenile and adult criminal courts.[39]

I have focused on Duncan's policies because he is the best guide for predicting the effect Obama's presidency might have on the course of American education should these initiatives go unchallenged. He is also a symbol of the contradictions and political missteps that characterize Obama's appeal to an ideological bankrupt notion of postpartisanship. As Obama's progressivism is increasingly called into question, the jury is still out on whether he will abandon his postpartisan politics for a bolder vision. Yet there remains a serious disconnect between his rhetoric and many of the policies he advocates for educational reforms and the appointments he has made to shape schooling during his first term. We can hope that the inspiration that Obama has ignited among the American public will fuel a deeply felt desire for change in education and help to create a progressive educational movement that may push Obama further than he may have planned. Obama is caught in a tug-of-war between corporate interests and democratic values, which is accentuated by an ongoing state of perpetual uncertainty in the economy and the crisis of deteriorating public and higher education. What the Obama administration must understand is that the crisis in education is not only an economic problem that requires funds to rebuild old and new schools but also a political crisis about the very nature of citizenship and democracy.

Currently, prospective changes for education under Obama's presidency are ambiguous. The postpartisan ideology Obama adopted has only weakened his ability to lead; he needs a social movement supporting him and pushing him in a more democratically inspired direction, one that connects educational theory, practice, and policy with his impassioned call for the "American people to accept some responsibility and reclaim the meaning of citizenship."[40] Educators have the strength, numbers, and courage to redefine the meaning and purpose of education to reflect the ideals and practices of a critical citizenry and a meaningful democracy. Let us hope they harness their collective insight and strength into an organized movement that demands a radical departure from the limited vision of education that has dominated the United States since Ronald Reagan and appears to be no less endorsed by President Obama and his new secretary of education, Arne Duncan.

Chapter 22
Educating the Rest of Us
Making Democracy Matter

✧

I do not believe that a student of human reality may be ethically neutral. The sole choice we face is one between loyalty to the humiliated and to beauty, and indifference to both. It is like any other choice a moral being confronts: between taking and refusing to take responsibility for one's responsibility.

—Zygmunt Bauman[1]

Barack Obama views education as a high priority in his administration. Unlike the Bush administration, his appears far more aware that public education and higher education are important sites of struggle with enormous implications for young people, the existing social order, and the future. Although President Obama and Secretary of Education Arne Duncan have focused on public education, they have done so by largely embracing the Bush administration's view of educational reform, which includes using more testing and more empirically based accountability measures, creating more charter schools and more military academies, defining the purpose of education in largely economic terms, and punishing public schools that do not measure up to high-stakes testing measures. For instance, Obama's recent reforms aimed at higher education consist of providing $12 billion to improve community colleges by developing new assessment tools and creating a standardized national curriculum. This piece of reform looks as if it is an attempt to upgrade bad secondary schools by adding computers and turning them into trade schools while producing an army of students prepared to take their place in low-skilled, low-paying service-sector jobs.

As Dianne Ravitch argues, educational reform for the Obama administration "starts with testing and ends with data and more testing."[2] She rightly insists that Obama is simply giving "Bush a 3rd term in Education."[3] Duncan is, by any educational standard, a hardwired disciple of free-market ideology who largely views schools as a business and defines educational reform within the language of market-driven values and social relations. Even though he sometimes insists that education represents the civil rights issue of this century, his view of education is as far removed as can be imagined from the discourse of the civil rights movement. In fact, his language largely echoes the conservative market-driven values of both the Bush administration and the Chamber of Commerce. There are no emancipatory or liberatory goals at work in this discourse. Like Obama, Duncan talks about education being important for democracy, but then he takes a right turn and reduces the purpose of education to preparing students almost exclusively for the workplace, defining students largely as foot soldiers in the race for the United States to be an economic leader in the global economy.

Of course, there is nothing wrong with students learning how to understand and engage with the growing demands of a global economy or learning vital work skills more generally. But a serious problem emerges when such a restrictive, instrumental goal becomes the only standard for defining the purpose of education. This is not merely a civically deprived vision of education; it is a dangerously narrow one as well. The discourse of standards and assessment dominates the Obama-Duncan language of reform and, in doing so, erases more crucial issues, such as inequitable school financing schemes, economic disinvestment in poor urban schools, widespread use of class- and race-based zero tolerance policies, reduction of teachers to testing technicians, an increase in racism and segregation of American schools, a turning of schools over to corporate interests, an ongoing modeling of schools after prisons, and a criminalization of young people. And these are only some of the problems.

Obama and Duncan want to treat teachers as low-skilled factory workers by creating market-based notions of reward and competitiveness, all based on a series of values that have been utterly discredited for causing the financial meltdown the country now faces. This market-based ideology being resurrected by Obama and Duncan has not only altered economic agendas throughout the world but also transformed politics, restructured social relations, and produced an array of reality narratives and disciplinary mea-sures that normalize this ideology's perverted view of citizenship, the state, and the supremacy of market relations.

In any concerted effort to reverse course, educators and others must take account of the profound emotional appeal and ideologi-cal hold of neoliberalism on the American public.[4] The success of a market ideology that has produced shocking levels of inequality and impoverishment, along with a market morality that makes greed and corruption ubiquitous, should raise fundamental questions about how viable such a philosophy is for educational reform in the United States. Obama's vision of education is largely centered on an economic discourse and rationality that are tied to the past, to the world and business values of investment bankers, insurance companies, and various other institutions in a market-driven culture that views social welfare largely with contempt. What the Obama administration must understand is that the crisis in education is not only an economic problem, but also a political and ethical crisis about the very nature of citizenship and democracy. Obama and Duncan on the issue of educational reform appear to be stuck on a relentless course to ensure the implementation of George W. Bush's vision of education.

We need a new language to define the meaning and purpose of public and higher education, one that makes democracy a defin-ing principle of both learning and everyday classroom practices. Part of such a challenge necessitates that educators, students, and others create organizations capable of mobilizing civic dialogue, provide an alternative democratic conception of the meaning and purpose of education, and develop political organizations that can influence legislation to challenge corporate power's ascendancy over the institutions and mechanisms of civil society. In strategic terms, revitalizing public dialogue suggests that parents, young people, teachers, students, and administrators take seriously the importance of defending public and higher education as institutions of civic culture whose purpose is to educate students for active and critical citizenship. Teaching strictly for tests, deskilling teachers, and turning administrators into CEOs actually devalue the teach-ing and learning of those crucial civic and social skills and forms of knowledge that allow students to learn how to govern rather than be governed. Obama's and Duncan's view of education may be good for creating ardent consumers and disengaged citizens who provide fodder for a growing cynicism and depoliticization of public life, but it does nothing to create the educational conditions in which young and old can exercise the critical judgment and understanding necessary to confront corporate corruption, financial mismanagement, poverty, collapse of the welfare state, militarism, ecological crisis, and a host of other problems that generations of young people are going to have to confront now and in the future.

Situated within a broader context of issues concerned with social responsibility, politics, and the dignity of human life, education should be engaged as a site that offers students the opportunity to involve themselves in the deepest problems of society—to acquire the knowledge, skills, and ethical vocabulary necessary for modes of critical dialogue and forms of broadened civic participation. This suggests developing classroom conditions for students to come to terms with their own sense of power and public voice as individual and social agents by enabling them to examine and frame critically what they learn in the classroom "within a more political or social or intellectual understanding of what's going on" in the interface between their lives and the world at large.[5] At the very least, students need to learn how to take responsibility for their own ideas, take intellectual risks, develop a sense of respect for others different from themselves, and learn how to think critically in order to function in a wider democratic culture. At issue here is providing students with an education that allows them to recognize the dream and promise of a substantive democracy, particularly the idea that as citizens they are "entitled to public services, decent housing, safety, security, support during hard times, and most importantly, some power over decision making."[6]

This is an understanding of education that treats teachers as critical and supportive intellectuals, not technicians; students as engaged citizens, not consumers; and schools as democratic public spheres, not training sites for the business world. It is also a view of education in which matters of power, equality, civic literacy, and justice are central to any viable notion of education that addresses the future in terms of its democratic possibilities rather than the bottom line.[7] I want to take up this challenge by focusing on higher education and what it means to define teachers as engaged public intellectuals. Even though this is a small part of the discourse of educational reform, it elucidates in important ways the kind of education that is a fundamental aspect of both democratization and politics itself. Although the context of academic labor differs from other work-related scenarios, the principles for defining educators as public intellectuals who critically connect learning to social change and make pedagogy central to any viable notion of politics have implications for all of us concerned about the fate and promise of a strong democracy.

In a sobering analysis of recent democratic decline, Sheldon Wolin rightly argues that in a "genuinely democratic system, as opposed to a pseudo democratic one in which a 'representative sample' of the population is asked whether it 'approves' or 'disapproves,' citizens would be viewed as *agents* actively involved in the exercise of power and in contributing to the direction of policy."[8] There is a long tradition of critical intellectuals in American higher education, extending from Thomas Jefferson to John Dewey, Edward Said, and Howard Zinn, who have all insisted that the university is one of the few spaces where the task of educating young people to become critical agents and socially engaged citizens is crucial to the meaning of education and an essential condition of academic labor and democracy itself. As a vast array of public spheres, including some of the nation's major newspapers, either fall prey to corporate control or simply disappear, higher education becomes one of the few remaining sites where a society might question itself, where it might reflectively consider how lived realities measure against democratic practices and ideals. Universities thus provide the pedagogical conditions for existing and future generations to defend democratic principles and to incorporate them into their own understanding of what it means to define themselves as engaged citizens and socially responsible adults.

Understanding higher education as a democratic public sphere means fully recognizing the purpose and meaning of education and the role of academic labor, which assumes among its basic goals promoting the well-being of students, a goal that far exceeds the oft-stated mandate of either preparing students for the workforce or engaging in a rigorous search for truth. Such objectives are not without merit, but they narrow the focus of human agency, depoliticize education, and ignore the issue of civic responsibility, among other generally unacknowledged shortcomings. Defining education as a search for the truth and preparing students for the workforce say little about the role that academics might play in influencing the fate of future citizens and the state of democracy itself. Surely academics are required to speak a kind of truth, but as Stuart Hall points out, "maybe not truth with a capital T, but ... some kind of truth, the best truth they know or can discover [and] to speak that truth to power."[9] Implicit in Hall's statement is an awareness that the priorities of big business and other powerful interests are not always, or even routinely, the priorities that shape intellectual commitment or pedagogical practice. To speak truth to power is not a temporary and unfortunate lapse into politics on the part of academics: It is central to opposing all those modes of ignorance, market-based, or instrumental rationalities and fundamentalist ideologies that make judgments difficult and democracy dysfunctional.

Amy Gutmann broadens the truth-seeking function of universities by insisting that education is always political because it is connected to the acquisition of agency and the ability to struggle with ongoing relations of power. It is a precondition for creating informed and critical citizens. For Gutmann, what is unique about academics is the crucial role they play in linking education to democracy and recognizing pedagogy as an ethical and political practice tied to modes of authority and "ways of life that are consistent with sharing the rights and responsibilities of citizenship in a democratic society."[10] Higher education, if it is to take its democratic ideals seriously, must be recognized as more than an outpost of business culture that simply does the bidding of corporate power.[11] Democratic societies need educated citizens who are steeped in more than workplace skills and the formal competencies of textual analysis. And it is precisely this democratic project that affirms the critical function of education and academic labor, while refusing to narrow their goals and aspirations to instrumental or methodological considerations. This is what makes critical pedagogy different from other provincial notions of teaching, which are largely restricted to teaching the canon or the conflicts, and other narrowly defined pedagogical commitments. And it is precisely the failure to connect learning to its democratic functions and possibilities that creates the conditions for those pedagogical approaches that ignore what it means to receive a critical education.[12]

The goals of higher education and the demands of academic labor must also include teaching students to be responsive to current issues and to learn how to identify antidemocratic forces in the wider society and connect knowledge, power, and critical modes of agency to the tasks of imagining a more just world and demonstrating a willingness to struggle for it. Academics have a moral and pedagogical responsibility to unsettle and oppose all orthodoxies, to make problematic the commonsense assumptions that often shape students' lives and their understanding of the world, and to energize students to come to terms with their own power as individual and social agents. Higher education, as Pierre Bourdieu, Paulo Freire, Stanley Aronowitz, and others remind us, cannot be removed from the hard realities of those political, economic, and social forces that both support it and consistently, though in diverse ways, attempt to shape its sense of mission and purpose.[13]

Politics is not alien to higher education but is central to comprehending the institutional, economic, ideological, and social forces that give it meaning and direction. Politics in this instance also refers to the outgrowth of historical conflicts that mark higher education as an important site of struggle. As Bourdieu argues, politics illuminates the complex ideological and institutional conditions that enable universities to function as democratic public spheres. At the same time, it makes visible the fact that such conditions are the outcome of "fragile social achievements that open up the possibility of more equality and justice, and to sacrifice them is to step backwards, whether this step is masked by a deterministic analysis of the 'market' or a naked assertion of self-interest by the wealthy and powerful."[14] Politics is thus not the bane of either education or academic research but rather a primary register of their complex relation to matters of power, ideology, freedom, justice, and democracy. The real enemies of education are those modes of politicizing education in which matters of critical dialogue, judgment, debate, and engagement are disabled through allegiance to domains of ideological purity, certainty, dogma, and assured knowledge—a species of fundamentalist thinking and practice that is not limited to any one ideological or political position or disciplinary terrain.

Nurturing critical agency is part of a pedagogical process that must be self-reflective, empowering, and directive, but not propagandistic. When the distinction between a political education and a politicizing education is collapsed or lost, the role of academics is reduced to that of either corporate clerks, hermetic specialists, or jargon-using, clever apologists for established power who justify their unthreatening combativeness by gleefully claiming "to profess nothing."[15] The smug call for academics to profess nothing or to save the world on their own time is not an educational virtue but a form of surrender, a corrosive cynicism parading as a form of professionalism—an ethical refusal to educate students to question official dogma, to create the pedagogical conditions for them to become moral agents and critical citizens, and to provide them with the knowledge and skills to engage the tension between existing reality and the promise of democracy. Critical sociologist C. Wright Mills penetrated as well as anyone the political ideology behind the disingenuous call for academics to retreat from matters of public engagement and the realm of politics:

Attempts to avoid such troublesome issues as I have been discussing are nowadays widely defended by the slogan that social science is "not out to save the world." Sometimes this is the disclaimer of a modest scholar;

sometimes it is the cynical contempt of a specialist for all issues of larger concern; sometimes it is the disillusionment of youthful expectations; often it is the pose of men who seek to borrow the prestige of The Scientist, imagined as a pure and disembodied intellect. But sometimes it is based upon a considered judgment of the facts of power. Because of such facts, I do not believe that social science will "save the world" although I see nothing at all wrong with "trying to save the world"—a phrase which I take here to mean the avoidance of war and the re-arrangement of human affairs in accordance with the ideals of human freedom and reason. Such knowledge as I have leads me to embrace rather pessimistic estimates of the chances. But even if that is where we now stand, still we must ask: If there *are* any ways out of the crises of our period by means of intellect, is it not up to the social scientist to state them? What we represent—although this is not always apparent—is man [*sic*] becoming aware of mankind. It is on the level of human awareness that virtually all solutions to the great problems must now lie.[16]

The save the world on your own time creed aligns too closely with the neoliberal incantation that "there is no alternative" and in the end means complicity with the established order. In this discourse, education as a fundamental basis for engaged citizenship, like politics itself, becomes a temporary irritant to be quickly removed from the hallowed halls of academia. In this stillborn conception of academic labor, faculty and students are scrubbed clean of any illusions about connecting what they learn to a world "strewn with ruin, waste and human suffering."[17]

Yet the commitments academics enact are distinctively political and civic, whether they deny or willingly embrace such roles. University educators cannot ignore politics, nor can they deny responsibility for acknowledging that the crisis of agency is at the center of the current crisis of democracy. At the very least, academics should be more responsible to and for a politics that raises serious questions about how students and educators negotiate the institutional, pedagogical, and social relations shaped by diverse ideologies and dynamics of power, especially as these relations mediate and inform competing visions regarding whose interests the university might serve, what role knowledge plays in furthering both excellence and equity, and how higher education defines and defends its own role in relation to its often stated, though hardly operational, allegiance to egalitarian and democratic impulses.

The view of higher education as a democratic public sphere committed to producing knowledge, skills, and social practices that enable young people to expand and deepen their sense of themselves, their moral imaginations, the public good, and the imperatives of a substantive democracy has been in a state of acute crisis for the last thirty years.[18] Harnessed to the needs and demands of corporate and military interests, higher education has increasingly abandoned even the pretense of promoting democratic ideals. The needs of corporations and the warfare state now define the nature of research, the role of faculty, the structure of university governance, and the type of education offered to students.[19] As federal and state funding for higher education is cut, universities are under more pressure to turn to corporate and military resources to keep themselves afloat. Such partnerships betray a more instrumental and mercenary assignment for higher education, a role that undermines the free flow of information, dialogue, and dissent. When faculty assume, in this context, their civic responsibility to educate students to think critically, act with conviction, learn how to make authority and power accountable, and connect what they learn in classrooms to important social issues in the larger society, they are often denounced for politicizing their classrooms and for violating professional codes of conduct, or, worse, for being unpatriotic.[20] In some cases, taking the risk of connecting what they teach to the imperative to expand the capacities of students to be critical and socially engaged agents may cost faculty their jobs, especially when they make visible the workings of power, injustice, human misery, and the alterable nature of the social order—all too evident in the firings of Norman Finkelstein, Ward Churchill, and others.

Educators need to defend what they do as political, support the university as a place to think, and create programs that nurture a culture of questioning and a willingness to fight for democratic values such as liberty, equality, and justice. But there is even more at stake here. It needs to be recognized on a broad scale that the very way in which knowledge is selected, pedagogies are defined, social relations are organized, and futures are imagined is always political, though these processes do not have to be politicized in a vulgar or an authoritarian way. Again, the conditions that make the university possible as a democratic public sphere are inescapably political and should be defended as such, but such a defense should take seriously the distinctive role that academics play not merely in preparing students for the world in which they work and live but also in enabling them to function as individual and social agents capable of critically understanding their own capacities and responsibilities in working to expand the promise of a democracy that is increasingly under assault.

The utterly privatized, if not reactionary, discourse through which academics with any sense of public commitment are now upbraided and told to save the world on their own time mimics both the logic of the market and the silencing forces of the corporate and warfare state. Within this discourse, there is a needless severing of the connection between the private and the public, theory and practice, learning and social change, and the university and the broader social contract, with its implied ethical and political foundations. Such a crude dismissal of academic responsibility is not merely theoretically weak and politically naïve; it is also part of an ongoing attack on the crucial civic and pedagogically responsible role that both the university and academics have in a society that—until the current global financial collapse—had aligned itself with the production of violence, greed, self-interest, cutthroat competitiveness, and a market-driven power bereft of ethical considerations.

In a society that remains troublingly resistant to or incapable of questioning itself, one that celebrates the consumer over the citizen (or simply reduces one to the other), and willingly endorses the narrow values and interests of corporate power, the importance of the university as a place of critical learning, dialogue, and social justice advocacy becomes all the more imperative. Moreover, the distinctive role that faculty play in this ongoing pedagogical project of democratization and learning, along with support for the institutional conditions and relations of power that make it possible, must be defended as part of a broader discourse of excellence, equity, and democracy. As Wolin points out: "For its part, democracy is ultimately dependent on the quality and accessibility of public education, especially of public universities. Education per se is not a source of *democratic* legitimacy: it does not serve as a justification for political authority, yet it is essential to the practice of citizenship."[21]

For education to be civic, critical, and democratic rather than privatized, militarized, and commodified, the work that academics do cannot be defended exclusively within the discourse of specialization, technological mastery, or a market-driven rationality concerned about profit margins. On the contrary, academic labor is distinctive by virtue of its commitment to modes of education that take seriously John Dewey's notion that democracy is a "way of life" that must be constantly nurtured and defended.[22] Or as Richard Bernstein puts it:

> Democracy, according to Dewey, does not consist exclusively of a set of institutions, formal voting procedures, or even legal guarantee of rights. These are important, but they require a culture of everyday democratic

cooperative *practices* to give them life and meaning. Otherwise institutions and procedures are in danger of becoming hollow and meaningless. Democracy is "a way of life," an ethical ideal that demands *active* and *constant* attention. And if we fail to work at creating and re-creating democracy, there is no guarantee that it will survive. Democracy involves a reflective faith in the capacity of all human beings for intelligent judgment, deliberation, and action if the proper social, educational, and economic conditions are furnished.[23]

Democracy is not cheap, and neither are the political, economic, and social conditions that make it possible. If academics believe that the university is a space for and about democracy, they need to profess more, not less, about eliminating the racial, economic, and political conditions that fill their ranks with adjuncts and that remove faculty from exercising power in university governance.[24] Instead, academics must work toward eliminating the economic conditions that prevent working-class and middle-class youth from getting a decent postsecondary education.

Both the responsibility that academics bear and the political nature of that responsibility are especially clear given the unprecedented economic meltdown the United States is now reeling from. As the financial crisis reached historic proportions, free-market fundamentalism lost both its claim to legitimacy and its pretense to democracy. Even a *Newsweek* cover declared, not without the expected confusion, "We Are All Socialist Now."[25] Despite this apparent growing recognition that market fundamentalism has fostered a destructive alignment among the state, corporate capital, and transnational corporations, there is little understanding that such an alignment has been constructed and solidified through a neoliberal disciplinary apparatus and corporate pedagogy partly produced in the halls of higher education and reinforced through the educational force of the larger media culture.

The economic Darwinism of the last thirty years has done more than throw the financial and credit systems into crisis; it has also waged an attack on all those social institutions that support critical modes of agency, reason, and meaningful dissent. And yet the financial Katrina we are now experiencing is rarely seen as part of an educational crisis in which the institutions of public and higher education have been conscripted into a war on democratic values through the endless reproduction of neoliberal beliefs, social relations, identities, and modes of understanding that legitimate the institutional arrangements of a cutthroat capitalism that has spawned rapacious greed, grotesque levels of inequality, the devaluation of any viable notion of the public good, and far-reaching levels of human suffering. There seems to be an enormous disconnect between the economic conditions that led to the financial meltdown and the call to action of a generation of young people and adults who have been educated for the last several decades in the knowledge, values, and identities of a market-driven society. Yet it has become clear that this generation of young people and adults will not solve this crisis if they do not connect it to the assault on an educational system that has been reduced to a lowly adjunct of corporate interests and the bidding of the warfare state.

This disconnect becomes clear in a recent article by Patricia Cohen in the *New York Times* in which she uncritically reports that in light of the current economic crisis, the humanities are going to have a harder time defending themselves because they are often found inadequate to the task of educating students for future employment in the workforce.[26] According to Cohen, who writes as if she were channeling Arne Duncan, Obama's secretary of education and a cheerleader for the free market, the humanities in these tough economic times have to "to justify [their] existence," by which she means they have to align themselves more closely still with the needs of the economy—a view closer to training than educating.[27] Rather than view the humanities, if not higher education in general, as one of the few public spheres left that can educate students to do more than reproduce a now widely condemned set of market-driven values, she wants universities to adopt them even more aggressively and do so in spite of broad public recognition that this mode of corporate-driven education has undermined the economy and sabotaged any viable notion of critical agency and democracy. Oddly, Cohen argues that the free-market rationality that has undermined, if not ruined, so many basic institutions in American society need not be jettisoned by higher education but rather should be applied more stringently. Couple this argument with the news that many prominent newspapers and hence critical public spheres are now failing, and it becomes clear that the faculty who inhabit the university can no longer downplay or "abandon the idea that life's most important questions are an appropriate subject for the classroom."[28]

Educators have a distinct and unique responsibility to make learning relevant, not merely to the imperatives of a discipline, scholarly method, or research specialization, but, more importantly, to the activation of knowledge, passion, values, and hope in the service of modes of agency that are crucial to sustaining a democracy in which higher education plays its rightful civic and critical pedagogical role. Academics bear a enormous responsibility in both reviving the rhetoric of democratic political culture and recognizing that to strengthen the public sphere, we must look at its most widespread institutions, especially higher education, both to undo their metamorphoses into means of surveillance, commodification, and control and to reclaim them as democratic spaces. By renewing such a commitment to critical teaching and learning, academic freedom, and the university as an autonomous sphere, academics will more easily defend their role as public and engaged intellectuals, while also enabling higher education to live up to its promise as a valuable and valued contributor to democratic relations, identities, and practices. It is time that we jettisoned antiquated notions of professionalism and subscribed to one that is alive to the challenges of the twenty-first century.

Notes

❧

Notes for the Introduction

1. Martin Luther King Jr., "I Have a Dream," *American Rhetoric.com,* http://www.americanrhetoric.com/speeches/mlkihaveadream.htm.

2. Barack Obama, "The Fierce Urgency of Now," speech delivered in South Carolina, November 3, 2007, *Rollingstone.com,* http://www.rollingstone.com/nationalaffairs/index.php/2007/11/03/the-fierce-urgency-of-now/.

3. Ibid.

4. Ibid.

5. Ibid.

6. All of these quotations are from Barack Obama, "This Is Your Victory—Speech," *CNN.com,* November 4, 2008, http://www.cnn.com/2008/POLITICS/11/04/obama.transcript/index.html.

7. Barack Obama, "Barack Obama's Inaugural Address," *New York Times,* January 20, 2009, http://www.nytimes.com/2009/01/20/us/politics/20text-obama.html.

8. "Obama's Speech to NAACP," *Washington Times,* July 17, 2009, http://www.washingtontimes.com/news/2009/jul/17/text-obamas-speech-naacp/.

9. Ibid.

10. "Cornel West and Carl Dix on Race and Politics in the Age of Obama," *Democracy Now,* July 22, 2009, http://www.democracynow.org/2009/7/22/cornel_west_and_carl_dix_on.

11. Zygmunt Bauman, *Liquid Times: Living in an Age of Uncertainty* (London: Polity Press, 2007), 3–4.

12. I am drawing here from Paul Street's useful list of structural determinants at work in promoting racism and class discrimination in the United

States. See Paul Street, "'Skip' Gates: A Curious Martyr in the Struggle Against Racism," *Black Agenda Report,* July 27, 2009, http://blackagendareport.com/?q=content/%E2%80%9Cskip%E2%80%9D-gates-curious-martyr-struggle-against-racism.

13. Zygmunt Bauman, "To Hope Is Human," *Tikkun* 19, no. 6 (November–December 2004): 65.

14. Bob Herbert, "Safety Nets for the Rich," *New York Times,* October 20, 2009, A27.

15. Ibid., Zygmunt Bauman, "To Hope Is Human," 65.

16. King, "I Have a Dream."

17. Paul Krugman, "Rewarding Bad Actors," *New York Times,* August 2, 2009, A21.

18. Bob Herbert, "Anger Has Its Place," *New York Times,* August 1, 2009, A17.

19. Bob Herbert, "Who Are We?" *New York Times,* June 23, 2009, A25.

20. Charles Savage, "Obama's Embrace of a Bush Tactic Riles Congress," *New York Times,* August 9, 2009, A18. See also Alissa J. Rubin, "Afghans Detail Detention in 'Black Jail' at U.S. Base," *New York Times,* November 29, 2009, A1, A18.

21. Frank Rich, "Is Obama Punking Us?" *New York Times,* August 9, 2009, WK8.

22. Glen Ford, "Another Obama Promise Broken—the Right to Organize Betrayed," *Black Agenda Report,* July 21, 2009, http://www.blackagendareport.com/?q=content/another-obama-promise-broken-right-organize-betrayed.

23. Julia Preston, "Staying Tough in Crackdown on Immigrants," *New York Times,* August 4, 2009, A1, A14.

24. Chris Hedges, "Nader Was Right: Liberals Are Going Nowhere with Obama," *Truthdig,* August 10, 2009, http://www.truthdig.com/report/item/20090810_nader_was_right_liberals_are_going_nowhere_with_obama/.

25. Ibid.

26. Peter Dreier, "We Need More Protests to Make Reform Possible," *The Nation,* August 7, 2009, http://www.thenation.com/doc/20090817/dreier?rel=emailNation.

27. See Godfrey Hodgson's evaluation of Obama's presidency up to the summer of 2009 in Godfrey Hodgson, "Barack Obama: A Six-Month Assessment," *OpenDemocracy,* July 7, 2009, http://www.opendemocracy.net/article/barack-obama-a-six-month-assessment.

28. C. Wright Mills, *The Sociological Imagination* (London: Oxford University Press, 2000), 187.

29. Glenn Greenwald, "Has Obama Lost the Trust of Progressives, as Krugman Says?" *Salon.com,* August 21, 2009, http://www.salon.com/opinion/greenwald/2009/08/21/obama/index.html.

30. Barack Obama cited in Macon Phillips, "Keeping Promises," *The Blog,* February 28, 2009, http://www.whitehouse.gov/blog/09/02/28/Keeping-Promises/.

Notes for Chapter 1

1. Ulrich Beck, "The Silence of Words and Political Dynamics in the World Risk Society," in *Planetary Politics: Human Rights, Terror, and Global Society*, ed. Stephen Eric Bronner (Lanham, MD: Rowman and Littlefield, 2005), 11.

2. Glenn Greenwald, "Another Brutal Year for Liberty," *Salon.com*, January 1, 2009, http://www.salon.com/opinion/feature/2009/01/01/civil_liberties/.

3. Equal Justice Initiative, *Cruel and Unusual: Sentencing 13- and 14-Year-Old Children to Die in Prison* (Montgomery, AL: Equal Justice Initiative, 2007), http://www.eji.org/eji/files/20071017cruelandunusual.pdf.

4. Ibid.

5. Ibid.

6. Ibid.

7. Marian Wright Edelman, "Juveniles Don't Belong in Adult Prisons," *Children's Defense Fund*, August 1, 2008, http://www.huffingtonpost.com/marian-wright-edelman/juveniles-don't-belong-in_b_116747.html.

8. Ibid.

Notes for Chapter 2

1. Mike Davis and Daniel Bertrand Monk, "Introduction," to *Evil Paradises*, eds. Mike Davis and Daniel Bertrand Monk (New York: New Press, 2007), ix.

2. Christine Haughney and Eric Konigsberg, "Despite Tough Times, Ultrarich Keep Spending," *New York Times*, April 14, 2008, A1.

3. Ibid.

4. Paul Krugman, "The Market Mystique," *New York Times*, March 27, 2009, A27.

5. Kenneth Saltman and David Gabard, eds., *Education as Enforcement: The Militarization and Corporatization of Schools* (New York: Routledge, 2003).

6. Orlando Patterson, *Slavery and Social Death: A Comparative Study* (Cambridge, MA: Harvard University Press, 1982), 42.

7. Zygmunt Bauman, "Happiness in a Society of Individuals," *Soundings* 38 (Winter 2008): 21.

8. Thomas Lemke, "Foucault, Governmentality, and Critique," *Rethinking Marxism* 14, no. 3 (Fall 2002): 49–64.

9. Nick Couldry, "Reality TV, or the Secret Theater of Neoliberalism," *Review of Education, Pedagogy, and Cultural Studies* 30, no. 1 (January–March 2008): 1.

10. Naomi Klein, *No Logo* (New York: Picador, 1999), 177.

11. Bill Moyers, "A Time for Anger, a Call to Action," *Common Dreams*, February 7, 2007, http://www.commondreams.org/views07/0322-24.htm.

12. I take this issue up in greater detail in Chapter 21.

13. Hannah Arendt, *Men in Dark Times* (New York: Harvest Books, 1970).

Notes for Chapter 3

1. Lizabeth Cohen, *A Consumer's Republic: The Politics of Mass Consumption in Postwar America* (New York: Vintage Books, 2003).

2. Lawrence Grossberg, *Caught in the Crossfire: Kids, Politics, and America's Future* (Boulder, CO: Paradigm Publishers, 2005), 264.

3. See Josh Golin, "Nation's Strongest School Commercialism Bill Advances Out of Committee," *Common Dreams Progressive Newswire,* August 1, 2007, http://www.commondreams.org/cgi-bin/newsprint.cgi?file=/news2007/0801-06.htm. Schor argues that total advertising and marketing expenditures directed at children in 2004 reached $15 billion (Juliet B. Schor, *Born to Buy* [New York: Scribner, 2005], 21).

4. Juliet Schor, "When Childhood Gets Commercialized, Can Childhood Be Protected?" in *Regulation, Awareness, Empowerment: Young People and Harmful Media Content in the Digital Age,* ed. Ulla Carlsson (Göteborg, Sweden: Nordicom, 2006), 114–115.

5. Kiku Adatto, "Selling Out Childhood," *Hedgehog Review* 5, no. 2 (Summer 2003): 40.

6. Schor, *Born to Buy,* 20.

7. Susan Linn, *Consuming Kids* (New York: Anchor Books, 2004), 8.

8. Benjamin R. Barber, *Consumed: How Markets Corrupt Children, Infantilize Adults, and Swallow Citizens Whole* (New York: Norton, 2007), 7–8.

9. Alex Molnar and Faith Boninger, "Adrift: Schools in a Total Marketing Environment," in *Tenth Annual Report on Schoolhouse Commercialism Trends: 2006–2007* (Tempe: Arizona State University, 2007), 6–7.

10. Schor, *Born to Buy,* 23.

11. Anup Shah, "Children as Consumers," *Global Issues,* January 8, 2008, http://www.globalissues.org/article/237/children-as-consumers.

12. Grossberg, *Caught in the Crossfire,* 88.

13. Linn, *Consuming Kids,* 54.

14. Molnar and Boninger, "Adrift," 9.

15. Schor, *Born to Buy,* 19–20.

16. Cited in Brooks Barnes, "Web Playgrounds of the Very Young," *New York Times,* December 31, 2007, http://www.nytimes.com/2007/12/31/business/31virtual.html?_r=1&oref=slogin.

17. Ibid.

18. Dan Harris, Suzanne Yeo, Christine Brouwer, and Joel Siegel, "Marketing Has Eye on Kids' Tastes for Food, 'Net,'" *ABC News,* November 1, 2009, http://abcnews.go.com/WN/w_ParentingResource/vigilant-parents-unaware-marketing-techniques-draw-teens-kids/story?d=8969255.

19. Editorial, "Clothier Pushes Porn, Group Sex to Youths," *WorldNetDaily.com,* November 15, 2003, http://www.wnd.com/news/article.asp?ARTICLE_ID=35604. See also Editorial, "Tell Nationwide Children's Hospital: No Naming Rights for Abercrombie & Fitch," *Campaign for a Commercial-Free Childhood,* June 2006, http://salsa.democracyinaction.org/o/621/t/5401/campaign.jsp?campaign_KEY=23662.

20. Tana Ganeva, "Sexpot Virgins: The Media's Sexualization of Young Girls," *AlterNet,* May 24, 2008, http://www.alternet.org/story/85977/.

21. Juliet Schor, "Tackling Turbo Consumption: An Interview with Juliet Schor," *Soundings* 34 (November 2006): 51.

22. This concept is developed in John Dewey, *Democracy and Education* (New York: Macmillan, 1966).

Notes for Chapter 4

1. Mark Halpern, "Obama Interview on CNBC," *Time,* June 15, 2008, http://thepage.time.com/obama-interview-on-cnbc/.

2. For further discussion of Disney culture, see Henry A. Giroux and Grace Pollock, *The Mouse That Roared: Disney and the End of Innocence,* rev. and exp. (Lanham, MD: Rowman and Littlefield, 2010).

3. Brooks Barnes, "Disney Expert Uses Science to Draw Boy Viewers," *New York Times,* April 14, 2009, A1.

4. Ibid.

5. Jonathan Rutherford, "Cultures of Capitalism," *Soundings* 38 (Spring 2008), http://www.lwbooks.co.uk/journals/soundings/cultures_capitalism/cultures_capitalism1.

6. Barnes, "Disney Expert," A14.

7. In fact, Kanner and some of his colleagues raised the issue in a letter to the American Psychological Association. See Miriam H. Zoll, "Psychologists Challenge Ethics of Marketing to Children," *American News Service,* April 5, 2000, http://www.mediachannel.org/originals/kidsell.shtml. See also Allen D. Kanner, "The Corporatized Child," *California Psychologist* 39, no. 1 (January–February 2006): 1–2; and Allen D. Kanner, "Globalization and the Commercialization of Childhood," *Tikkun* 20, no. 5 (September–October, 2005): 49–51. Kanner's articles can be found at http://www.commercialfreechildhood.org/articles/.

8. For a list of the Walt Disney Company's vast holdings, see "Who Owns What," *Columbia Journalism Review,* April 14, 2009, http://www.cjr.org/resources/?c=disney.

9. Giroux and Pollock, *The Mouse That Roared.*

10. Victoria Rideout, Donald F. Roberts, and Ulla G. Foehr, *Generation M: Media in the Lives of 8–18 Year-Olds* (Washington, DC: Kaiser Family Foundation, March 2005), 4.

11. Ibid., 4.

12. Jeff Chester and Kathryn Montgomery, *Interactive Food and Beverage Marketing: Targeting Children in the Digital Age* (Berkeley, CA/Washington, DC: Media Studies Group/Center for Digital Democracy, 2007), 13, http://digitalads.org/documents/digiMarketingFull.pdf.

13. Barnes, "Disney Expert," A14.

14. Brooks Barnes, "Disney's Retail Plan Is a Theme Park in Its Stores," *New York Times,* October 13, 2009, A1.

15. Editorial, "The Role of Media in Childhood Obesity," *Issue Brief,* February 2004, http://www.kaiserfamilyfoundation.org/entmedia/upload/

The-Role-Of-Media-in-Childhood-Obesity.pdf. See also Zoe Williams, "Commercialization of Childhood," *Compass: Direction for the Democratic Left,* December 1, 2006, http://www.criancaeconsumo.org.br/downloads/commercialization%20of%20childhood%20from%20britain.pdf. Williams estimates that children in both the United States and the United Kingdom are "exposed to between 20,000 and 40,000 ads a year." Juliet B. Schor, *Born to Buy* (New York: Scribner, 2005), 25.

16. Rideout, Roberts, and Foehr, *Generation M,* 6, 9.

Notes for Chapter 5

1. For an excellent analysis of this issue, see Christopher Robbins, *Expelling Hope: The Assault on Youth and the Militarization of Schooling* (Albany: State University of New York Press, 2008); William Lyons and Julie Drew, *Punishing Schools: Fear and Citizenship in American Public Education* (Ann Arbor: University of Michigan Press, 2006); and Henry A. Giroux, *The Abandoned Generation* (New York: Palgrave, 2004).

2. Jonathan Simon, *Governing Through Crime: How the War on Crime Transformed American Democracy and Created a Culture of Fear* (New York: Oxford University Press, 2007), 209.

3. Bob Herbert, "School to Prison Pipeline," *New York Times,* June 9, 2007, A29.

4. Ibid.

5. Randall R. Beger, "Expansion of Police Power in Public Schools and the Vanishing Rights of Students," *Social Justice* 29, no. 1 (2002): 120.

6. This term "crime complex" comes from David Garland, *The Culture of Control: Crime and Social Order in Contemporary Society* (Chicago: University of Chicago Press, 2002). See also David Garland, "The Culture of Control After 9/11," *Cosmopolis,* no. 2. (2008), http://www.cosmopolisonline.it/20081215/garland.php. See, especially, Kenneth Saltman, *Education as Enforcement: The Militarization and Corporatization of Schools* (New York: Routledge, 2003).

7. Some of the best books analyzing all aspects of zero tolerance policies are Robbins, *Expelling Hope*; Giroux, *The Abandoned Generation*; and William Ayers, Bernadine Dohrn, and Rick Ayers, eds., *Zero Tolerance* (New York: New Press, 2001).

8. Yolanne Almanzar, "First Grader in $1 Robbery May Face Expulsion," *New York Times,* December 4, 2008, A26.

9. Advancement Project in partnership with Padres and Jovenes Unidos, Southwest Youth Collaborative, *Education on Lockdown: The Schoolhouse to Jailhouse Track* (Chicago: Children and Family Justice Center, Northwestern University School of Law, March 24, 2005), 11.

10. Ibid., 33.

11. Ibid., 7.

12. Bernadine Dohrn, "'Look Out, Kid, It's Something You Did': The Criminalization of Children," in *The Public Assault on America's Children,* ed. Valerie Polakow (New York: Teachers College Press, 2000), 158.

13. See Paul Street, *Segregated Schools: Educational Apartheid in Post–Civil Rights America* (New York: Routledge, 2005). See also Henry A. Giroux, *Youth in a Suspect Society: Democracy or Disposability?* (New York: Palgrave Macmillan, 2009).

14. Advancement Project, *Education on Lockdown,* 17–18.

15. Ibid.

16. Sam Dillon, "Study Finds High Rate of Imprisonment Among Dropouts," *New York Times,* October 9, 2009, A12.

17. Advancement Project, *Education on Lockdown,* 17–18.

18. Ibid., 31.

19. Elora Mukherjec, *Criminalizing the Classroom: The Over-policing of New York City Schools* (New York: American Civil Liberties Union and New York Civil Liberties, March 2008), 9.

20. Adam Liptak, "Strip-Search of Girl Tests Limit of School Policy," *New York Times,* March 24, 2009, A1.

21. Beger, "Expansion of Police Power," 120.

22. Victor M. Rios, "The Hypercriminalization of Black and Latino Male Youth in the Era of Mass Incarceration," in *Racializing Justice, Disenfranchising Lives,* eds. Manning Marable, Ian Steinberg, and Keesha Middlemass (New York: Palgrave Macmillan, 2007), 40–54.

23. For a superb analysis of urban marginality of youth in the United States and France, see Loïc Wacquant, *Urban Outcasts* (London: Polity Press, 2008).

24. Children's Defense Fund, *America's Cradle to Prison Pipeline* (Washington, DC: Children's Defense Fund, 2007), 77.

25. David Sirota, "Columbine Questions We Still Don't Ponder," *CommonDreams.Org,* April 17, 2009, http://www.commondreams.org/view/2009/04/17-6.

26. For an informative analysis of the history and struggle over youth since the 1970s, see Lawrence Grossberg, *Caught in the Crossfire: Kids, Politics, and America's Future* (Boulder, CO: Paradigm Publishers, 2005).

27. Bob Herbert, "Stacking the Deck Against Kids," *New York Times,* November 28, 2009, A19.

Notes for Chapter 6

1. Charles Isherwood, "Chaotic Household? Sell the Kids," *New York Times,* April 22, 2009, C1.

2. For an insightful analysis of the myth of innocence, see Marina Warmer, *Six Myths of Our Time* (New York: Vintage, 1995), especially chap. 30. Of course, the concept of childhood innocence as a historical invention has been pointed out by a number of theorists. See, for example, Philip Aries, *Centuries of Childhood* (Harmondsworth, UK: Penguin, 1979); and Lloyd deMause, ed., *The Evolution of Childhood* (New York: Psychohistory Press, 1974). I take up this issue in Henry A. Giroux, *America on the Edge* (New York: Palgrave, 2006).

3. Daniel Thomas Cook, "When a Child Is Not a Child, and Other Conceptual Hazards of Childhood Studies," *Childhood* 16, no. 5 (2009): 8.

4. Frank Rich, "Let Me Entertain You," *New York Times,* January 18, 1997, A23.

5. Richard Goldstein, "The Girl in the Fun Bubble: The Mystery of JonBenet," *Village Voice,* June 10, 1997, 41.

6. Jane Treays, "The Child Beauty-Pageant Queens Who Grew Up," *Sunday Times Online,* May 25, 2008, http://women.timesonline.co.uk/tol/life_and_style/women/article3997487.ece.

7. Rich, "Let Me Entertain You."

8. Stacy Weiner, "Goodbye to Girlhood," *Washington Post,* February 20, 2007, HE01.

9. This paragraph relies heavily on comments by pediatric psychologists quoted in Rebecca A. Eder, Ann Digirolamo, and Suzanne Thompson, "Is Winning a Pageant Worth a Lost Childhood?" *St. Louis Post-Dispatch,* February 24, 1997, 7B.

10. David Elkind, "The Family in the Postmodern World," *National Forum* 75 (Summer 1995): 24–28.

11. I take this issue up in greater detail in Henry A Giroux, *Stealing Innocence: Corporate Culture's War on Children* (New York: Palgrave, 2001); Henry A. Giroux, *The Abandoned Generation* (New York: Palgrave, 2004); and Henry A. Giroux, *Youth in a Suspect Society* (New York: Palgrave Macmillan, 2009).

Notes for Chapter 7

1. For a brilliant analysis of the racist state, see David Theo Goldberg, *The Racial State* (Malden, MA: Wiley-Blackwell, 2001).

2. Joe Klein, "Obama's Victory Ushers in a New America," *Time.com,* November 5, 2008, http://www.time.com/time/politics/article/0,8599,1856649,00.html.

3. George Will, "Obama Judges a Judge," *The Cagle Post,* August 12, 2007, http://www.caglepost.com/column/George+Will/2264/Obama+Judges+a+Judge.html.

4. Paul Ortiz, "On the Shoulders of Giants: Senator Obama and the Future of American Politics," *Truthout.Org,* November 25, 2008, http://www.truthout.org/112508R?print.

5. Jonathan Simon, *Governing Through Crime: How the War on Crime Transformed American Democracy and Created a Culture of Fear* (New York: Oxford University Press, 2007), 59.

6. On homelessness, see National Alliance to End Homelessness, "Homelessness Looms as Potential Outcome of Recession," January 23, 2009, http://www.endhomelessness.org/files/2161_file_Projected_Increases_in_Homelessness.pdf. For figures on children on food stamps, see Jason DeParle and Robert Gebeloff, "Across U.S., Food Stamp Use Soars and Stigma Fades," *New York Times,* November 29, 2009, A1. For some interesting figures on children living in poverty, see Susan Campbell, "Bad Economy Hard On Children

in Poverty," *Chicago Tribune*, November 4, 2009, www.chicagotribune.com/news/breaking/hc-campbellct1104.artnov04-col,0,4419883.column.

7. Jason DeParle, "The American Prison Nightmare," *New York Review of Books* 54, no. 6 (April 12, 2007): 33.

8. Paul Street, *Segregated Schools: Educational Apartheid in Post–Civil Rights America* (New York: Routledge, 2005), 82.

9. Angela Y. Davis, *Abolition Democracy: Beyond Empire, Prisons, and Torture* (New York: Seven Stories Press, 2005), 98.

10. "Barack Obama's Speech on Race," *New York Times*, March 18, 2008, http://www.nytimes.com/2008/03/18/us/politics/18text-obama.html?_r=1&scp=1&sq=%22Barack%20Obama's%20Speech%20on%20Race%22&st=cse.

11. Adam Nossiter, "With Jobs to Do, Louisiana Parish Turns to Inmates," *New York Times*, July 5, 2006, http://www.nytimes.com/2006/07/05/us/05prisoners.html.

12. Ibid.

Notes for Chapter 8

1. I have taken the term "torture factories" from Angela Y. Davis, *Abolition Democracy: Beyond Empire, Prisons, and Torture* (New York: Seven Stories Press, 2005), 50. The United States had 2,319,258 people in jail or prison at the start of 2008—1 out of every 100 and more than any other nation. See Associated Press, "A First: 1 in 100 Americans Jailed," *MSNBC.com*, February 28, 2008, http://www.msnbc.msn.com/id/23392251/print/1/displaymode/1098/.

2. Mike Davis and Daniel Bertrand Monk, "Introduction," to *Evil Paradises*, eds. Mike Davis and Daniel Bertrand Monk (New York: New Press, 2007), ix.

3. See Marian Wright Edelman, "Now Is the Time to Bail Our Poor Children and Families Out of Poverty," *Children's Defense Fund*, January 25, 2009, http://www.childrensdefense.org/child-research-data-publications/data/marian-wright-edelman-child-watch-column/bail-our-poor-children-and-families-out-of-poverty.html.

4. Alliance for Excellent Education, "Fact Sheet," February 2009, http://www.all4ed.org/files/GraduationRates_FactSheet.pdf.

5. http://www.bls.gov/news.release/pdf/youth.pdf.

6. Bob Herbert, "The Danger Zone," *New York Times*, March 15, 2007, A25.

7. These figures are taken from Children's Defense Fund, *America's Cradle to Prison Pipeline* (Washington, DC: Children's Defense Fund, 2007), http://www.childrensdefense.org/site/DocServer/CPP_report_2007_summary.pdf?docID=6001.

8. Lawrence Grossberg, *Caught in the Crossfire* (Boulder, CO: Paradigm Publishers, 2005), 16.

9. "Kindergarten Girl Handcuffed, Arrested at Fla. School," *WFTV.com*, March 30, 2007, http://www.wftv.com/news/11455199/detail.html.

10. Adam Liptak, "Lifers as Teenagers, Now Seeking a Second Chance," *New York Times*, October 17, 2007, A1.

11. Ibid.

Notes for Chapter 9

1. Ian Urbina and Sean D. Hamill, "Judges Plead Guilty in Scheme to Jail Youths for Profit," *New York Times*, February 13, 2009, A1, A20.

2. Ibid.

3. Jean Comaroff and John Comaroff, "Reflections of Youth, from the Past to the Postcolony," in *Frontiers of Capital: Ethnographic Reflections on the New Economy*, eds. Melissa S. Fisher and Greg Downey (Durham, NC: Duke University Press, 2006), 267.

4. David Garland, *The Culture of Control: Crime and Social Order in Contemporary Society* (Chicago: University of Chicago Press, 2001); Jonathan Simon, *Governing Through Crime: How the War on Crime Transformed American Democracy and Created a Culture of Fear* (New York: Oxford University Press, 2007). See also Phil Scraton, *Power, Conflict, and Criminalization* (New York: Routledge, 2007).

5. Loïc Wacquant, "From Slavery to Mass Incarceration: Rethinking the 'Race Question' in the U.S.," *New Left Review*, January–February 2002, 57.

6. Alex Koroknay-Palicz, "Scapegoating of Youth," *National Youth Rights Association*, December 2001, http://www.youthrights.org/scapegoat.php.

7. Children's Defense Fund, *2007 Annual Report* (Washington, DC: Children's Defense Fund, 2008), http://www.childrensdefense.org/site/DocServer/CDF_annual_report_07.pdf?docID=8421.

8. See Bob Herbert, "Head for the High Road," *New York Times*, September 2, 2008, A25; Sam Dillon, "Hard Times Hitting Students and Schools," *New York Times*, September 1, 2008, A1, A9; and Erik Eckholm, "Working Poor and Young Hit Hard in Downturn," *New York Times*, November 9, 2008, A23.

Notes for Chapter 10

1. For a critical summary of the racist and sexist smear campaign waged against Judge Sotomayor, see Faiz Shakir, "Right-Wing Hate Machine Launches Vicious Campaign of Racist and Sexist Attacks on Sotomayor," *AlterNet*, May 30, 2009, http://www.alternet.org/story/140248.

2. Sonia Sotomayor, "A Latina Judge's Voice," *New York Times*, May 14, 2009, http://www.nytimes.com/2009/05/15/us/politics/15judge.text.html?_r=1.

3. Jack Tapper, "Gingrich Calls Sotomayor a Racist," *Political Punch*, May 27, 2009, http://blogs.abcnews.com/politicalpunch/2009/05/gingrich-calls.html.

4. Charles Murray, *Losing Ground: American Social Policy, 1950–1980* (New York: Basic Books, 1985).

5. Joy James, "The Dead Zone: Stumbling at the Crossroads of Party Politics, Genocide, and Postracial Racism," *South Atlantic Quarterly: Africana Thought* 108, no. 3 (Summer 2009): 464–465.

6. This issue is taken up brilliantly in David Theo Goldberg, *The Racial State* (Malden, MA: Blackwell, 2002); and in David Theo Goldberg, *The Threat of Race: Reflections on Racial Neoliberalism* (Malden, MA: Wiley-Blackwell, 2009).

7. Manning Marable, "Beyond Color-Blindness," *The Nation*, December 14, 1998, 29.

8. For specific figures in all areas of life, see Eduardo Bonilla-Silva, *White Supremacy and Racism in the Post–Civil Rights Era* (Boulder, CO: Lynne Rienner, 2001), esp. 89–120.

9. I address these issues in detail in Henry A. Giroux, *Youth in a Suspect Society: Democracy or Disposability?* (New York: Palgrave Macmillan, 2009).

10. Loïc Wacquant, "From Slavery to Mass Incarceration: Rethinking the 'Race Question' in the U.S.," *New Left Review*, January–February 2002, 44.

11. Quoted in Paul Street, "Mass Incarceration and Racist State Priorities at Home and Abroad, *DissidentVoice*, March 11, 2003, 6–7, http://www.dissidentvoice.org/Articles2/Street_MassIncarceration.htm. See also Jennifer Warren, *One in 100: Behind Bars in America 2008* (Washington, DC: PEW Center on the States, 2008).

12. All of these quotes can be found in Bob Herbert, "The Howls of a Fading Species," *New York Times*, June 2, 2009, A23.

13. See "Fox Host Glenn Beck: Obama Is a Racist," *Huffington Post*, July 28, 2009, http://www.huffingtonpost.com/2009/07/28/fox-host-glenn-beck-obama_n_246310.html.

14. Frank Rich, "Small Beer, Big Hangover," *New York Times*, August 1, 2009, http://www.nytimes.com/2009/08/02/opinion/02rich.html.

15. Ibid.

16. Ibid.

17 . Bob Herbert, "The Howls of a Fading Species," *New York Times*, June 2, 2009, A23.

Notes for Chapter II

1. Claude Brown, *Manchild in the Promised Land* (New York: Signet Books, 1965).

2. Ibid., 419.

3. Quoted in Bob Herbert, "Children in Peril," *New York Times*, April 21, 2009, A25.

4. Kenneth C. Land, *Education for Homeless Children and Youths Program* (New York: Foundation for Child Development, April 2009), http://www.fcd-us.org/usr_doc/Final-2009CWIReport.pdf.

5. See Marian Wright Edelman, "Now Is the Time to Bail Our Poor Children and Families Out of Poverty," *Children's Defense Fund*, January 25, 2009, http://www.childrensdefense.org/child-research-data-publications/

data/marian-wright-edelman-child-watch-column/bail-our-poor-children-and-families-out-of-poverty.html.

6. Robert Weissman, "The Shameful State of the Union," *Common Dreams.org*, January 30, 2008, http://www.commondreams.org/archive/2008/01/30/6725.

7. Dorothy Roberts, *Shattered Bonds: The Color of Child Welfare* (New York: Basic Civitas Books, 2008), 268.

Notes for Chapter 12

1. Paul Krugman, "Barack Be Good," *New York Times*, December 26, 2008, A25.

2. Bob Herbert, "Stop Being Stupid," *New York Times*, December 27, 2008, A19.

3. Thomas L. Friedman, "Time to Reboot America," *New York Times*, December 24, 2008, A21.

4. Deborah Jones Barrow, "Greenspan Shrugged? Did Ayn Rand Cause Our Financial Crisis?" *WowOwow*, October 24, 2008, http://www.wowowow.com/post/greenspan-shrugged-did-ayn-rand-cause-our-financial-crisis-128286.

5. I take up in great detail the philosophy and effects of neoliberalism in Henry A. Giroux, *Against the Terror of Neoliberalism* (Boulder, CO: Paradigm Publishers, 2008).

6. Thomas Lemke, "Foucault, Governmentality, and Critique," paper presented at the Rethinking Marxism Conference, University of Amherst, Massachusetts, September 21–24, 2000, http://www.thomaslemkeweb.de/publikationen/Foucault,%20Governmentality,%20and%20Critique%20IV-2.pdf.

7. Ellen Willis, "Escape from Freedom: What's the Matter with Tom Frank (and the Lefties Who Love Him)?" *Situations* 1, no. 2 (2006): 9.

8. This issue is taken up in great detail in Henry A. Giroux, *Youth in a Suspect Society: Democracy or Disposability?* (New York: Palgrave Macmillan, 2009).

Notes for Chapter 13

1. See, for example, Chris Hedges, "It's Not Going to Be OK," *TruthDig.com*, February 2, 2009, http://www.commondreams.org/view/2009/02/02-0.

2. See Henry A. Giroux, *Against the Terror of Neoliberalism* (Boulder, CO: Paradigm Publishers, 2008).

3. Fulvia Carnevale and John Kelsey, "Art of the Possible: An Interview with Jacques Rancière," *Artforum* (March 2007): 264.

4. Frank Rich, "No Time for Poetry," *New York Times*, January 25, 2009, WK10.

5. Sheldon Wolin, *Democracy, Inc.: Managed Democracy and the Specter of Inverted Totalitarianism* (Princeton, NJ: Princeton University Press, 2008), 260–261.

6. Ibid., 261.

7. See also Chapter 18.

8. Zygmunt Bauman, *Liquid Life* (London: Polity Press, 2005), 14.

9. Sally Kohn, "Real Change Happens Off-Line," *Christian Science Monitor,* June 30, 2008, http://www.csmonitor.com/2008/0630/p09s01-coop.html.

10. Jacques Derrida, "Intellectual Courage: An Interview," trans. Peter Krapp, *Culture Machine* 2 (2000): 9.

Notes for Chapter 14

1. Bill Readings, *The University in Ruins* (Cambridge, MA: Harvard University Press, 1996), 11, 18.

2. Zygmunt Bauman, *In Search of Politics* (Palo Alto, CA: Stanford University Press, 1999), 170.

3. Lynn Worsham and Gary A. Olson, "Rethinking Political Community: Chantal Mouffe's Liberal Socialism," *Journal of Composition Theory* 19, no. 2 (1999): 178.

4. Stuart Hall quoted in Les Terry, "Travelling 'The Hard Road to Renewal,'" *Arena Journal,* no. 8 (1997): 55.

5. Sheldon Wolin, "Political Theory: From Vocation to Invocation," in *Vocations of Political Theory,* eds. Jason Frank and John Tambornino (Minneapolis: University of Minnesota Press, 2000), 4.

Notes for Chapter 15

1. A typical example is Noam Cohen, "Twitter on the Barricades: Six Lessons Learned," *New York Times,* June 21, 2009, WK4. Although acknowledging the role Twitter is playing in the Iranian uprisings, Cohen is content to analyze Twitter solely as a communication tool, suggesting, for instance, that we cannot believe everything posted on Twitter.

2. Two interesting articles on the relationship between the Internet and democracy are Evgeny Morozov, "Texting Towards Utopia," *Boston Review,* March–April 2009, http://bostonreview.net/BR34.2/morozov.php; and Linda Jean Kenix, "The Internet as a Tool for Democracy?" *First Monday* 13, no. 7 (July 2008), http://www.uic.edu/htbin/cgiwrap/bin/ojs/index.php/fm/article/view/2124/1984. For some important work on the new media, see Nick Dyer-Witheford, *Cyber-Marx: Cycles and Circuits of Struggle in High-Technology Capitalism* (Chicago: University of Illinois Press, 1999); Manuel Castells, *The Internet Galaxy* (New York: Oxford University Press, 2001); Nick Couldry, *Media Rituals* (New York: Routledge, 2003); Mark Poster, *Information Please: Culture and Politics in the Age of Digital Machines* (Durham, NC: Duke University Press, 2006); and Megan Boler, ed., *Digital Media and Democracy* (Cambridge, MA: MIT Press, 2008).

3. Herbert Marcuse, *One-Dimensional Man* (Boston: Beacon Press, 1964).

4. Zygmunt Bauman, *Wasted Lives* (London: Polity Press, 2004), 130.

5. I take up the issue of screen culture and the challenge of the new media in Henry A. Giroux, *Beyond the Spectacle of Terrorism: Global Uncertainty and the Challenge of the New Media* (Boulder, CO: Paradigm Publishers, 2006).

6. I want to thank Tony Kashani for these figures and for his help with some questions raised by this chapter.

7. Robert F. Worth, "Security Forces and Protesters Clash in Tehran," *New York Times,* June 21, 2009, A1.

8. Nazila Fathi, "Protesters Defy Iranian Efforts to Cloak Unrest," *New York Times,* June 18, 2009, A1.

9. Editorial, "Canada Will Not 'Stay Out' of Iranian Politics: Cannon," *CBC News,* June 18, 2009, http://www.cbc.ca/world/story/2009/06/18/iran-canada-foreign-affairs-meeting847.html.

10. Brian Stelter and Brad Stone, "Stark Images of the Turmoil in Iran, Uploaded to the World on the Internet," *New York Times,* June 18, 2009, A14.

11. Ibid.

12. Thomas Keenan, "Mobilizing Shame," *South Atlantic Quarterly* 103, nos. 2–3 (2004): 447. Keenan explores the relationship between ethics and responsibility in even greater detail in his *Fables of Responsibility* (Palo Alto, CA: Stanford University Press, 1997).

13. Jacques Derrida cited in Michael Peters, "The Promise of Politics and Pedagogy in Derrida," *Review of Education/Pedagogy/Cultural Studies* (in press).

14. Allen Feldman, "On the Actuarial Gaze: From 9/11 to Abu Ghraib," *Cultural Studies* 19, no. 2 (March 2005): 212.

15. Jürgen Habermas, *Theory of Communicative Action,* vol. 2: *Lifeworld and System: A Critique of Functionalist Reason,* trans. Thomas McCarthy (Cambridge: Polity Press, 1987), 390.

16. Nick Couldry, "Media and the Problem of Voice," unpublished paper (2009).

17. Angela Y. Davis, *Abolition Democracy: Beyond Empire, Prisons, and Torture* (New York: Seven Stories Press, 2005), 128–129.

Notes for Chapter 16

1. Glenn Greenwald, "The Neda Video, Torture, and the Truth-Revealing Power of Images," *Salon.com,* June 24, 2009, http://www.commondreams.org/view/2009/06/24-10.

2. Fulvia Carnevale and John Kelsey, "Art of the Possible: An Interview with Jacques Rancière," *Artforum,* March 2007, 259–260.

3. Tabassum Zakaria, "Obama Calls Neda Video 'Heartbreaking,'" *Reuters Blogs: Front Row,* June 23, 2009, http://blogs.reuters.com/frontrow/tag/barack-obama-iran-protests-neda/.

4. Randy Cohen, "Moral of the Story," *New York Times,* June 29, 2009, http://ethicist.blogs.nytimes.com/2009/06/29/the-power-of-pictures/.

5. Greenwald, "The Neda Video."

6. Scott Wilson, "Obama Shifts on Abuse Photos," *Washington Post*, May 14, 2009, http://mobile.washingtonpost.com/detail.jsp?key=387026&rc=wo&npc=wo.

7. Glenn Greenwald, "Defeat of the Graham-Lieberman Bill (H.R. 2892) and the Ongoing War on Transparency," *Salon.com*, June 9, 2009, http://www.salon.com/opinion/greenwald/2009/06/09/transparency/.

8. Mark Danner, "US Torture: Voices from the Black Sites," *New York Review of Books*, April 9, 2009, 77.

9. Judith Butler, *Frames of War: When Is Life Grievable?* (London: Verso, 2009), 74.

10. Roy Eidelson, "How Americans Think About Torture—and Why," *TruthOut.com*, May 11, 2009, http://www.truthout.org/051209C.

Note for Chapter 17

1. Nicholas D. Kristof, "Obama and the War on Brains," *New York Times*, October 9, 2009, WK10.

Notes for Chapter 18

1. David Labaree quoted in Alfie Kohn, "The Real Threat to American Schools," *Tikkun*, March–April 2001, 25. For an interesting commentary on Obama and the struggle over school reform, see Alfie Kohn, "Beware School 'Reformers,'" *The Nation*, December 29, 2008, http://www.thenation.com/doc/20081229/kohn/print.

2. The term "crime complex" comes from David Garland, *The Culture of Control: Crime and Social Order in Contemporary Society* (Chicago: University of Chicago Press, 2002). I have modified it somewhat by highlighting "youth."

3. For a brilliant analysis of the "governing through crime" complex, see Jonathan Simon, *Governing Through Crime: How the War on Crime Transformed American Democracy and Created a Culture of Fear* (New York: Oxford University Press, 2007).

4. Advancement Project in partnership with Padres and Jovenes Unidos, Southwest Youth Collaborative, *Education on Lockdown: The Schoolhouse to Jailhouse Track* (New York: Children and Family Justice Center, Northwestern University School of Law, March 24, 2005), 31. On the broader issue of the effect of racialized zero tolerance policies on public education, see Christopher G. Robbins, *Expelling Hope: The Assault on Youth and the Militarization of Schooling* (Albany: State University of New York Press, 2008). See also Henry A. Giroux, *The Abandoned Generation* (New York: Palgrave, 2004).

5. Yasmin Nair, "Duncan Draws Mixed Reactions from LGBTAs," *Catalyst*, January 7, 2009, http://www.catalyst-chicago.org/news/index.php?item=2514&cat=5.

6. See http://www.atkearney.com.

7. Nair, "Duncan Draws Mixed Reactions."

8. Renaissance Schools Fund, "Creating a New Market of Public Education: The Renaissance Schools Fund 2008 Progress Report," http://www.rsfchicago.org.

9. Kenneth J. Saltman, *Capitalizing on Disaster: Taking and Breaking Public Schools* (Boulder, CO: Paradigm Publishers, 2007), chap. 3. See also David Hursh and Pauline Lipman, "Renaissance 2010: The Reassertion of Ruling-Class Power Through Neoliberal Policies in Chicago," *Policy Futures in Education* 5, no. 2 (2007): 160–178.

10. Sarah Karp and Joyn Myers, "Duncan's Track Record," *Catalyst Chicago*, December 15, 2008, http://www.catalyst-chicago.org/news/index.php?item=2514&cat=5&tr=y&auid=4336549.

11. See Chicago Public Schools, Office of New Schools, "2006/2007 Charter School Performance Report Executive Summary" (Chicago: CPS, 2008).

12. See Dorothy Shipps, *School Reform, Corporate Style: Chicago 1880–2000* (Lawrence: University of Kansas Press, 2006).

13. See, for example, Children's Defense Fund, *America's Cradle to Prison Pipeline* (Washington, DC: Children's Defense Fund, 2007), http://www.childrensdefense.org/site/DocServer/CPP_report_2007_summary.pdf?docID=6001. See also Elora Mukherjee, *Criminalizing the Classroom: The Over-policing of New York City Schools* (New York: American Civil Liberties Union and New York Civil Liberties, March 2008), 1–36.

14. Donna Gaines, "How Schools Teach Our Kids to Hate," *Newsday*, April 25, 1999, B5.

15. As has been widely reported, the prison industry has become big business, with many states spending more on prison construction than on university construction. See Jennifer Warren, *One in 100: Behind Bars in America 2008* (Washington, DC: PEW Center on the States, 2007), http://www.pewcenteronthestates.org/news_room_detail.aspx?id=35912.

Notes for Chapter 19

1. Jeffrey Brainard, "U.S. Defense Secretary Asks Universities for New Cooperation," *Chronicle of Higher Education*, April 16, 2008, http://chronicle.com/news/article/4316/us-defense-secretary-asks-universities-for-new-cooperation.

2. Michael Geyer, "The Militarization of Europe, 1914–1945," in *The Militarization of the Western World*, ed. John Gillis (New Brunswick, NJ: Rutgers University Press, 1989), 79.

3. William G. Martin, "Manufacturing the Homeland Security Campus and Cadre," *ACAS Bulletin* 70 (Spring 2005): 1.

4. Chalmers Johnson, *The Sorrows of Empire: Militarism, Secrecy, and the End of the Republic* (New York: Metropolitan Books, 2004), 291.

5. See Cary Nelson, "The National Security State," *Cultural Studies* 4, no. 3 (2004): 357–361.

6. Chalmers Johnson, "Empire v. Democracy," *TomDispatch.com*, January 31, 2007, http://www.commondreams.org/cgi-bin/print.cgi?file=/views07/0131-27.htm.

7. Jacques Rancière, "Democracy, Republic, Representation," *Constellations* 13, no. 3 (2006): 299.

Notes for Chapter 20

1. Marc Bousquet, "An Education President from Wal-Mart," *Chronicle of Higher Education*, July 23, 2009, http://chronicle.com/blogPost/An-Education-President-From/7434/.

2. See Stanley Aronowitz, *Against Schooling: For an Education That Matters* (Boulder, CO: Paradigm Publishers, 2008); John Wilson, *Patriotic Correctness: Academic Freedom and Its Enemies* (Boulder, CO: Paradigm Publishers, 2008); Christopher Newfield, *Unmaking the Public University: The Forty-Year Assault on the Middle Class* (Cambridge, MA: Harvard University Press, 2008); Mark Bousquet, *How the University Works: Higher Education and the Low-Wage Nation* (New York: New York University Press, 2008); Frank Donoghue, *The Last Professors: The Corporate University and the Fate of the Humanities* (New York: Fordham University Press, 2008); Evan Watkins, *Class Degrees: Smart Work, Managed Choice, and the Transformation of Higher Education* (New York: Fordham University Press, 2008); and Henry A. Giroux and Susan Searls Giroux, *Take Back Higher Education* (New York: Palgrave, 2004).

3. Jennifer Washburn, *University, Inc.: The Corporate Corruption of Higher Education* (New York: Basic Books, 2006), 227.

4. Bill Moyers, "A Time for Anger, a Call to Action," *CommonDreams.org*, February 7, 2007, http://www.commondreams.org/views07/0322-24.htm. I take up the issue of the increasing militarizing of the university in Henry A. Giroux, *The University in Chains: Confronting the Military-Industrial-Academic Complex* (Boulder, CO: Paradigm Publishers, 2007).

5. On the relationship between education and hope, see Mark Coté, Richard J. F. Day, and Greig de Peuter, eds., *Utopian Pedagogy: Radical Experiments Against Neoliberal Globalization* (Toronto: University of Toronto Press, 2007); and Henry A. Giroux, *Public Spaces/Private Lives: Democracy Beyond 9/11* (Boulder, CO: Rowman and Littlefield, 2003).

6. Cited in Burton Bollag, "UNESCO Has Lofty Aims for Higher Education Conference, but Critics Doubt Its Value," *Chronicle of Higher Education*, September 4, 1998, A76.

7. Sheldon Wolin, *Democracy, Inc.: Managed Democracy and the Specter of Inverted Totalitarianism* (Princeton, NJ: Princeton University Press, 2008), 43.

8. Ibid., 66.

9. Ibid., 65.

10. Ibid., 68.

11. Giroux and Giroux, *Take Back Higher Education*.

12. Jacques Derrida, "The Future of the Profession or the Unconditional University," in *Derrida Down Under*, eds. Laurence Simmons and Heather Worth (Auckland, New Zealand: Dunmore Press, 2001), 245; Fulvia Carnevale and John Kelsey, "Art of the Possible: An Interview with Jacques Rancière," *Artforum*, March 2007, 260–261.

13. Peter Seybold, "The Struggle Against Corporate Takeover of the University," *Socialism and Democracy* 22, no. 1 (March 2008): 2.

14. John Dewey quoted in Elizabeth L. Hollander, "The Engaged University," *Academe*, July–August 2000, http://www.aaup.org/publications/Academe/2000/00ja/JA00Holl.htm.

15. Wolin, *Democracy, Inc.*, 147. I am not arguing that young people should not serve in the military. Rather, I am calling on all citizens to serve, thereby sharing the military sacrifices a country has to make.

16. See, especially, Bousquet, *How the University Works*; and Donoghue, *The Last Professors*.

Notes for Chapter 21

1. George Packer, "The New Liberalism," *New Yorker*, November 17, 2008, http://www.newyorker.com/reporting/2008/11/17/081117fa_fact_packer.

2. Judith Butler, "Uncritical Exuberance?" *IndyBay.org*, November 5, 2008, http://www.indybay.org/newsitems/2008/11/05/18549195.php.

3. Richard Lichtman, "Myths of the Marketplace: The Terrible Violence of Abstraction," *Capitalism, Nature, Socialism* (in press).

4. For an excellent account of how the Bush administration played fast and loose with the truth, see Frank Rich, *The Greatest Story Ever Told* (New York: Penguin, 2006).

5. I analyze these issues in Henry A. Giroux, *The University in Chains: Confronting the Military-Industrial-Academic Complex* (Boulder, CO: Paradigm Publishers, 2007).

6. See Rich, *The Greatest Story Ever Told.*

7. Frank Rich, "Slumdogs Unite!" *New York Times*, February 8, 2009, A10.

8. Zygmunt Bauman, "Has the Future a Left?" *Soundings* 35 (March 2007): 9.

9. V. Dion Haynes and Michael Birnbaum, "D.C. Tries Cash as a Motivator in School," *Washington Post*, August 22, 2008, A1.

10. See, for example, Larissa MacFarquhar, "The Conciliator," *New Yorker*, May 7, 2007, http://www.newyorker.com/reporting/2007/05/07/070507fa_fact_macfarquhar; Packer, "The New Liberalism"; Christopher Hayes, "The Pragmatist," *The Nation*, December 29, 2008, 13–16; Simon Critchley, "The American Void," *Harper's Magazine*, November 2008, 17–20; and Paul Krugman, "Stuck in the Middle," *New York Times*, January 23, 2009, http://www.nytimes.com/2009/01/23/opinion/23krugman.html.

11. Hayes, "The Pragmatist," 15.

12. Paul Krugman, "On the Edge," *New York Times*, February 6, 2009, A23.

13. Obama's emphasis on coddling the political center got a black eye when his "pick for commerce secretary, the Republican Senator Judd Gregg, refused to vote for Obama's stimulus bill, abstaining instead" (Maureen Dowd, "Post-partisan Depression," *New York Times*, February 8, 2009, A11). Frank Rich has issued an insightful but tempered statement about Obama's postpartisan-

ship: "The new president who vowed to change Washington's culture will have to fight much harder to keep from being co-opted by it instead. There are simply too many major layers in the Obama team who are either alumni of the financial bubble's insiders' club or of the somnambulant governmental establishment that presided over the catastrophe" (Rich, "Slumdogs Unite!" A10).

14. Critchley, "The American Void," 17.

15. Paul Krugman, "Republican Death Trip," *New York Times*, August 14, 2009, A19.

16. David Sirota, "A Team of Zombies," *Truthdig.com*, February 6, 2009, http://www.truthdig.com/report/item/20090206_a_team_of_zombies/.

17. Barack Obama, "A 21st Century Education," speech to the United Federation of Teachers, September 10, 2008, http://www.uft.org/member/today/political/news/obama_speech.

18. I have taken up the issue of schooling as a public good in a number of books, including Henry A. Giroux, *Schooling and the Struggle for Public Life* (Boulder, CO: Paradigm Publishers, 2005); Henry A. Giroux and Susan Searls Giroux, *Take Back Higher Education* (New York: Palgrave, 2004); and Henry A. Giroux, *The University in Chains: Confronting the Military-Industrial-Academic Complex* (Boulder, CO: Paradigm Publishers, 2008).

19. Obama has outlined his reform efforts in a number of speeches. See David Mark, "Obama Interview," *Politico*, February 12, 2008, http://www.politico.com/news/stories/0208/8457.html; Obama: "A 21st Century Education"; "Obama Speech on Education in South Carolina," *Think on These Things*, November 2, 2008, http://thinkonthesethings.wordpress.com/2007/11/02/full-text-obama-speech-on-education-in-south-carolina; and "Barack Obama's Inaugural Address," *New York Times*, January 20, 2009, http://www.nytimes.com/2009/01/20/us/politics/20text-obama.html?scp=1&sq=Obama's%20Inaugural%20address&st=Search.

20. Sam Dillon, "Stimulus Plan Would Provide Flood of Aid to Education," *New York Times*, January 28, 2009, A1, A16.

21. All of these figures are from Derrick Z. Jackson, "Shovel-Ready Stimulus Buries Schools," *Boston Globe*, February 10, 2009, http://www.boston.com/bostonglobe/editorial_opinion/oped/articles/2009/02/10/shovel_ready_stimulus_buries_schools/.

22. Paul Krugman, "The Destructive Center," *New York Times*, February 9, 2009, A23.

23. Obama, "A 21st Century Education."

24. Stephen Metcalf, "Reading Between the Lines," *The Nation*, January 28, 2002, 18.

25. Barack Obama, "What's Good for Our Children," *Denver Post*, December 2, 2008, http://www.denverpost.com/news/ci_9405199.

26. Chris Hedges, "It's Not Going to Be OK," *TruthDig.com*, February 2, 2009, http://www.commondreams.org/view/2009/02/02-0.

27. Obama's call for educational reform embraces many of the same arguments made by George W. Bush, who maintained that schools should make sure "our children are prepared for the jobs of the future, and our country

is more competitive, by strengthening math and science skills" (George W. Bush, "Full Text of 2007 State of the Union Address," *MSNBC*, January 23, 2007, http://www.msnbc.msn.com/id/16672456/).

28. Maria Glod, "Education Pick Is Called 'Down-to-Earth' Leader," *Washington Post*, December 17, 2008, A03; Dillon, "Stimulus Plan." For a devastating critique of Duncan, see Paul Street, "Arne Duncan and Neoliberal Racism," *ZNet.org*, December 25, 2008, http://www.nybooks.com/articles/20056.

29. Kelly Field, "Hearing Offers Insight into Education-Secretary Nominee's Priorities for Higher Education," *Chronicle of Higher Education*, January 14, 2009, http://chronicle.com/daily/2009/01/9550n.htm.

30. David Hursh and Pauline Lipman, "Renaissance 2010: The Reassertion of Ruling-Class Power Through Neoliberal Policies in Chicago," *Policy Futures in Education* 5, no. 2 (2007): 160–178. I discuss this education plan in detail in Chapter 18.

31. Alfie Kohn, "Beware School Reformers," *The Nation*, December 29, 2008, 7.

32. Linda Darling-Hammond, "Evaluating 'No Child Left Behind,'" *The Nation*, May 21, 2007, http://www.thenation.com/doc/20070521/darling-hammond.

33. Street, "Arne Duncan and Neoliberal Racism."

34. Jesse Sharkey, "Arne Duncan's Privatization Agenda," *CounterPunch.org*, December 18, 2008, http://www.counterpunch.org/sharkey12182008.html.

35. Andy Kroll, "Will Public Education Be Militarized?" TomDispatch.com, January 18, 2009, http://www.tomdispatch.com/post/175022. See also Sophia Tareen, "Chicago Leads in Public Military Schools," *USA Today*, November 2, 2007, http://www.usatoday.com/news/nation/2007-11-02-2738760309_x.htm.

36. On the role of schools in governing through crime and the adoption of a militarized security culture to contain young people, see Jonathan Simon, *Governing Through Crime: How the War on Crime Transformed American Democracy and Created a Culture of Fear* (New York: Oxford University Press, 2007).

37. Jean Comaroff and John Comaroff, "Criminal Obsessions, after Foucault: Postcoloniality, Policing, and the Metaphysics of Disorder," *Critical Inquiry* 30 (Summer 2004): 808.

38. Advancement Project in partnership with Padres and Jovenes Unidos, Southwest Youth Collaborative, *Education on Lockdown: The Schoolhouse to Jailhouse Track* (Children and Family Justice Center, Northwestern University School of Law, March 24, 2005), http://www.advancementproject.org/reports/FINALEOLrep.pdf.

39. For an excellent discussion of the schools' increasing criminalization of student behavior, see Christopher G. Robbins, *Expelling Hope: The Assault on Youth and the Militarization of Schooling* (Albany: State University of New York Press, 2008). See also Bernadine Dohrn, "'Look Out, Kid, It's Something You Did': The Criminalization of Children," in *The Public Assault on America's Children: Poverty, Violence, and Juvenile Justice*, ed. Valerie Polakow (New York: Teachers College Press, 2000), 157–187.

40. Quoted in Frank Rich, "No Time for Poetry," *New York Times,* January 25, 2009, WK10.

Notes for Chapter 22

1. Zygmunt Bauman and Keith Tester, *Conversations with Zygmunt Bauman* (Malden, MA: Polity Press, 2001), 47.

2. Diane Ravitch, "Obama Gives Bush a 3rd Term in Education," *Common-Dreams.org,* June 15, 2009, http://www.commondreams.org/print/43399.

3. Ibid.

4. I take up this issue in great detail in Henry A. Giroux, *Youth in a Suspect Society: Democracy or Disposability?* (New York: Palgrave Macmillan, 2009).

5. A Conversation Between Lani Guinier and Anna Deavere Smith, "Rethinking Power, Rethinking Theater," *Theater* 31, no. 1 (Winter 2002): 36.

6. Robin D. G. Kelley, "Neo-cons of the Black Nation," *Black Renaissance Noire* 1, no. 2 (Summer–Fall 1997): 146.

7. See Henry A. Giroux and Susan Searls Giroux, *Take Back Higher Education* (New York: Palgrave, 2004); and Henry A. Giroux, *Schooling and the Struggle for Public Life,* 2nd ed. (Boulder, CO: Paradigm Publishers, 2005).

8. Sheldon Wolin, *Democracy, Inc.: Managed Democracy and the Specter of Inverted Totalitarianism* (Princeton, NJ: Princeton University Press, 2008), 60.

9. Stuart Hall, "Epilogue: Through the Prism of an Intellectual Life," in *Culture, Politics, Race, and Diaspora: The Thought of Stuart Hall,* by Brian Meeks (Miami: Ian Rundle, 2007), 289–290.

10. Amy Gutmann, *Democratic Education* (Princeton, NJ: Princeton University Press, 1998), 42.

11. Ian Angus, "Academic Freedom in the Corporate University," in *Utopian Pedagogy: Radical Experiments Against Neoliberal Globalization,* eds. Mark Coté, Richard J. F. Day, and Greig de Peuter (Toronto: University of Toronto Press, 2007), 64–75.

12. This position is brilliantly articulated in Edward Said, *Humanism and Democratic Criticism* (New York: Columbia University Press, 2004).

13. See also Giroux and Giroux, *Take Back Higher Education.*

14. Craig Calhoun and Loïc Wacquant, "Social Science with Conscience: Remembering Pierre Bourdieu (1930–2002)," *Thesis Eleven* 70 (August 2002): 10.

15. Stanley Fish, *Save the World on Your Own Time* (New York: Oxford University Press, 2008).

16. C. Wright Mills, *The Sociological Imagination* (London: Oxford University Press, 2000), 193.

17. Said, *Humanism and Democratic Criticism,* 50.

18. See, especially, Christopher Newfield, *Unmaking the Public University: The Forty-Year Assault on the Middle Class* (Cambridge, MA: Harvard University Press, 2008).

19. I take up the issue of the emerging of the academic-military-industrial complex in Henry A. Giroux, *The University in Chains: Confronting the Military-Industrial-Academic Complex* (Boulder, CO: Paradigm Publishers, 2008).

20. See Henry A. Giroux, "Academic Unfreedom in America: Rethinking the University as a Democratic Public Sphere," in *Academic Freedom and Intellectual Activism in the Post-9/11 University*, ed. Edward J. Carvalho, a special issue of *Work and Days* 51–54 (2008–2009), 45–72. This may be the best collection yet published on intellectual activism and academic freedom.

21. Wolin, *Democracy, Inc.*, 161.

22. John Dewey, *Democracy and Education: An Introduction to the Philosophy of Education* (New York: Free Press, 1966 [1916]).

23. Richard J. Bernstein, *The Abuse of Evil: The Corruption of Politics and Religion Since 9/11* (Malden, MA: Polity Press, 2005), 25–26.

24. On the crucial issue of the erosion of tenure-track jobs and the growing casualization of academic labor, see Marc Bousquet, *How the University Works: Higher Education and the Low-Wage Nation* (New York: New York University Press, 2008). For a more pessimistic account, see Frank Donoghue, *The Last Professors: The Corporate University and the Fate of the Humanities* (New York: Fordham University Press, 2008).

25. See the February 7, 2009, issue of *Newsweek* and the accompanying story: Jon Meacham and Evan Thomas, "We Are All Socialists Now," *Newsweek*, February 7, 2009, http://www.newsweek.com/id/183663/output/print.

26. Patricia Cohen, "In Tough Times, the Humanities Must Justify Their Worth," *New York Times*, February 25, 2009, C1, C7.

27. Ibid., C1.

28. Anthony Kronman, "Why Are We Here? Colleges Ignore Life's Biggest Questions, and We All Pay the Price," *Boston Globe*, September 16, 2007, http://www.boston.com/news/globe/ideas/articles/2007/09/16/why_are_we_here/.

Index

〜∞

Index

Obama, Barack (continued): Neda
video, 126–128; neoconservatives'
racist labeling, 89; suppressing
photos of torture and abuse,
127–131; symbolizing social state
renewal, 65–66
Ortiz, Paul, 66

Palin, Sarah, 65–66
Parties, creation of a third, 12
Partisanship, 166–168
Patriot Act, 164
Patriotism, 20
Patterson, Orlando, 25
Pay-for-performance educational
objectives, 112
Pay-to-play mentality, 103
Pena, Kelly, 40–41
Philadelphia Public Schools, 47
Phillips, Kevin, 36
Photos, torture, 127–128, 130
Political conditions for democracy, 13,
101
Political order, 13
Political participation, 81, 108
Politics: antipolitics of postpartisanship,
167–168; citizens' removal from
the arena of, 154; discourse of
hope linking education and, 136;
education as cultural politics,
103, 108–110; higher education
as a democratic public sphere,
181–183, 185–187; Iranian youth
challenging authoritarianism
through electronic media, 119–
122; role of higher education, 156
Poll ratings, Obama's, 7
Pollock, Grace, 41
Popular consent, 101–102
Pornography, 57
Possible and impossible, concepts of,
156
Postpartisanship, 166–168
Postracial state, 65–70
Poverty: Chicago's Renaissance 2010
plan, 141; child poverty figures, 73,
83, 93; increasing suffering and
visibility of youth, 93–95; poverty
reduction programs, 12–13;
privatization of, 26; as violation of
social order, 21

Power relations: democratic reforms,
103; higher education, 158; Iranian
protest, 123; Obama's antipolitics,
167
Preventive detention, 9
Prison culture, school discipline
mirroring, 45–47
Prison system/prison-industrial
complex: black male high-
school dropouts, 67; children's
disappearances into the prison
system, 21; corrupt judges filling
private detention centers, 80–81;
education and political reform,
95–96; incarceration rates for
minority youth, 74; labor force, 69;
life sentences for youth, 75–76; new
racism in, 87; Obama ignoring, 6;
school-to-prison pipeline, 48–49;
statistics for minority youth, 83;
war on youth replacing investment
in the public good, 74
Privatization: Chicago's Renaissance
2010 plan, 139–142; cloaking new
racism, 87; corporate co-optation
of higher education, 185–186;
educated hope opposing, 111–112;
juvenile detention centers, 80;
neoliberal cultural transformation,
102; Obama's era of responsibility,
12; screen culture promoting
culture of, 117–118; of self,
163; of social problems, 26–27;
technology, 110
Product placement, 34
Progressive movement, 136
Public disclosure, 129
Public good: Chicago's Renaissance
2010 plan, 141; Disneyfication of
culture, 43; transformation of
schools to security risk, 46–47; war
on youth, 73–74
Public pedagogy, 102
Public sphere: education as,
113–114; higher education as
democratic, 181–187; institutional
strengthening of, 27
Punishing state: Bush's corporate
model of education, 138; Duncan's
endorsement of, 173; increasing
suffering of poor minority youth,

About the Author

⤴

Henry A. Giroux holds the Global TV Network Chair in English and Cultural Studies at McMaster University in Canada. His most recent books include *The University in Chains: Confronting the Military-Industrial-Academic Complex* (2007), *Against the Terror of Neoliberalism: Politics Beyond the Age of Greed* (2008), and *Youth in a Suspect Society: Democracy or Disposability?* (2009).